ROADS

NOT

TAKEN

ROADS NOT TAKEN

Rereading Robert Frost

Edited with an Introduction by
Earl J. Wilcox and Jonathan N. Barron

UNIVERSITY OF MISSOURI PRESS
COLUMBIA AND LONDON

Copyright © 2000 by
The Curators of the University of Missouri
University of Missouri Press, Columbia, Missouri 65201
Printed and bound in the United States of America
All rights reserved
5 4 3 2 1   04 03 02 01 00

Library of Congress Cataloging-in-Publication Data

Roads not taken : rereading Robert Frost / edited with an introduction
by Earl J. Wilcox and Jonathan N. Barron.
    p. cm.
    Includes index.
    ISBN 0-8262-1305-7 (alk. paper)
    1. Frost, Robert, 1874–1963—Criticism and interpretation.
I. Wilcox, Earl J., 1933–   II. Barron, Jonathan N.
PS3511.R94 Z9156 2000
811'.52—dc21   00-062891

♾™ This paper meets the requirements of the
American National Standard for Permanence of Paper
for Printed Library Materials, Z39.48, 1984.

Text design: Stephanie Foley
Jacket design: Susan Ferber
Typesetter: BOOKCOMP, Inc.
Printer and binder: Edwards Brothers, Inc.
Typefaces: Adobe Caslon and Snell Roundhand

    Excerpts from the poems of Robert Frost from *The Poetry of Robert Frost*, edited by
Edward Connery Lathem, © 1969 by Henry Holt and Co. Reprinted by permission of
Henry Holt & Co., L.L.C.
    Excerpts from previously unpublished lectures by Robert Frost used by permission of
the Estate of Robert Lee Frost, © 2000, Estate of Robert Lee Frost; quotations from
transcripts courtesy of Dartmouth College and Amherst College.

For Elizabeth, Michael, Sara Elizabeth, Geoffrey, and Virginia because
"Earth's the right place for love: / I don't know where it's likely to go better."
EARL J. WILCOX

For Ellen, and for Liana and Raphael   ·
JONATHAN N. BARRON

CONTENTS

POETICS AND THEORY

ACKNOWLEDGMENTS

It is a pleasure to acknowledge colleagues, friends, and family members who contributed in significant ways to my part in the making of this book. First, thanks go to my colleagues in the English department at Winthrop University who gave so generously of their time by participating in the international Frost conference in 1997, an event which was the origin of several of the essays appearing in this volume. Without their support, confidence, and enthusiasm, the conference simply could not have taken place. Kudos are especially fitting for William Sullivan, chair, president Anthony DiGiorgio, Dean Betsy Brown, and Becky McMillan, vice president for university development, all of whom have helped make Winthrop University the center for Robert Frost studies for the past decade. Thanks also to other university colleagues who organized music, theater, and other events to make the international conference a remarkably successful undertaking. Finally, words of praise are inadequate to express my deepest thanks to my family for their love and support. To them this book is dedicated.

Earl J. Wilcox

So much goes into the making of a fine book. My first thanks are to my coeditor, Earl Wilcox. No thanks can begin to express what Earl has, through the years, done for Frost studies in this country. Founding editor of the *Robert Frost Review*, longtime organizer of the Robert Frost Society and of two of the most important conferences on Frost in recent memory. Generous, warm, kind, he has made this book possible. I also take this occasion to thank him publicly for the guidance, help, and advice he has given to me over the years. Here at the University of Southern Mississippi, I thank Michael Salda, chair of the English department, for providing research assistants and for his support of this project. Without them this book could not have been. At the University of Missouri Press, I thank the director, Beverly Jarrett, for her willingness to take this project, and I thank Sara Davis for working so carefully on it. Mostly, though, I thank my children, Liana and Raphael, for understanding why their father was so often buried in his study when he should have been playing with them. In truth, no support, however earnest, would have been of any consequence had it not been for the help, advice, comfort, and cajoling of my wife, Ellen Weinauer. I dedicate this book to her.

Jonathan N. Barron

NOTE TO THE READER

Each of the following essays refers to the poetry of Robert Frost as found in Richard Poirier and Mark Richardson, *Robert Frost: Collected Poems, Prose, and Plays* (New York: Library of America, 1996.) References appear parenthetically in the text.

Other books referred to in many of the essays will be identified in the footnotes by the following abbreviations:

Brodsky, Joseph, Seamus Heaney, and Derek Walcott. *Homage to Robert Frost.* New York: Farrar, Straus and Giroux, 1996. (**Homage**)

Cox, Sidney. *A Swinger of Birches: A Portrait of Robert Frost.* New York: Collier Books, 1961. (**Cox**)

Faggen, Robert. *Robert Frost and the Challenge of Darwin.* Ann Arbor: University of Michigan Press, 1997. (**Faggen**)

Frost, Robert. *Selected Prose of Robert Frost.* Edited by Hyde Cox and Edward C. Lathem. New York: Holt, Rinehart and Winston, 1949. (**Prose**)

————. *Selected Letters of Robert Frost.* Edited by Lawrance Thompson. New York: Holt, Rinehart and Winston, 1964. (**Letters**)

Lathem, Edward C. *Interviews with Robert Frost.* New York: Holt, Rinehart and Winston, 1966. (**Lathem**)

Meyers, Jeffrey. *Robert Frost.* New York: Houghton Mifflin Co., 1996. (**Meyers**)

Oster, Judith. *Toward Robert Frost: The Reader and the Poet.* Athens: University of Georgia Press, 1991. (**Oster**)

Poirier, Richard. *Robert Frost: The Work of Knowing.* New York: Oxford University Press, 1977. (**Poirier**)

Pritchard, William. *Frost: a Literary Life Reconsidered.* 2d ed. Amherst: University of Massachusetts Press, 1993. (**Pritchard**)

Richardson, Mark. *The Ordeal of Robert Frost.* Champaign: University of Illinois Press, 1997. (**Richardson**)

Tharpe, Jac, ed. *Frost: Centennial Essays I.* Jackson: University Press of Mississippi, 1974. (**Tharpe I**)

————. *Frost: Centennial Essays II.* Jackson: University Press of Mississippi, 1976. (**Tharpe II**)

————. *Frost: Centennial Essays III.* Jackson: University Press of Mississippi, 1978. (**Tharpe III**)

Thompson, Lawrance. *Robert Frost: The Early Years: 1874–1915.* New York: Holt, Rinehart and Winston, 1963. (**Early Years**)

————. *Robert Frost: The Years of Triumph, 1915–1938.* New York: Holt, Rinehart and Winston, 1970. (**Triumph**)

————. *Robert Frost: The Later Years, 1938–1963.* New York: Holt, Rinehart and Winston, 1976. (**Later Years**)

Untermeyer, Louis. *The Letters of Robert Frost to Louis Untermeyer.* New York: Holt, Rinehart and Winston, 1963. (**Untermeyer**)

ROADS

NOT

TAKEN

INTRODUCTION

OF ALL THE MAJOR twentieth-century American poets, Robert Frost remains the most well known, the most public, and the least understood. While Frost's intellectual and artistic credentials need no defending, his work, compared to that of his generational peers, is still the least explored. Rather than bringing Frost's work into line with current discussion of the work of such fellow poets as T. S. Eliot, Wallace Stevens, Marianne Moore, H.D., and Ezra Pound, the past decade has seen a new burst of attention to just those elements that make Frost's work so singular.

In the early 1980s, the Robert Frost Society was founded to perpetuate and encourage study of the poet's life and work. Since that time, the society has been the principal force in organizing programs, forums, and freelance discussion in cities, on university campuses, and on the World Wide Web. At major academic gatherings, such as the annual meetings of the Modern Language Association and the American Literature Association, the society has sponsored gatherings in cities as diverse as New York, Chicago, San Francisco, and Toronto. The enthusiasm with which these programs were greeted in turn led to at least two notable events: the founding in 1991 of the *Robert Frost Review* and, in 1997, the first major international academic conference devoted exclusively to Frost in more than a decade.

This conference, held at Winthrop University, was sponsored in large part by the society and organized by its director and the founding editor of the *Robert Frost Review,* Earl J. Wilcox. The symposium marked the culmination of a decade of remarkably innovative work on Frost's poetry. There scholars and laymen alike from as far away as China, Japan, Norway, Italy, Scotland, Israel, England, and India joined with Americans from all over the country for a four-day "revival." Indeed, much of the new work presented at this conference had been encouraged, fostered, and debated in the pages of the *Robert Frost Review.*

With this essay collection, we, the editors of the *Robert Frost Review,* mean to bring this new work on Frost to the attention of a wider academic audience. Specifically, Frost scholarship in the past ten years has examined the poet's work from perspectives as various as critical hermeneutics, cultural studies, feminism, postmodernism, and textual editing. Despite this resurgence of scholarly work on Frost no book yet exists that accounts for its wide variety. The variety, moreover, is not just theoretical. For instance, in the past three years alone, there has been a great deal of new textual and biographical research into the poet as well. Specifically, the Library of America in 1995 published a new scholarly edition of the poet's collected works, *Robert Frost: Collected Poems, Prose, and Plays*. Furthermore, a number of significant biographical studies have been published, including a best-selling volume by Jeffrey Meyers. Additional new evidence of sustained and vigorous attention to Frost is reflected in entirely new studies such as Robert Faggen's provocative book *Robert Frost and the Challenge of Darwin* (1997), Karen L. Kilcup's insightful treatise *Robert Frost and Feminine Literary Tradition* (1999), and a widely praised biography, *Frost: A Life* (1999), by Jay Parini. Frost continues to attract contemporary criticism in international circles; two new studies by Italian scholars and one by a Japanese critic have appeared within the past year alone. Meyers's controversial biography suggests that even outside the literary criticism community there is enthusiasm for the poet.

Indeed, contemporary poets and the world of creative writing have shown an equally unfailing and renewed interest in Frost in recent years. In 1995 three Nobel laureates—Joseph Brodsky, Derek Walcott, and Seamus Heaney—paid unusual attention to Frost as a major force behind their successful and productive careers. Quite coincidentally, these three laureates published separate essays in leading literary journals; a publishing house saw the significance and brought out the essays in a collection, *Homage to Robert Frost* (1997). And, at the 1997 Winthrop conference, both Richard Wilbur and Galway Kinnell offered their own homage in major public speeches and readings. The 1999 poet laureate of the United States, Robert Pinsky, conducted a yearlong survey of Americans, asking for their favorite poet, and Frost has won this national poll by a large and impressive margin. Meanwhile, an anthology entitled *After Frost* (1996) collects the work of a variety of American poets who write in the mode made possible by Frost's poetry.

Given this interest among scholars, the general public, and contemporary poets, we believe that, as one scholar at the Winthrop conference put it, the poet will soon prove to be the Trojan horse of the modern era. The new attention to Frost proves that the poet's work more often upsets our conventional understanding of both modernism and romanticism. Frost's work is now seen as decidedly open-minded, polyvalent, and dialogic.

To present these new approaches to the poet, we have gathered together groups of scholars; some will bring to bear on Frost's work the specific theoretical paradigms that have, until the past ten years, been entirely ignored with regard to Frost. Others will single out the still woefully understudied or underrecognized elements in Frost's own work. Together, the articles we assemble will reintroduce Robert Frost to the literary community and will also suggest ways of thinking about the poet that may well change the current discussion about both modernism and American poetry's development after modernism.

The contributors to this volume have been in the vanguard in exploring new ways to look at Frost, and almost all have published book-length studies of the poet; all have written extensively on Frost. Mark Richardson, for example, is coeditor of the Library of America volume; George Monteiro, a preeminent scholar, has published widely on many significant writers and cultures; thanks to her focus on gender in Frost, Katherine Kearns's book *Robert Frost and a Poetics of Appetite* has already changed the way an entire generation will read Frost's poems. As another indication of continuing interest in Frost, Peter J. Stanlis was recently featured in the Sunday *New York Times*. Short of presenting here the extended resumes of all our contributors, we would add only that they have already devoted scholarly careers to the study of Frost and, in so doing, have now opened up Frost studies in ways previously unimaginable.

Specifically, we have noticed in these essays four new roads to travel: gender, biography and cultural context, the intertext, and rhetorical and cultural poetics. We believe that their publication here together will shape the new century's sense of the poetry of Robert Frost. Also, in these essays, one will find new readings of old poems and new readings of still unremarked yet nonetheless remarkable poems; for example, such understudied poems as "The Black Cottage," "Beech," and "There Are Roughly Zones" get extended treatment. Similarly, in these essays readers are invited to consider Frost in light of such intellectual traditions as women's sentimental poetry, the American liberal tradition, and the cultural context of the Cold War as well as through the new lens of gender.

By dividing our collection into four sections, then, we do not mean to limit approaches to Frost to these four roads. Rather, we, as editors, mean to tell a story we have seen emerge in recent Frost scholarship. As this collection presents it, the biggest news in recent years is the insistence by scholars that Frost's interest in gender be taken far more seriously than had been done before. The first section's essays explore a variety of gender issues that circulate throughout Frost's work and that, until now, have gone mostly undiscussed in Frost scholarship. Karen Kilcup's essay begins this section with a description of the gendered environment of American poetry at the turn of the century, when Frost first began to write. Rather than read that historical context in terms of the now familiar war between an aggressively antisentimental masculine modernism and a far too sentimentalized and feminized genteel era, Kilcup returns us to the far more nuanced intersection of masculine and feminine codes that so often defined the poems of both men and women in the 1880s and 1890s. Kilcup focuses on an "unexpected literary connection" between Frost and late-nineteenth-century feminist and nature poet Lucy Larcom. In doing so, Kilcup not only offers a strikingly new reading of "Birches," but also shows that it depends on "the imaginative freedom that domestic ideology . . . describes and enacts." In other words, Kilcup reminds us that in the work of poets like Larcom, the domestic, feminized gender codes associated with sentimentalism do a great deal of cultural work. Frost's poem, by invoking such complex sentimental traditions and contexts, shares in tone, person, and important connections with Larcom's earlier poem "Swinging on a Birch-Tree."

In contrast with Kilcup, Katherine Kearns's challenging and creative essay, "Frost on the Doorstep and Lyricism at the Millennium," reads these same masculine and feminine codes in negative terms. According to her, neither system satisfied Frost; despite his cultural, and perhaps emotional, investment in traditional masculinity he was hardly content with these codes. Says Kearns, "lyricism stands for something entirely other, which is why . . . it is so often felt as 'femaleness.'" The lyric is not a cultural space for the domestic sphere, the feminine. Rather, it is the expression of all that we mean by uncontained, uncontainable, true and pure individuality. Do the masculine gender codes of Frost's day war against more traditional ideas of the feminine lyric? Then, says Kearns, this genre allows Frost to war against those codes. However, Kearns believes it will not suffice to think that the lyric is some kind of feminine antidote to the masculine; rather than read lyricism as the space for the feminine, Kearns sees it in a more phenomenological setting as the site for the fragmented self. Kearns concludes that Frost returned us to the wildness and freedom of the lyric by showing just how often it liberated him, despite his own best wishes, from masculinity and its codes even if, in going there, he risked identifying himself as female.

In the second section of our collection, we highlight both new biographical takes on Frost and new approaches to his work through the cultural context that surrounds it. This section opens with Mark Richardson's essay. Robert Frost's famous reading at President John F. Kennedy's inauguration was an epiphanic moment in the poet's public career. In truth, however, the poet's presence on the occasion was but a climactic ceremony to ideas he had nurtured for at least two decades before 1960. In "Frost and the Cold War: A Look at the Later Poetry," Richardson demonstrates that the complex mind-set of Frost began much earlier with the publication of *Steeple Bush* (1947); it continued with essays such as "The Future of Man," (1959), and the collection near the end of his life, *In the Clearing* (1962). Richardson's analysis of the sexualized language of a little-noticed sonnet, "Bursting Rapture" (*Steeple Bush*), draws attention to Frost's concerns for the "bomb" and all things relevant to the Cold War. Similar "sexualized" language in portions of "Kitty Hawk" and the very late poem, "Does No One at All Ever Feel This Way in the Least?" and "A Cabin in the Clearing" illustrate awareness of the "military invulnerability that American geography used to provide" before World War II.

Following this revealing view of Frost as a political force, Peter Stanlis offers evidence of Frost as an innovator in education. Stanlis's assertion that a "strong shift in perspective" is needed to perceive Robert Frost as primarily teacher, rather than poet, is the deftly understated premise of his essay. In "Robert Frost's Philosophy of Education: The Poet as Teacher," Stanlis explores his thesis with a comprehensive survey of the major intellectual milieu of Frost, the poet's family, teachers, students, of course, and the poet's own vast knowledge of the world's great thinkers. As Stanlis points out, Frost himself, in "Education by Poetry" (and elsewhere in numerous forms), said the "essence of both poetry and education is to teach readers . . . how to think . . . in metaphor." Maturing in the Victorian era, which showcased the conflict between Huxley, Newman, and Arnold, the poet developed a philosophy that he articulated throughout his life, a philosophy that, as Stanlis argues, made Frost America's unique teacher/poet.

Lisa Seale, too, returns to a little-discussed yet fundamental feature of Frost's "canon"—his various impromptu lectures, talks, and discussions. As it turns out, an enormous number of these talks were recorded, and they provide a rich mine for further understanding Frost's intellectual and poetic interests and concerns. Based on heretofore unpublished materials—tapes of two hundred or so talks he gave before his many public readings—Seale introduces a radically new dimension for understanding Frost's creative process. By examining the poet's introductory remarks given over a period of nearly five decades, from 1915 until the year of his death, she demonstrates how Frost blended his talking and reading. Examination of poems such as "Cluster of Faith" and portions of "Kitty Hawk," reveals, among other new insights, how Frost approaches answers and questions to topics ranging from poetic originality to the design of the universe. Seale persuasively argues that the poet's remarks are "extended examples of how Frost's talks illuminate . . . aspects of his poetry and of his ideas about the origins of thinking."

The third and fourth sections of our book, "The Intertext" and "Poetics and Theory," open up still-unexplored theoretical, textual, and poetic facts of Frost's work. While it is commonplace to associate the work of Frost's high modernist peers with dense allusions to the world literary tradition, it will come as a surprise to those who have not studied Frost to learn that his work, as much as Eliot's or Pound's, also contains a dense allusive, textual web. The three essays printed in "The Intertext" explore the ways Frost invoked Dante, Wordsworth, and Arnold.

In David Hamilton's essay, for example, the familiar "Stopping by Woods" becomes both an invocation of Dante and a response both to T. S. Eliot's *The Waste Land* and to Frost's own counter-*Waste Land*, "New Hampshire." By opening the field of this poem to include Dante, Eliot, and himself, Frost, says Hamilton, further "darkens" his poem. Hamilton's "The Echo in Frost's Woods" offers a fascinating and provocative reading of the perennially popular sixteen-line poem along two fronts: Frost and Eliot's admiration and assimilation of Dantean devices and Frost's awareness of Eliot's landmark poem. Both poets knew Dante's use of overlapping incremental advance to create a canto effect. Using Dante as a kind of signature engages both poets in complex artistic processes. Hamilton distances Frost from Eliot by noting the "apparent ease" with which Frost composed his most famous poem in contrast to Eliot's dictum that poetry should arise out of "intensity." Thanks to Hamilton's insights, this poem is removed from the pervasive psychological context in which it is so often exclusively read.

Jonathan Barron's essay, by contrast with Hamilton's, does not return to a well-known poem but rather revives a long-neglected one: "The Black Cottage." In his essay, Barron argues for that poem's merit by returning to the textual heritage it invokes: William Wordsworth's "The Ruined Cottage." Barron shows that Frost not only invoked Wordsworth's poem but actively intervened and further revised Wordsworth's own poetic theories. In doing so, Frost was able to speak not only to his cultural moment—the few months before World War I—but also to a continuing problematic theoretical issue: the cultural association of nationalism and religion, politics, and theology. As much a critique of immanence as an invocation of it, Frost's "The Black Cottage" questions the long line of American lyrics (from those of the Puritans through Emerson's) that have evoked, in the land, a kind of incarnate spirituality.

George Monteiro adds even more critical and cultural context to Frost's work by associating that poet with a surprising forebear, Matthew Arnold, and a surprising near contemporary, Lionel Trilling. Reading "Neither Out Far Nor In Deep" as a response to Arnold's "Dover Beach," Monteiro finds the poem to be far more sympathetic to Arnold than critical of him. As he says, "Frost's 'people,' like Arnold's, do not look out far or in deep . . . because they cannot do so, for no one can look out far or in deep." This bleak democracy of limitation is the sort of liberalism that Lionel Trilling found in Arnold, which, says Monteiro, explains why Trilling would find such "terror" in Frost as well. In his essay, Monteiro further tightens the textual web by reading as one the works of Arnold, Frost, and Trilling. In doing so, he offers new insight into Frost's own liberalism.

Our final section, "Poetics and Theory," investigates the more theoretical issues at stake in Frost's poetry. Beginning with Walter Jost's essay, we return to Frost's poetics as an experiment in rhetoric and hermeneutics. Jost contends that Frost's poetry marks a triumph of intellectual activity, a poetic response, even a counter to both philosophy and classical rhetoric. In his dialogues, says Jost, Frost offers an original hermeneutics that inserts itself somewhere between the claims of philosophy on the one hand and rhetoric on the other. Frost's poetry as "informal conversation," says Jost, manages to present a "more social orientation for a democratic nation." Reminding us of Frost's own skepticism toward any conclusive system, Jost returns us to the hermeneutic strategy of Frost's work in the little-studied poem, "There Are Roughly Zones." In doing so, Jost shows us a Frost who invites investigation into, rather than mere agreement with, the often totalizing claims he is so often said to have made.

Andrew Lakritz, meanwhile, reflects on Frost's "Americanness" by investigating his nationalism. According to Lakritz, Frost is said to be the quintessentially American poet. This was certainly the view of the poet Joseph Brodsky, who claimed that Americans have escaped history's net; they face the darkness alone and without context. In their poetry, particularly in Frost's, he argues, one does not find tragedy; one finds pure terror. Taking his cue from Brodsky's distinction, Lakritz examines Frost's 1942 poem "Beech" in order to question the very idea of an American land, a territory. In the terror located by Brodsky one no longer finds a territory. At the heart of such poems as "Beech," one finds no ground. Where is

Frost's America? As Lakritz asks, "Is it an empty space to be filled with human culture and the spiritual quest of the Puritans?" Ultimately arguing against that reading, Lakritz adds that such poems as "Home Burial" and "The Road Not Taken" also "prove our contingency with the place marked out and possessed."

In our final essay, Richard Calhoun explores the technical element to Frost's poetics. Calhoun examines Frost's use of the sonnet, and in so doing, he offers new readings of Frost's poems based on the sonnet's structural form. Furthermore, Calhoun emphasizes the tension between extravagance and conformity that marks not only Frost's thematic interest, but also the very definition of the sonnet. According to Calhoun, Frost's sonnets play with "the tension between a need for form and the corresponding need for a freedom from form." Frost, in Calhoun's reading of the sonnets, becomes a poetic innovator, intellectual "devil," and grand experimenter—as fine a set of terms as any with which to enter the new millennium of Frost study.

GENDER

"Something of a Sentimental Sweet Singer"

Robert Frost, Lucy Larcom, and "Swinging Birches"

Karen L. Kilcup

WORDSWORTH, WHITMAN, Keats, Arnold, Emerson, Virgil: these are the poets with whom Robert Frost is customarily associated and with whom his work is regularly compared. Yet in completing the research for *Robert Frost and Feminine Literary Tradition,* which focuses on his transformations of nineteenth-century American traditions, I found another, entirely unexpected literary connection with the poet: Lucy Larcom (1824–1893). This essay will delineate that connection more fully and, in particular, will explore the gendered relationship between the sentimental and the modern as that relationship evolves in the lyric poem, undertaking in some sense a backward extension of what Suzanne Clark has called "sentimental modernism."[1] In the process, I hope to illuminate both the interconnections between the two modes and the limitations of current conceptions of "the sentimental." To pursue this goal, the first section of this essay will follow a cultural-historical trajectory for this pairing of poets, aiming to complicate readers' understanding of "the sentimental" and to explore the interpretive context into and out of which each was writing; the second will interrogate in more direct and analytical fashion the poets' lyric links, focusing attention on the poems that sparked this discussion, Larcom's "Swinging on a Birch-Tree" and Frost's "Birches."

OF "SENTIMENTAL SWEET SINGERS"

I should not have been surprised at Frost's echo of Larcom's work, given the latter's New England connections. A feminist, abolitionist, intellec-

---

1. The studies that associate Frost with romantic and classical writers are too numerous to mention here; among the best known are **Poirier** and George F. Bagby, *Frost and the Book of Nature* (Knoxville: University of Tennessee Press, 1993).
   Suzanne Clark, *Sentimental Modernism: Women Writers and the Revolution of the Word* (Bloomington: Indiana University Press, 1991).

tual, and naturalist and a friend of Whittier's, Larcom was born and raised in northeastern Massachusetts. Paralleling the pattern of many contemporaries, she and her family moved to Lowell from rural Beverley, Massachusetts, after her father's untimely death, which plunged the family into the economic distress that propelled Larcom's mother to open a boardinghouse for the "mill girls" of the city. Larcom herself worked in the mills from the age of eleven. She began her writing career by contributing to the *Lowell Offering,* a magazine founded and edited by the mill girls. As Cheryl Walker notes, the poet "received only slight notice in the anthologies compiled by [Rufus] Griswold and [Edmund Clarence] Stedman"; but Larcom's work was popular and widely disseminated in the nineteenth century, appearing in a "Household Edition" in 1884. Although she interests today's readers as a poet of working-class experience and as a feminist, she was, like Frost, primarily a nature poet, and she wrote many effective poems in this vein, including "Fern-Life," "November," and "Flowers of the Fallow." Like Frost, Larcom was also a powerful children's poet, and from 1865 to 1870 she edited *Our Young Folks,* one of the most influential periodicals of the time, ostensibly for children but popular with readers and listeners of all ages. Larcom's work disappeared from critical view early in the twentieth century and has only recently been rediscovered as part of the general recovery of nineteenth-century American women's writing. In the past widely regarded as "merely" a "sentimental" poet, Larcom often exceeds or complicates this genre, as her biographer Shirley Marchalonis observes.[2] Her work merits renewed attention, especially in the context of the poet's influence, conscious or

2. For Larcom's autobiography, see her *A New England Girlhood: Outlined from Memory* (1889; rpt. Boston: Northeastern University Press, 1986); for other biographical sources, see Nancy Cott, foreword to *A New England Girlhood,* xi–xvii; Shirley Marchalonis, "*Legacy* Profile: Lucy Larcom," *Legacy* 5.1 (1988): 45–52; Shirley Marchalonis, *The Worlds of Lucy Larcom* (Athens: University of Georgia Press, 1989). On Larcom's "Household Edition," see Cheryl Walker, "Lucy Larcom," *American Women Poets of the Nineteenth Century* (New Brunswick: Rutgers University Press, 1992), 216.

On Larcom and sentimentalism, see Emily Stipes Watts, *The Poetry of American Women from 1632 to 1945* (Austin: University of Texas Press, 1977), 191n.; Marchalonis, *Worlds,* 3.

For a discussion of Frost's children's writing, see my *Robert Frost and Feminine Literary Tradition* (Ann Arbor: University of Michigan Press, 1998), 202–12. I suggest other connections between Frost and Larcom (see 92–93, 276 n. 86) and argue that the term *sentimental* requires much more unpacking than it has received (see ch. 1, esp. 17–22); see also, Cheryl Walker, introduction to *American Women Poets of the Nineteenth Century;* Walker, *The Nightingale's Burden: Women Poets and American Culture before 1900* (Bloomington: Indiana University Press, 1982); Paula Bennett, "'The Descent of

otherwise, on poets of the late nineteenth and early twentieth centuries such as Frost.

To understand Larcom and Frost's invocation and transformation of sentimentalism we need first to look briefly at the genre or mode itself. Readers will be familiar with the groundbreaking work of Jane Tompkins, who attempts to recover "the cultural work of American fiction" done by sentimentalism, and Cheryl Walker, who seeks to identify characteristics of sentimental poetry. Many critics have argued, like Nina Baym, that sentimentalism was fundamentally involved with social change, a domestic ideal elaborated as "a value scheme for ordering all of life, in competition with the ethos of money and exploitation that is perceived to prevail in American society." In spite of modernist critics' association of sentimental poetry exclusively with women, even a casual glance at nineteenth-century anthologies reveals the fallaciousness of such a connection, for men too wrote sentimental poetry in vast quantities. In Tompkins's important account, "twentieth-century critics have taught generations of students to equate popularity with debasement, emotionality with ineffectiveness, religiosity with fakery, domesticity with triviality, and all of these, implicitly, with womanly fakery." As Joanne Dobson has observed, such criticisms are based in "modes of definition and evaluation developed exclusively within the framework of a critical valorization of romantic, individualistic, culturally dissenting, self-consciously artistic aspects of the classic masculine texts." Described in Shirley Samuels's more general terms, sentimentalism is "a set of cultural practices designed to evoke a certain form of emotional response, usually empathy, in the reader or viewer."[3]

To conceive of sentimentalism as a popular mode emerging from religious conviction, centered around domestic experience, and aiming at an

---

the Angel': Interrogating Domestic Ideology in American Women's Poetry, 1858–1890," *American Literary History* 7.4 (1995): 591–610; and Clark, *Sentimental Modernism*.

3. Nina Baym, *Woman's Fiction: A Guide to Novels by and about Women in America, 1820–1870* (Ithaca: Cornell University Press, 1978), 27. On sentimental men's poetry, see Paula Bennett, introduction to *Nineteenth-Century American Women Poets: An Anthology* (Malden, Mass.: Blackwell, 1997), xxxiv, xxxvi. Some of the most recent discussions of sentimentalism have been even more damning than Ann Douglas's important early study *The Feminization of American Culture* (New York: Discus-Avon, 1977); see Laura Wexler, "Tender Violence: Literary Eavesdropping, Domestic Fiction, and Educational Reform" in *The Culture of Sentiment, Race, Gender, and Sentimentality in Nineteenth-Century America*, ed. Shirley Samuels (New York: Oxford University Press, 1992), 15. Joanne Dobson, "The American Renaissance Reenvisioned," in *The (Other) American Traditions: Nineteenth-Century Women Writers*, ed. Joyce Warren (New Brunswick: Rutgers University Press, 1993), 168; see 171, 175. Shirley Samuels, introduction to *The Culture of Sentiment*, 4.

emotional engagement with the reader is, however, insufficiently precise. Paula Bennett has distinguished between the "high sentimentalism" of earlier women poets such as Lydia Sigourney, Elizabeth Oakes Smith, and Frances Sargent Osgood and the merely conventional work of later writers: "High sentimentalism (c. 1825–1850) is an epistemologically based discourse. It claimed that the intimations of the heart could serve as reliable guides to moral and spiritual truths. Low sentimentalism is the kind of sentimentalism still with us today. It is loose, subjective, personal, and makes no claims to knowledge, only to feeling." In *Robert Frost and Feminine Literary Tradition*, I question this distinction for several reasons: the difficulty of distinguishing between the two modes, the participation of many earlier poets in what I call "ironic sentimentalism" (as Bennett's important anthology *Nineteenth-Century American Women Poets* itself demonstrates), and the potential for hierarchization in the terms themselves, leading literary critics once again to a devaluing of emotion as an element of critical response.[4] This hierarchization is especially problematic in view of the continuing negative resonances of the term *sentimental*.

Unpacking this term remains difficult; for one thing, sentimentality and emotion are not identical, and sentimentality can be inflected in a variety of ways, suggesting anger as well as despair. We need to investigate not only the diverse emotions elicited by a range of sentimental texts, but also the heterogeneity of readers' responses according to such variables as age, class, race, and personal experience, as well as "the textual or aesthetic qualities that can lead to the perception (or prevention) of 'excess' or inauthenticity in affective literature; and the historical and generic variations that occur." One such variation occurs in the activist poetry of Lydia Sigourney, where, in a poem like "Indian Names," the writer engages Christian values to provoke not sympathetic weeping but understanding, shame, and action. Sigourney's work intimates some of the bedrock concerns associated with sentimentalism; especially as it was (re)constructed by "beleaguered avant-garde intellectuals" of the modern era who used sentimentalism (and the domestic culture that it putatively embodied) as a touchstone against which to define themselves as "a discourse community." As Suzanne Clark argues, "multiple issues of gender, of power and desire, were contained in this

---

4. Paula Bennett, "'The Descent of the Angel,'" 606 n. 2; see 592, 594. See Kilcup, *Robert Frost and Feminine Literary Tradition*, 17–22. On the constraint of emotion in critical discourse, especially by women, see *The Intimate Critique: Autobiographical Literary Criticism*, ed. Diane P. Freedman, Olivia Frey, and Frances Murphy Zauhar (Durham: Duke University Press, 1993).

opposition to the sentimental," which "calls up the repressed involvement of literature with power—literature as a rhetorical instrument, literature used in the interests of economy and politics, literature as locus of pleasure and transgression."[5]

This matrix of power, gender, and desire figures significantly in the apparent translation of sentimentalism from Larcom's time to Frost's. To understand more fully their interwoven character we must acknowledge the situation of individual poems in periodicals and recognize the critical norms for poetry articulated in the time of each writer. One of the earlier reviews of Larcom's *Poems* (1868) appeared in the *Atlantic Monthly* in 1869. It begins ambiguously with an implicit criticism of "Skipper Ben" in contrast to "Hannah Binding Shoes," the poem that made Larcom famous. The reviewer emphasizes the latter's "perfect simplicity and self-control" as well as its realism. Genuineness—especially genuineness of emotion— and realism (a "life-like" quality) are simultaneously valued; such a pairing seems impossible in light of current views of sentimentalism, where realism and emotion cannot mix. The reviewer concludes by praising Larcom's "gift to move and please, which certainly does not come from the poetic culture of our age, and which we do not mind calling genius." At least initially, Larcom was not perceived in sentimental terms, even though by this time "sentimental" was as likely to be a term of disparagement as one of praise. For example, Harriet Prescott Spofford, herself a famous and well-paid writer, reviewed Larcom's work in terms that separated her unequivocally from the familiar mode and emphasized her originality: "In conclusion, it may be said of these verses that there is not one syllable to be found in them of that maudlin sentimentality which sickens on the pages of so many poets, nor is there any trace of imitation of another."[6]

To understand the full import of such remarks, it is crucial to examine briefly the poem around which they centered, "Hannah Binding Shoes,"

---

5. On the heterogeneity of readers' responses, see Kilcup, *Robert Frost and Feminine Literary Tradition*, 19. On "Indian Names," see Nina Baym, "Reinventing Lydia Sigourney," in *The (Other) American Traditions*, 54–72; Kilcup, *Robert Frost and Feminine Literary Tradition*, 51–59; Suzanne Clark, *Sentimental Modernism*, 1, 2.

6. Review of *Poems* by Lucy Larcom, *Atlantic Monthly* 23 (January 1869): 136. Harriet Prescott Spofford [writing as H. P. S.], "Lucy Larcom's Poems," *Galaxy* 7 (1869): 299. On Spofford's own career and work, see Alfred Bendixen, introduction to *The Amber Gods and Other Stories* (New Brunswick: Rutgers University Press, 1989); Paula Bennett, "'Pomegranate-Flowers': The Phantasmic Productions of Late-Nineteenth-Century Anglo-American Women Poets," in *Solitary Pleasures: The Historical, Literary, and Artistic Discourses of Autoeroticism*, ed. Paula Bennett and Vernon A. Rosario II (New York: Routledge, 1995), 189–213.

which made Larcom a household name. Hannah marries her young lover and remains at home when he leaves for a fishing voyage from Marblehead, Massachusetts. Twenty years later, we see her still asking for news of her lost husband, as she sits overlooking the harbor at her work. From a modern (and contemporary) perspective, the poem participates in a sentimental discourse, engaging the domestic values of love and home in a drama of loss. From another perspective, the poem encodes the suffering of a women who, in the absence of her husband's economic support, must labor ceaselessly at a poorly paid occupation to support herself: "Twenty winters / Bleach and tear the ragged shore she views."[7] Although it follows the rhetorical and substantive conventions of sentimental discourse, Larcom's poem could as readily be construed as a political poem that critiques domestic ideology for its unreality and for the powerlessness and implied poverty that it imposes on the waiting wife.

By 1875, Larcom had published a book-length poem based on her experiences in the Lowell Mills. *An Idyl of Work* attracted another notice in the powerful *Atlantic,* which, although it referred to the *Lowell Offering* in slighting terms, compared American working-class "girls" favorably to their British counterparts ("the vicious and stupid operative class of the Old World") and again praised Larcom's work for its realism ("faithfulness to the life it depicts") and its "sincerity," "boldness," and ability to "move one to a compassionate sympathy with girlhood struggling to keep life pretty and nice and even noble in circumstances so adverse." Although the reviewer wishes that the poet had undertaken "something more decided and dramatic than she has done," he praises the "Wordsworthian courage" of her realism. As with earlier reviews, Larcom's work emerges in the valorized context of realistic, not sentimental, discourse, perhaps because an investigation of class relations is deeply embedded in the poem, the first section of which, for example, interrogates the cultural definition of "lady."[8]

Reflecting the diminished cultural authority of poetry, by 1885 the *Dial* would review Larcom's collected poems in terms that were at best ambiguous: "The three hundred closely printed pages which are needed to contain the verse of Lucy Larcom bear unmistakable witness to the industry of one of our most estimable women of letters. Her verses are simply written, and are such as may have a strong hold upon simple

---

7. Larcom, *Poetical Works,* 2.
8. For a review of Larcom's *An Idyl of Work,* see "Recent Literature" *Atlantic Monthly* 36 (August 1875): 242. Lucy Larcom, *An Idyl of Work* (1875; rpt. Westport, Conn.: Greenwood Press, 1970), 14, 19.

minds." Here the writer emphasizes Larcom's hard work (with "industry" perhaps a snide reference to Larcom's situation as a factory worker) and her "simplicity," which here becomes not a positive term like "accessibility" but instead connects the poet with a broad, "popular" (read female) audience. Already we see the affiliation between the feminine and the popular that would condemn nineteenth-century women poets in the minds of modern(ist) poets and critics.[9] The reviewer continues by asserting that her work has nothing of "the heights and depths of poetry": "Most regions of the imagination and most phases of passion are entirely unknown to her; but she has a considerable facility in the expression of a mild form of religious sentiment, and of the gentler aspect of nature as seen in her New England home." "Religion," "sentiment," and a limp (rather than a hard, passionate, romantic) presentation of nature all characterize the female poet here: "A refined and delicate fancy is her substitute for imagination, and kindly feeling what she has to give in the place of passion. While these offer nothing to the true lover of poetry, there are many who, lacking the artistic perceptions needed for its enjoyment, may find in such verse as this a pleasure analogous at least—though far lower—to that which persons of acuter sensibilities find in the works of genuine poets." Once again, readers are separated into "elite" and "common" categories, with the assertion that Larcom appeals only to the latter. Well before "the modernist new critics used aesthetic antisentimentality to make distinctions, to establish a position of authority against mass culture," this reviewer rebelled against Larcom's cultural power and authority.[10] Most noteworthy in all of these critiques is the reviewers' refusal to acknowledge (or their inability to perceive) the political thrust of her work, for they emphasize only its affiliation with the realistic or romantic lyric.

This description of Larcom's work did not deter her numerous "ordinary" (if deluded) readers. At the same time, however, the continuing value of sentimental writing for many readers is evident in a nearly contemporary (1888) review of the poems of Oliver Wendell Holmes, Rose Terry Cooke, and others. Of Holmes, the reviewer observes, "We wonder at him almost as much as we delight in him, and when his pretty little volume comes to us, bright and dainty without and within, we almost suspect that in his professional researches he must have stumbled upon the secret of eternal youth. . . ." At the same time that the reviewer asserts that Holmes "is

---

9. Andreas Huyssen, *After the Great Divide: Modernism, Mass Culture, Postmodernism* (Bloomington: Indiana University Press, 1986), vii, 47.
    10. Anonymous review, *Dial* 5 (1885): 265. Clark, *Sentimental Modernism,* 5.

not a great poet," he praises the work of John James Piatt for its "peculiar sub-melancholy," "peculiar charm," and "plaintive tone" in "verse which is in other respects sturdy and strong." Cooke, on the other hand, is praised for her emotional impact: "Among all our women singers there is none with a sweeter note. Her lyrics are spirited, picturesque, and effective. Her songs of sentiment are never artificial or affected, but mirror the deeper feelings which visit all unspoiled hearts." In this reviewer's eyes "feelings" (apparently interchangeable with "sentiment") are not necessarily negative, but they must be natural and authentic. From another perspective in this broader critical context, however, the criticisms of sentimentalism that had appeared earlier from both men and women, poets and reviewers, had by 1890 gathered sufficient force for Helen Gray Cone to remark disparagingly in *Century Magazine* that "sentimentalism has infected both continents" and to denigrate "the flocks of quasi-swan singers."[11]

At the time that Frost was coming to think of himself as a poet, these critical standards retained significant elements of ambivalence about the value, place, and form of emotion in poetry. The anxiety expressed by Cone seems much more muted in Susan Hayes Ward's review of the time, "A Decade of Poetry: 1889–1899," published in the *Independent,* of which Ward was then coeditor. One of Frost's early supporters, Ward discusses a range of individual poets, reflecting on the condition of poetry in general and indicating the expected shape and content of poems that will appear in her journal. Ward expected poets to write "serious" poems that combined such qualities as "strength, thoughtfulness and grace." The former quality appears especially important, for she observes of Edith Thomas's work that it "exhibits that nobility, strength and grasp of thought that are usually called masculine." On the role of emotion in poetry, Ward appreciates work that conveys the poet's "spiritual and emotional" state, his or her "moods," at least as much as "intellectual discernment." Perhaps more than any other quality, Ward values genuineness or authenticity; though she does not use these terms, they provide a subtext for remarks like the following: "The composing of verse is more an art and less an inspiration than formerly. . . . [A poem's] structure is erected and completed after the latest and best approved rules of the profession." She concludes this section by criticizing those who write because of "an empty purse rather than an overflowing heart." Emotion, then, is actually central to the best poetry, but it cannot be planned and executed; it must be spontaneous. Ward's

---

11. Anonymous review of poetry collections, *New York Daily Tribune,* July 8, 1888, p. 10. Helen Gray Cone, "Woman in American Literature," *Century Magazine* 40.6 (1890): 922.

emphasis, as Frost would have acknowledged, was on the lyrical elements of poetry, not its investment in political, cultural, or economic power. In fact, Ward reveals a strong bias against writers who have to earn their living by writing, preferring those with the freedom and leisure to be at least open to true "inspiration"—an ironic attitude for Frost, given both his poverty at this time and Ward's affirmative mention of his work in her review. Ward assigns to "the poet" a position of economic privilege from which he can create lyrics uncontaminated by the constraints of everyday life.

Ward's remarks become even more interesting when we juxtapose them to the observations of Edmund Clarence Stedman, whose massive, influential *American Anthology* (1901) attracted Frost's attention. After constructing a version of American literary history, Stedman describes the current moment in terms that themselves seem sentimental: "a twilight interval, with minor voices and their tentative moods and tones; still, the dusk is not silent, and rest and shadow with music between the dawns are part of the liturgy of life, no less than passion and achievement." Depending on one's state of mind, this "twilight" could promise obscurity or provide opportunity to an aspiring poet. Stedman echoes Ward's criticism of contemporary poetry: "Poetry being a rhythmical expression of emotion and ideality, its practice as a kind of artistic finesse is rightly deprecated. . . . Our recent verse has been subjected to criticism as void of true passion, nice but fickle in expression, and having nothing compulsive to express."[12] Again intensity of emotion is acceptable only if it is not forced—that is, if it is not merely "sentimental." Like Ward, Stedman seems in fact to desire a return to the ideal of the romantic lyric praised by many of Larcom's critics. Most noteworthy in the criticism during the period with which we are concerned, 1867–1915, is not a turn from emotion but the judgment of emotion as occurring on a continuum from false ("feminine," sentimental) to authentic ("masculine," romantic).

Two other sections of the introduction to *An American Anthology* have particular relevance for Frost. The first is Stedman's rather defensive remarks about male poets: "The work of [women writers'] brother poets is not emasculate, and will not be while grace and tenderness fail to make men cowards, and beauty remains the flower of strength." Grace, tenderness, and beauty, he claims, do not render men effeminate but actually stronger; this expression will be "lyric" in form (rather than narrative or dramatic,

---

12. On Frost's reading of Stedman, see Reginald Cook, *Robert Frost: A Living Voice* (Amherst: University of Massachusetts Press, 1974), 157. Edmund Clarence Stedman, *An American Anthology 1787–1900* (1900; rpt. New York: Glenwood Press, 1968), xxviii, xxix.

for example). Calling on literary nationalism throughout this introduction, Stedman also insists that regional writing is "a secondary value in art," and he insists that "the method and spirit peculiar to a region make for an 'addition to literature,' but a work conveying them must have the universal cast to be enduring." Stedman's observations about poetry are carefully attuned to the tenor of the times; regionalism or "local color" was falling out of favor, and there was renewed attention to the idea of a national literature. Significantly for Frost, lyric was privileged as the dominant form of poetic expression, and, Stedman suggests, the nature lyric was particularly valued in contrast to the ostensibly "political" work of his sentimental precursors. Bennett describes the change from an earlier mode: "a movement in poetry toward greater concrete detail, more ambiguous and flexible stylistic expression, and toward a much wider—and more disturbing—range of themes and voices than high sentimentalism, with its commitment to religiously based domestic and cultural values, allowed."[13] In this process of transformation, writers became increasingly attentive to the situation of art *as art,* in part because *critics* urged them to do so and defined poetry's project in aesthetic rather than political and cultural terms. As these criteria for poetry at the turn of the century suggest, Frost wrote out of—in both senses—his historical and aesthetic moment. As we shall see, he asserted his place in a relyricized poetic tradition while he retained his connection with powerful earlier norms and values that continue to resonate—though perhaps ambivalently—for many readers today.

BOYS AT PLAY: THE WORK OF THE POET

Even if we assume the absence of personal connections with Larcom, an avid reader like Frost could not have been unaware of such a precursor, whose influence and reach were profound and whose works appeared in numerous influential nineteenth-century periodicals and can be readily found even today in many large used bookshops. Larcom wrote many poems worthy of contemporary consideration, including many on New England and its natural environment. Beyond the affiliation between Frost and Larcom as New England nature poets, however, is a more personal connection, for Larcom was the teacher of Frost's lifelong supporter (and

---

13. On the privilege of lyric, see Marjorie Perloff, *The Dance of the Intellect: Studies in the Poetry of the Pound Tradition* (Cambridge: Cambridge University Press, 1985), 178. Bennett, " 'The Descent of the Angel,' " 592.

publisher of what he saw as his "real" first poem) Susan Hayes Ward. According to Lesley Lee Francis, "Frost's lifelong friendship with . . . Ward was unusual in the depth of reciprocal caring." For Christmas 1911, Frost sent her a collection of seventeen pieces of his early work, confirming indirectly his debt to the work of his precursors in his admission two months later that "[I am] something of a sentimental sweet singer myself." The continuities between Larcom, Ward, and "Birches," the central concern of this essay, become even more direct when we recognize that Ward was the "source of inspiration for 'Wild Grapes'"; Frost acknowledged his debt to Ward in a letter to her nephew in December 1923: "I wish I had published the fact that it was written by request of Susan Hayes Ward as a companion piece of another poem of mine called Birches. She said Birches was for boys and she wanted me to do another like it on nearly the same subject for girls. For all we so seldom saw each other we were great friends. My wife and I cared for her more than I can tell you."[14]

Although many of Larcom's poems may have served as an (at least) unconscious influence for Frost, "Swinging on a Birch-Tree" stands out. The title obviously resonates for Frost's readers, because "Birches" was originally titled "Swinging Birches," but Larcom's poem itself will seem to many to have little connection with his evocative modernist meditation and to embody—at least on the surface, on a quick reading—precisely the term *sentimental*. Yet this poem, and its conjunction with Frost's, merits more careful investigation. "Swinging on a Birch-Tree" was published in *Our Young Folks* in 1867 and included in the "Household Edition" of Larcom's collected poems in 1884.[15] Some discussion of the context in which the poem was published will be important for understanding its ambitions and effects. *Our Young Folks* (subtitled *An Illustrated Magazine for Boys and Girls*) published a wide range of literature for children and (indirectly) their parents. The issue in which Larcom's poem appeared

14. For a discussion of Ward and Larcom's relationship, see Marchalonis, *Worlds*, 246–47, 262–63; Daniel Dulany Addison, *Lucy Larcom: Life, Letters, and Diary* (Boston: Houghton Mifflin, 1895), 53, 223–24, 238. On Frost and Ward's relationship, see Lesley Lee Francis, "Robert Frost and Susan Hayes Ward," *Massachusetts Review* 26 (1985): 341–50. **Letters**, 45. The last letter in this paragraph is quoted in Francis, "Robert Frost and Susan Hayes Ward," 349–50. See also Robert Frost, *Robert Frost at 100* (Boston: David R. Godine, 1974), 71.

15. Frost mentions the early title of his poem in a letter to John Bartlett of August 7, 1913. **Letters**, 89. Lucy Larcom, "Swinging on a Birch-Tree," *Our Young Folks* 3 (June 1867): 355–56; reprinted in *The Poetical Works of Lucy Larcom, Household Edition* (Boston: Houghton Mifflin, 1884), 140–41. The text below is from the first publication; the two versions differ only in punctuation.

contained such work as the humorous instructional story "A Batrachian Romance, with Zoölogical Overture," by "Vieux Moustache"; a fairy story about a stolen sister saved by her brother; Harriet Beecher Stowe's "What Pussy Willow Did," a religiously inflected story about internal and external beauty; an Orientalist adventure story on the lines of Melville's *Typee;* and a poem, "Flower Secrets for Fan." One of the most noteworthy contributions is another poem, "The Motherless Turkeys," which on the surface appears humorous but attacks a lazy mother of only one child unwilling to help others in need. The "Hen with one chicken" complains of her unending chores to the Duck with eight offspring and the Goose with nine: "'Half my care, I suppose, there is nobody knows,— / I'm the most overburdened of mothers!'" Her conclusion is that the four orphaned turkeys will have to "learn . . . how to scratch for themselves."[16] Such warnings to negligent mothers alternate with cautionary tales for their children. "Daddy's Man" offers an implied moral admonishing children not to wander from home; "Good Old Times" is an ethnocentric story about the impending French and Indian War in which the European-American mother worries about her children becoming savages. Other features of the magazine include the informative essay, "Archery and Archers"; a printed song, with music; and "Round the Evening Lamp, A Treasury of Charades, Puzzles, Problems," a regular feature to which subscribers contributed that encouraged family activities.

What insight can we gain from this context? First, we learn that the magazine is hardly dominated by what we would now call sentimental materials, even when the stories are "fairy tales." The essays and some stories are more or less realistic, while other works are comic (though, as in the case of "The Motherless Turkeys," with more ominous overtones about the social safety net for orphans, and women's domestic responsibilities).[17] Religion continues to occupy a central role in domestic life, and ethnocentrism is prominent; for example, we are told in "The Wonderful Beads: Or, King Fu-Ti and Nathaniel Nye" that Nye's goal is to "Christianize

16. Marian Douglass, "The Motherless Turkeys," *Our Young Folks* 3 (June 1867): 376–77.
17. I disagree with Nancy A. Walker's contention that humor and sentimentality are incommensurate. Nancy Walker, "Wit, Sentimentality, and the Image of Women in the Nineteenth Century," *American Studies* 22.2 (1981): 6; see Walker, *A Very Serious Thing: Women's Humor and American Culture* (Minneapolis: University of Minnesota Press, 1988) 27; Kilcup, "'Quite unclassifiable': Crossing Genres, Crossing Genders in Twain and Greene," in *New Directions in American Humor,* ed. David E. E. Sloane (Tuscaloosa: University of Alabama Press, 1998), 129–47; Gregg Camfield, *Necessary Madness: The Humor of Domesticity in Nineteenth-Century American Literature* (New York: Oxford University Press, 1997).

and civilize" the South Sea "savages" whom he meets. The story concludes: "Idleness and war were forsaken for industry and thrift, and before long the nation was metamorphosed."[18] As a whole, the issue performs a subtextual anxiety about national, domestic, and spiritual certainties; a desire for a return to a state of childlike innocence; and, paradoxically, a realism about the menace of contemporary culture.

To this bricolage "Swinging on a Birch-Tree" adds a relatively affirmative note. Removing Larcom's poem from its first published context virtually assures its reception today as a "sentimental" poem: putatively invested in the precious values of domesticity and too confident (in modernist and contemporary terms) of safety and contentment.[19] But recovering the context enables a more informed reading and a clearer appreciation of the poet's self-conception and her understanding of the poetic enterprise. To foster a sense of the poem's overall project requires that we see it as a whole:

> Swinging on a birch-tree
>   To a sleepy tune,
> Hummed by all the breezes
>   In the month of June!
> Little leaves a-flutter
>   Sound like dancing drops
> Of a brook on pebbles,—
>   Song that never stops.
>
> Up and down we seesaw:
>   Up into the sky;
> How it opens on us,
>   Like a wide blue eye!
> You and I are sailors
>   Rocking on a mast;
> And the world's our vessel:
>   Ho! She sails so fast!
>
> Blue, blue sea around us;
>   Not a ship in sight;
> They will hang out lanterns

18. William Wirt Sikes, "The Wonderful Beads: Or, King Fu-Ti and Nathaniel Nye," *Our Young Folks* 3 (June 1867): 347.

19. Another important feature of this first published context is the moody Winslow Homer etching facing the poem.

When they pass, to-night.
We with ours will follow
    Through the midnight deep;
Not a thought of danger,
    Though the crew's asleep.

O, how still the air is!
    There an oriole flew;
What a jolly whistle!
    He's a sailor, too.
Yonder is his hammock
    In the elm-top high:
One more ballad, messmate!
Sing it as you fly!

Up and down we seesaw:
    Down into the grass,
Scented fern, and rose-buds,
    All a woven mass.
That's the sort of carpet
    Fitted for our feet;
Tapestry nor velvet
    Is so rich and neat.

Swinging on a birch-tree!
    This is summer joy,
Fun for all vacation,—
    Don't you think so, boy?
Up and down to seesaw,
    Merry and at ease,
Careless as a brook is,
    Idle as the breeze.

The obvious differences of this poem from Frost's are too numerous to recount; for example, the ostensibly light and carefree, "merry and at ease" stance of Larcom's narrator diverges sharply from the contemplative and moody one of Frost's self-reflective speaker. While Larcom's speaker possesses a youthful voice, Frost's articulates an exhausted maturity; and while Larcom's represents a more participatory perspective, Frost's is more detached and formal. Nevertheless, acknowledging the construction of "Swinging on a Birch-Tree" as a children's poem printed first in a popular periodical, I invite contemporary readers to suspend for a moment their sense of the poem's limitations, to hold in abeyance their prejudices about tone and image, and to consider the several ways in which this poem anticipates Frost's.

The most immediate connection is the gender of the swinger; in line three of his poem, Frost's speaker muses of the birches, "I like to think some boy's been swinging them" (and later in the poem he returns to the imagination of the boy "too far from town to learn baseball, / Whose only play was what he found himself, / Summer or winter, and could play alone"), while Larcom's concluding stanza suggests a similar depiction.[20] Connecting "Birches" with a passage from Thoreau's *Journals,* George Monteiro notes of Frost's poem, "In some ways it is unfortunate that Frost stopped calling the poem by this title ["Swinging Birches"]. I say unfortunate because the activity at the heart of the poem—the activity that generates whatever cohesion the poem has—is the boy's swinging of birches and the poet's ruminations on the possibility that the birches he sees have been bent by boys at play." "Boys at play" is a central subject of both Larcom's and Frost's poems, not least, as I will discuss in a moment, in the "play" of the poets' imaginations. What is important to observe about Larcom's, however, is the poet's necessary transgendering to achieve this play. Larcom's poems about women, spoken from explicitly female perspectives, characteristically focus on work: "Weaving" and "A Little Old Girl" come to mind. Like Emily Dickinson, Larcom appropriates a masculine persona to achieve the freedom, both physical and creative, that "Swinging on a Birch-Tree" celebrates.[21]

If we emphasize this playful element it is possible to argue that both poems are on one level "about" the writing of poetry itself and that the lines of the birches figure the flexibility and tension of the poem's own lines. Larcom's self-conscious reference to the making of verse appears first in stanza one, where she suggests a mother's lullaby ("a sleepy tune" and "song

20. While some today might protest that girls would be unlikely to participate in such activities, gender roles were often suspended for children on farms, as "Wild Grapes" and numerous other stories in nineteenth-century American literature suggest. See, for example, Sarah Orne Jewett's "Woodchucks" (1878), in Kilcup, *Nineteenth-Century American Women Writers: An Anthology,* 379. See also Lesley Frost's recollections about swinging on birches in *New Hampshire's Child: The Derry Journals of Lesley Frost.* (Albany: State University of New York Press, 1969), 2, 5–6.

21. George Monteiro, *Robert Frost and the New England Renaissance* (Lexington: University Press of Kentucky, 1988), 104–5 and see 99–111. This strategy was one that Larcom's contemporaries used regularly. In addition to Emily Dickinson, see Harriet Beecher Stowe's *Oldtown Folks,* ed. Elizabeth Ammons (1869; rpt. New Brunswick: Rutgers University Press, 1987). On Larcom's desire for freedom, see Cheryl Walker, *Nightingale's Burden,* 73, 76; and Larcom, *A New England Girlhood,* 183, 124.

that never stops"), then reappears in stanza four, where she invokes the song of the boy (and herself as his coconspirator): "One more ballad, messmate! / Sing it as you fly!" Written in ballad stanza, the poem's structure parallels the poet's musical intentions at another level. The slower tempo of Frost's iambic pentameter implies a different, less physically active kind of music, as the speaker conjures the tinkling of the melting ice on the birch branches and its noisy fall to the ground in his broken, consonantal meditation:

> They click upon themselves
> As the breeze rises, and turn many-colored
> As the stir cracks and crazes their enamel.
> Soon the sun's warmth makes them shed crystal shells
> Shattering and avalanching on the snow-crust—
> Such heaps of broken glass to sweep away
> You'd think the inner dome of heaven had fallen. (117–18)

In different ways, both Larcom and Frost remain attentive to aesthetic concerns; Larcom's indirect cultural dissent is complemented by Frost's mourning of the loss of community and religious comfort ("You'd think the inner dome of heaven had fallen") of the sentimental era and the achievement of an isolating individualism. Just as Larcom's speaker imagines herself and her boy ("Up and down we seesaw"), Frost's insistence on "going and coming back" underscores as it delineates the poem's larger structural pattern. In its invocation of the lullaby, Larcom's poem intimates a ("sentimental") safety net that paradoxically enables the imaginative freedom from domestic ideology that it describes and enacts, in a pre-modern declaration of independence. While Frost's, on the other hand, appears much more amenable to (recalling Joanne Dobson) "modes of definition and evaluation developed exclusively within the framework of a critical valorization of romantic, individualistic, culturally dissenting, self-consciously artistic aspects of the classic masculine texts," it retains an element of nostalgia that suggests, if it does not perform, the consolations of the domestic (the "heaps of broken glass to sweep away"; "Like girls on hands and knees that throw their hair / Before them over their heads to dry in the sun").

Although the tone of the two poems differs, like Frost, Larcom imagines at the opening the "sleepy," buzzing state of a hot June day. It is this state of dreaminess and suspension, both literal and figurative, that seems most noteworthy. Like Frost, Larcom renders the experience entirely accessible; "Swinging on a Birch-Tree" seeks to evoke an imaginative journey and, like "Birches," works largely through association (and, we might argue, dissociation). In the first stanza, Larcom invokes "dancing drops / Of a brook on pebbles,—" an image that propels the narrator toward a fantasy of departure from the ordinary, both of time and place. At first she envisions the boy and the narrator as sailors for whom "the world's our vessel." Flying above the treetops, they acquire an "oriole" with "a jolly whistle" (everything seems musical in this poem) and a "hammock" in the elm tree above their heads. Upon landing, they encounter a natural carpet that suggests both release from domestic restraint imagined in the last stanza ("summer joy," "fun for all vacation") and safety.

Safety is something that Frost's narrator has been forced to relinquish; the boy who "subdued his father's trees . . . until . . . not one but hung limp, not one was left to conquer," faces a new challenge: "He learned all there was / To learn about not launching out too soon." Of course we can read these lines both as an erotic Oedipal drama and as further instructions on the composition of a poem, but they also resonate further in the context of Larcom's emphasis on play: the boy seeking adulthood "too soon" will fall short, and in his "adult" manifestation will find himself "weary of considerations," where

> life is too much like a pathless wood
> Where your face burns and tickles with the cobwebs
> Broken across it, and one eye is weeping
> From a twig's having lashed across it open.

This stunning image of vulnerability, absence, loss, and pain contrasts sharply with those of Larcom's poem; nevertheless, what Judith Oster notes so astutely of "Birches" is true for "Swinging on a Birch Tree" as well: "The dividing lines between identification with experience and figure enlarging it, between contemplative detachment and emotional nearness, are simply not there." As I have suggested is true for much of Frost's earlier writing, the feminine poetic subjectivity that frames "Birches" is freely dispersed and hospitably available to the reader.[22]

The cultural work in which Frost's poem engages becomes more visible if we contextualize it, like Larcom's, within the scene of its first publication. The *Atlantic Monthly* was a northeastern periodical published for an elite

22. **Oster,** 59. Kilcup, *Frost and Feminine Literary Tradition* (see especially chapters 1 and 2); Annie Finch, "The Sentimental Poetess in the World: Metaphor and Subjectivity in Lydia Sigourney's Nature Poetry," *Legacy* 5.2 (1988): 3–15.

audience of "highbrow" readers.[23] In spite of these editorial ambitions, the August 1915 issue reveals that if we delete the putative age difference between its audience and that of *Our Young Folks* from 1869, some of the *Atlantic*'s unwritten agenda appears to be remarkably similar to its predecessor's. The opening piece, "Hepaticas," is an intensely sentimental war story centered on the mother of an English soldier; it concerns the soldier's loss of innocence in his marriage to a dancer—presumably a woman of loose morals—whom he has gotten pregnant. The mother suppresses her desire to reject her new daughter-in-law and grandchild, instead inviting her son to bring them home, where they can be more readily assimilated into mainstream life. The son, of course, is killed in action, and the mother is on some level relieved, because his death enables her to reaffirm their familial connection over his bond with his wife and child. Not surprisingly, military matters dominate the content of the issue as a whole, including an essay, "Questions for Pacifists"; an autobiographical series of letters by an American woman in France, "The Coming of the English: Adventures in the Little House on the Marne"; "After Seeing Young Soldiers in London," a poem; a biographical portrait entitled "Von Hindenburg, General and Man"; and an essay on pacifism by Bertrand Russell entitled "War and Non-Resistance." Even the nonwar items are inflected with severe anxiety, like the essays on poverty in New York City ("The House on Henry Street VI") and on college women ("A New Profession for Women"), whom the (male) author urges to become booksellers. Located in virtually the center of the issue is Edward Garnett's famous essay on Frost, "A New American Poet," and "A Group of Poems" by the poet, including (in this order) "Birches," "The Road Not Taken," and "The Sound of Trees." Garnett provides a context within which readers will be able to appreciate the poet, emphasizing three elements of his work that distinguish it from others': originality, realism, and nationalism. Originality is the sine qua non, the alpha and omega with which the review implicitly begins and explicitly concludes. Garnett appears to discover this newness in Frost's amalgamation of prose and poetry, from which emerge a "quiet passion and spiritual tenderness." Denigrating work that is "orthodox in tone and form," he valorizes a psychological realism that he directly opposes to both romanticism and sentimentalism. Not surprisingly, the latter is intimately connected with market appeal; "sufficiently orthodox . . . [poetry] may

23. Lawrence Levine, *Highbrow/Lowbrow: The Emergence of Cultural Hierarchy in America* (Cambridge: Harvard University Press, 1988).

impress itself on that public which reads poetry as idly as it looks at pictures, with sentimental appetite or from a vague respect for 'culture.'" Deriding mass culture, Garnett privileges an elite audience of educated readers who—paradoxically—value novelty remarketed as originality.[24]

Not only is the elite reader removed from a contaminating affiliation with popular (and by extension, working-class) culture, but the poet himself is elevated by his emergence from English rather than American literature. Acknowledging that Frost has "a genuine New England voice," Garnett again affirms that "originality of tone and vision is always the stumbling-block to the common taste when the latter is invited to readjust its accepted standards." Although he claims that "I take it that just as Hawthorne owed a debt to English influence, so Mr. Frost owes one also," he highlights Frost's participation in "the best and oldest American tradition," in spite of his probable disjunction with "cosmopolitan clamor of New York." In Garnett's account, Frost appears not just as a New England poet, or an American poet, but an international poet who appeals "neither to the interests nor caprices of the market." Emerging in these literary and interpretive contexts, Frost's poems seem at once intensely anxious about modern life and virtually detached from its mundane and menacing concerns.

The secondary publication contexts of both Larcom's and Frost's poems offer us further understanding of how much the label "sentimental" is determined by contextual cues and interpretive (as well as historical) moment. In *Our Young Folks*, "Swinging on a Birch-Tree" is noteworthy in part for its distance from the religious consolation offered (unevenly) by other contributors, even though Spofford's review underscores Larcom's commitment to a Christian worldview in which the poet "seems to value nature only for its spiritual interpretations." Reading *The Poetical Works of Lucy Larcom*, one is struck by both the accuracy of Spofford's assertion and its inaccuracy. Many of the children's poems among which it appears value the consolations of nature at least as much as those of religion; moreover, a poem like "A Little Old Girl" dissents strongly from domestic cultural norms. The protagonist Prudence imitates her adult female counterparts, "knitting stockings, / Sweeping floors, and baking pies." Prudence's world is "a world that women work in . . . a world where men grow rich." A poignant counterpoint to the boy's freedom in "Swinging on a Birch-Tree,"

24. Edward Garnett, "A New American Poet," *Atlantic Monthly* (August 1915): 214–21. Huyssen points out that elite culture itself contained a strong element of consumerism (*After the Great Divide*, vii, 47).

"A Little Old Girl" not only critiques the patriarchal-capitalist status quo, but also offers a biting commentary on women's collusion with this state of affairs, for at the end of the poem, it is the "gossips" who smilingly approve Prudence's work: "'What a good wife she will make!'"[25]

Frost's "Birches" enjoys a similarly provocative context in *Mountain Interval*, his third book. Following poems that echo sentimental and domestic concerns, such as "In the Home Stretch," "The Telephone," and "Meeting and Passing," it is preceded by "Bond and Free" and followed by "Pea Brush," each of which elaborates in significant ways on "Birches" itself. "Bond and Free" proposes an opposition between "Love" and "Thought," which represent variations on "emotion" and "reason." In Western tradition these concepts are gendered female and male, respectively; here we see the imaginative priority of "Love" who, "by being thrall / And simply staying possesses all / In several beauty that Thought fares far / To find fused in another star" (116, 117). "Pea Brush" juxtaposes the wild ("many a trillium") and the domesticated ("garden things"), celebrating the liberation of those wild things, which occupy an intimate relationship to the erotic. In some sense, this set of three poems performs a movement from the affirmation of the rooted and domestic in "Bond and Free," to anxiety about release from the pleasures that it entails (and reaffirmation of a return to "earth" and "love") in "Birches," to a liberation of the wild from the domestic in "Pea Brush," where "someone" must remove the birch brush from "off the wild flowers' backs." Cut down, the birches are only "good for garden things / To curl a little finger round, / The same as you seize cat's-cradle strings": that is, for offering a strong, parental support around which little things can grow. In both "Bond and Free" and "Birches," we see masculinity not attenuated by but complementary to femininity and realism complementary to sentimentalism.[26]

Finally, when we compare "Birches" to Larcom's "Swinging on a Birch-Tree," what becomes apparent is Frost's continuing reference to the sentimental (in its comforting, ordinary, innocent, and playful aspects) and his simultaneous fracture from it. From one perspective, when we see them in the critical and literary contexts of their first publication, *both*

25. Spofford, "Lucy Larcom's Poems," 298. Larcom, *Poetical Works,* 154–55. For Larcom's attitude toward housework, see *New England Girlhood,* 192–93; Walker, *Nightingale's Burden,* 73, 78, 163 n. 10.

26. For a different view of "Birches" and the demasculinization of the phallic birch tree, see Katherine Kearns, *Robert Frost and a Poetics of Appetite* (New York: Cambridge University Press, 1994) 126. For views more closely aligned with my own, see George Monteiro, *Robert Frost and the New England Renaissance,* 106–10; **Oster,** 61–63.

Larcom's and Frost's poems appear to avoid engagement with the realities and urgencies of their historical moments—one modern criteria for "universal" and "lyric" poetry. Yet these same contexts provide us with another angle of vision, from which it is possible to discern that the sentimental is not necessarily sentimental (at least in the modern, derogatory sense) and that the modern is not unambiguously modern. In particular, Frost's poem becomes inflected with the "feminine," emotional resonances that often empowered the work of precursors like Larcom. This concept of poetry enables Frost to reject Amy Lowell's poems as too detached, too hard, too masculine, and, in some sense, too "modern." It enables him to write the great dramatic poems of female suffering and survival like "Home Burial" and "A Servant to Servants." And it enables him to affirm sentimentalism transformed as a discourse still available to him, as it was to his precursors, male and female. When independence and individuality are taken for granted, "connection, commitment, community" recur as terms of value, however inaccessible.[27] Both Frost and Larcom affirm the necessary freedom of art, where poetry becomes analogous to "boys at play," although ironically, such freedom seems even less possible for Frost than for Larcom.

Composed (or at least published) in the wake of the Civil War, Larcom's poem also represents a kind of willed happiness, or at least a desire that childhood might still be possible for another generation. Written in a time of impending war, Frost's poem bears differently the burden of its historical moment. However direct or indirect his awareness of "Swinging on a Birch-Tree" was, the retrospective, longing view of "Birches" represents Frost's postlapsarian response to his precursor, as he muses, "So was I once a swinger of birches, / And so I dream of going back to be." Wishing he could reclaim the innocence, energy, certainty, and even imagination of her boy, along with the love that the boy receives, both from the speaker of Larcom's poem and the mother whose presence she invokes ("Not a thought of danger, / Though the crew's asleep"), Frost reminds us, and finally himself, that "Earth's the right place for love," an observation at once sentimental and modern.

27. Robert Frost, "The Poetry of Amy Lowell," *Robert Frost: Collected Poems, Prose, and Plays,* 712. Joanne Dobson, "The American Renaissance Reenvisioned," 167.

Frost on the Doorstep and Lyricism at the Millennium

Katherine Kearns

"Nature within her it self divides
To trouble men with having to take sides.
"From Iron: Tools and Weapons"

"Science cannot be scientific about poetry, but
poetry can be poetical about science. It's bigger,
more inclusive. Get that right, you know."
Robert Frost

GENES, GENEALOGY, GENRE, GENDER, GENUS

ALMOST 1999. A room in the Whitney Humanities Center at Yale University, a gathering of people, mostly from the humanities and the social sciences but a few rare interdisciplinary spirits from the sciences, and a lunchtime talk by one of the Fellows. Today a real honest-to-god scientist, chair of ecology and evolutionary biology, will speak, his title, "The Meaning of Homology."[1] The group couldn't be more receptive. It would be hard to imagine a gathering of people more learned, but these meetings are also marked by a certain pleasurable childish excitement when a new dessert or some other unexpected addition—soup, for example— appears to leaven the regular fare, secret relief when the speaker has brought slides or a tape player, open anticipation when there is a VCR or some slightly fancier piece of technology to keep language in its place. The

---

1. The speaker was Professor Guenter Wagner, who is completely absolved of all my poetic licenses and worse but whose talk was too provocatively interesting to leave entirely to the scientists.

Fellows expect their equipment and their talks to be neither too archaic nor too radically individualistic, and one violates those reasonably generous parameters at one's peril. The millennium may be at hand, but Yale, at least, will not be untoward.

Today everyone is a little confused, because there is an overhead projector in the room to go with the scientist who will speak. A piece of equipment whose place in the evolutionary chain is obscure, the overhead projector squats in the corner, head down, waiting to be hoisted up when the talk starts. Taxonomically, where does this familiar, always already outclassed mechanism fit, with its innocent, boxy glare? Except for the lone molecular biologist in the group, every one of us is prepared out of necessity to emblematize this talk, since conceptual homologies are our only avenue into and out of the pure science that underwrites the subject at hand. Our scientist is about to speak, presumably about something evolutionary, and already we are off balance because of this platypus of a machine that will mediate between his much more thorough way of knowing and our relative innocence.

(Robert Frost: if it walks like a duck and quacks like a duck, then it is most likely a duck. Except, of course, when there's a platypus in the mix. Robert Frost, whose poetry always announces itself as taxonomically straightforward even though it never actually is, whose nicely crafted and shaped formalisms intercede for us as we, in our relative innocence, prepare to make our way through the intricate ironies of his way of knowing. His is poetry that seems to occupy some ontologically distinct place between the phylogenous transmission of encoded inevitabilities and the morphologically distinct manifestations of generic types. "We dance around in a ring and suppose / But the secret sits in the middle and knows.")

The scientist's talk is revolutionary; it makes "postmodernism" look positively tame because it dismantles the bipolar legitimacy of particularisms and metaphysics all at once. Take birds' feet, for example. Already—and this is said by him only in passing as a given—we've got the wonderful incongruity that proves birds the closest living link to dinosaurs; then add to that the fact that alligators' and birds' feet have more in common, phylogenetically speaking, than any other pairing one could make.

(Robert Frost—one wonders if somehow he sensed that all the little birds, lyric mascots, rose from the Tyrannosaurus Rex and the Archeoptyrix and walked on alligator feet. Certainly now the Oven Bird can finally lumber up into the air unashamed. At any rate, this familial dinosaur-bird-alligator group puts a new twist on the blithe Spirit that sings with clear, keen joyance, and on all those other fleet-winged singers that metaphorize poetic inspiration. Connect birds to dinosaurs and then talk about the poet's anxiety of influence: think *Jurassic Park* and the moment when that glass of water starts to quiver. For once, then, the something that disturbs the reflective surface is about to make itself manifest, its birdlike footprint the least of one's worries in a situation where one stands to be flattened or ripped to shreds.)

Homology: "a fundamental similarity due to community of descent," the idea that there is some inalienable connectedness that can make developmental sense of both point A and point C even when point C neither looks like nor functions the same as point A. But what the speaker tells us, basically, is this: everything scientists think they've known about the developmental continuum—about "community," about "sameness"—is underinflected, and homology's most typical ontological categories are insufficient. He says that some of what have always been seen as mere epiphenomena along the developmental way are—must be—actual states of being (as a conceptual possibility, this wouldn't surprise, say, most feminists, who know firsthand what it means to be perpetually mistaken for an epiphenomenon of the ontologically stable category "man," bone of my bone, flesh of my flesh. Nor would it surprise many lyric poets, Frost in particular, since writing lyrically more than proves that the forms lyricism takes are limited relative to the moments of being that bring them about: between "A," the poetic impulse and "C," the formal product of that impulse as a sonnet, or blank verse, or terza rima, or hendecasyllables, and so on, there are any number of different "Be's"). Our scientist tells us that the ontological status that homology accords only to genes, to cells, and to what has been seen as their final morphological products is based on a wishful assumption of straight-line cause and effect and is insufficient as an explanatory tool. This homological rage for pure lines of descent, this ontological elitism fails to recognize the possibility of some intact other thing that enters the process, not as epiphenomenon but as a distinct ontological category.

(Robert Frost: The figure a poem makes is the same as for love, but of its lineage, a thing most contestable on the one hand and most imperatively important on the other, one can never be certain. Paternal doubt as a theme riddles the poetry and becomes the parable by which one comes to suspect, with Frost, that his lyricism is born discontinuously, not from one stable self but from many. No wonder he claims to have written only two poems without speakers, that his poetry is so thoroughly peopled, that so many strangers wander through: each poem is a rebound off a new ontological middleman. No wonder there are so many childless women in Frost's poetry; with this infinitely promiscuous crew of masculine selves there's no telling how their progeny might end up. And no wonder his women are born of maples, pulled as dry pith out of trees; no wonder they are hill wives and witches and maenads: for Frost "woman" constitutes the essence of the epiphenomenal, which surely must be defined in part as a manifestation that can arise out of not one source, from which it may claim itself as a stable endpoint, but from any number of very different sources back into which it may subside. For Frost, masculinity must commit itself to its placedness in history, to a genealogically, homologically, and Oedipally stable relationship to the past. And in this logic (and it is precisely and importantly that) it must by extension commit itself to a formal (bodily) integrity, one so impermeable that it can impose its symmetries on an "outside" that its own willful shapeliness necessitates and demands. It is no surprise, then, that femaleness rises endlessly in his poetry, like vapor, like mist in a vale, or, more ominously, with the chthonic heaviness of witches and hill wives. No wonder, then, that he says in *A Masque of Reason* that "It comes down to a doubt about the wisdom / Of having children—after having had them, / So there is nothing we can do about it / But warn the children they perhaps should have none" (291–94). Lyric birth, within Frost's Ovidian world of metamorphoses, reflects his sense of "being" as polytropic, the product of an infinite succession of couplings and thus always inclined toward catachresis.)

So developmentally, there are ontological categories that trip up the morphologist on the one hand and the geneticist and the molecular biologist on the other. The bird's foot proves it, and the alligator's, too. Somehow the bird's foot comes to be an efficient predatory appendage, one thumblike, opposable digit and another two fingers for snatching, for holding on. If it developed according to expectation, it would be all thumbs (or more precisely, no thumbs), because, morphologically speaking, usually the last things to pop out are the first to go. Fingers always bud out starting with digit two, then three, then four, and only after that come the crucial, opposable one and the dainty five. But somehow the bird ends up with digits one, two, and three, talons that grab. It is as if some new player has come into the game, one substantial enough to wrest development out of its inertial tendency toward first-come, first-serve.

(Robert Frost and the visceral genius of "Mending Wall," homology's nightmare: one begins over time to apprehend this poem more and more intimately. In growing old with it, making it one's own, it seems to get under the skin and into the bones. The poem sitting on the page becomes the objective correlative of some internal process of making and undoing and mending and coming undone; and this respiration comes to feel both physical and existential. The wall, like Frost's houses, gradually becomes more than merely a wall and more than merely a metaphor. Laid across a physical landscape already dense with metamorphic bodies, it seems sinewy, muscular. The wall holds things together by keeping things apart—and of course the formal and the prosodic structure seeks to include the poem itself in this willed order. But it is itself vulnerable to random force and must suffer interventions by whatever comes along—dogs, hunters, frost, gravity, and, standing in for a world of ontological possibilities that cannot be named, "Elves," but not elves exactly. This poem is encrypted with evidence of itself as lyric poem, one that rides on the "frozen ground-swell" of Frost's invention: the stones may be the same stones, it seems to say, and the hands that build the wall back up may be the same hands, but the wall never becomes the same wall it was before, even if it looks precisely the same as before. This mending-wall poem tells Frost's lyric secret: that the "same" formal manifestations of his lyricism are produced, not from a stable self but from a series of strangers, alienated forms who perpetually contest the fiction of an intact, single human soul and who also dispute the fiction of his masculinity.)

"If a lion could talk, we could not understand him."[2] All of us in the room, products of a liberal arts education, believe that this "sameness" of origin will have left its traces on each of us, no matter what our disciplines. Here we are in this room, listening, having coffee, educated people operating on the assumption that we are hearing and talking about the same thing, more or less. The overhead projector sits on the table throwing simple images onto the back of the cave, while we imagine ourselves making some secondhand, metaphorical sense of this hard science. Homology says that looks and functions don't matter but only the community of descent; no comfort there for the existentially paranoid, since the converse would say (and the scientist did say) that similar looks and functions are absolutely no guarantee of pure descent. And what if what the scientist says is true? What if the pathways from phylogenetic beginning to morphological end may be infinitely diverse, with always (unless you are a newt or a salamander) another hidden, unnamed, potentially capricious agency set to deflect straight-line assumptions? This is an existential crap-shoot, in fact, all of us looking more or less homologous but having arrived there by radically different paths.

2. Ludwig Wittgenstein, *Philosophical Investigations*, trans. G. E. M. Anscombe (New York: MacMillan, 1958), 223.

(Robert Frost: yet another meaning to squeeze from "The Road Not Taken." "Two roads diverged in a yellow wood, / And sorry, I could not travel both / And be one traveler. . . ." I have never liked this poem much, but, as with "Mending Wall," which I do like, I can't stay away. I seem to be caught in some pattern of infinite regress and return; it is as if Frost managed, remarkably, to create a poem that endlessly enforces one's own relentless intuition of sameness and difference, that feeling of being utterly mundane and prosaic and utterly alien at the same time, of looking and sounding and acting like every other regular Joe, of suffering from a conviction of indistinguishability, while in the same instance suffering an isolation beyond which it is impossible to go. And this could be said to be the dilemma of the lyric poet as well. Frost never explicitly sings the modernist lament that brings this alienation from self and from language to light; we need, for example, Eliot, to solemnize the bipolarities whose middle ground is a dark chasm: "Between the idea / And the reality / Between the motion / And the act / Falls the shadow. . . . / Between the conception / And the creation / Between the emotion / And the response / Falls the shadow." Instead, all the roads in Frost's poetry seem to lead back to "The Road Not Taken" sooner or later, back to the same homely enigma packed in the same seemingly banal package. The speaker—he could be standing here talking to us—tells a story about two nearly identical roads, both grassy and covered in fallen leaves. Only a Martian wouldn't know by now that he "took the one less traveled by" and that " . . . that has made all the difference." But think about the lethal irony of the last stanza—"I shall be telling this with a sigh / Somewhere ages and ages hence, . . ."— consisting of a prediction whose truth is prefigured in the present by the poem itself: he already *knows* where he will end up, and "all the difference" can have made no difference. Will he be lying, do you think, in the retelling down the road? In this Oedipal world the answer is, of course, yes and no.)

What if neither end predicts the other? What if there really is no metaphysics sufficient to the task of explanation, no first causes and no sustained unilateral causality? Taken at the level of the minute, there would be no necessary progression outward from genetic inevitability. Homology is predicated on the idea that some fundamental thing can give rise to manifestations of itself that are "same," not by virtue of form or function but by virtue of the connectedness itself. One could say that homology plagues itself with the question of being, or that caught in some generative myth it seeks to claim, always retroactively, that there are no bastard children in the lot, no inconvenient and embarrassing intrusion, at some secret moment, by an unknown third party. It is willing to accept all sorts of conditions to keep this fiction intact—monstrosity, biformity, you name it. "Homology" sets itself up, in fact, precisely to be disputed at the ontological level, with the presumption of "same" carrying with it a conviction of genealogical inevitability. Legitimation is reciprocal but always fraught with the necessity for arguable difference, without which "same" is simply uninteresting. Neither state of being is complete without the other. One could say, then, that the conception "homology" is quintessentially Oedipal; homology erects itself as an embattled authority that, by virtue of its announcing its name, can never go down to defeat. It is this, perhaps, that makes the scientist's millennial story of "The Meaning of Homology" so familiar and so compelling. Made to be challengeable from within, the only force that could ever supersede it would have to come from outside, but there is no outside since the invocation, "homology," includes the property of infinite assimilation. (The overhead projector remains on the table, light out, after the talk is finished.)

HISTORY, HOMOLOGY, LYRICISM

Based on an assumption of demonstrable cause and effect and on a preference for reciprocal legitimation, homology and history entail each other, but lyricism, a concept in resistance to assimilations, may be felt as doing without the comfort and the burden of either.[3] "Lyricism" presumes Being—a core self from which genuineness may rise and declare itself— and, if in so presuming it also suggests that the lyric poem, the artifact of this genuineness, will always stand in a symptotic relationship to the ideal, this only more certainly reinforces the fantasy of an unmediated, noncontingent self. This is not to say, of course, that lyricism is itself outside

---

3. Given the next-to-impossible task of claiming a sufficient and sufficiently nuanced definition of what constitutes lyric poetry, and the impossible task of doing the same for "lyricism," and given the fact that any working definition of these terms is forced to beg any number of questions, I am simply claiming a representative, contemporary "we" for whom lyricism presupposes thoughts about genuineness and the idea of "self." For a thoughtful synopsis of what "lyric" has been taken to mean and to represent, see Alex Preminger and T. V. F. Brogan, eds. *Princeton Encyclopedia of Poetry and Poetics* (Princeton: Princeton University Press, 1995). We are reminded there of the canonical definitions that inform even postmodernist rewritings of the modern idea of the lyric: that the poem be brief (Poe), that it "be one, the parts of which mutually support and explain each other . . ." (Coleridge), that it be "the spontaneous overflow of powerful feelings" (Wordsworth), that it be an intensely subjective and personal expression (Hegel), that it be an "inverted action of mind upon will" (Schopenhauer), that it be "the utterance that is overheard" (Mill).

of history, or that the lyric self is not always overdetermined by history. But it is to make the fairly extravagant claim that the concept "lyricism" may be a placeholder for some shared but purely anticommunitarian, ahistorical impulse and that a lyric poem may actually rise like a spark, its tie to history as ephemeral as a flake of fire. Nor is it to suggest that the lyric poet escapes from the anxiety of influence that any writer possessed of something other than a purely private language (and thus a language that no one else could understand) must suffer. There will always be an implied homology, in part because its audience predicates its intellectual understanding of the poem on homology and will find it, or something like it, out. No matter how strange or new it looks, no matter how radically different its functions, the poem will share in some "fundamental similarity due to community of descent." Yet even so, this homologous extension may be discovered as a merely retroactive fact, after the poem has had its flight. The receiver, in other words, may for a brief moment be thrown beyond her own ponderous, always distracted self, beyond history and beyond the lyric poet's history, to some Hyperborean place behind the north wind.

One also comes to feel in reading poetry—and Frost's poetry most particularly—that this apotheosis will be forever denied to the poet who creates the poem and is, at best, available only to the others who hear it. ("The conviction closes in on me that I was cast for gloom as the sparks fly upward . . . ," said Frost, "I am of deep shadow.")[4] If the poem can temporarily escape its history, the poet cannot. It is as if the very act of attempting to verify a self in language—to write lyric poetry—is born of negational energy:[5] "I am x" seems to arise as the necessary but always partial antidote to "I am not x" (or perhaps it is, rather, that "I am" arises as the always partial antidote to "I am not"). Perhaps it is this apprehension of his own necessary habit of negation that overtakes the good Yankee realist of "West-Running Brook" as he sets his wife straight through an appeal to history and reason: "That wave's been standing off this jut of shore / Ever since rivers . . . / Were made in heaven. It wasn't waved to us." A figure for Frost if there ever was one, the speaker uses poetic language—

---

4. **Triumph,** 114.

5. Sigmund Freud, "Negation," in *The Standard Edition of the Complete Psychological Works of Sigmund Freud,* trans. James Strachey (London: Hogarth Press, 1961), 235–39. "The content of a repressed image or idea can make its way into consciousness, on condition that it is *negated.* Negation is a way of taking cognizance of what is repressed. . . . With the help of symbol of negation, thinking frees itself from the restriction of repression and enriches itself with material that is indispensable for its proper functioning" (235–36).

white water like a bird's feathers—and jocular allusion—woman like an Amazon off to lady-land—to correct his wife's fancies even as he falls into his own, much darker reverie. The parenthetical darkness of lines nineteen through twenty-six could be an allegory for the poet's impossible task of lyric affirmation, for if the white water rides the black forever, "Not gaining but losing," the lyric bird fights against something inside its own heart that wants it down: this white water over black is "like a bird / White feathers from the struggle of whose breast / Flecked the dark stream and flecked the darker pool / Below the point, and were at last driven wrinkled / In a white scarf against the far-shore alders." And, as if the parentheses have burst, the swell of lines thirty-eight through seventy-two marks a dark epiphany that sees everything that holds a self in time and space, in history, spilling away.

"West-Running Brook," which wrests itself in the end back to cheerful domesticity and communal language ("Today will be the day of what we both said."), seems to me to speak and to perform its lyric anxiety with painful candor. For to speak oneself, not in parentheses, not with jocularity, not conversationally, not in masculine-speak, to forget for a moment the dogma of the measured sentence sounds that forbid hysteria—to speak oneself in lyric poetry, and as lyric poet is, for any man of moderation and communal goodwill, likely to be felt at some level as a punishable offense. It would mean that all barriers are down, all safety protocols off-line (I think this fantasy is at the heart of the ominously beautiful "Spring Pools" or in "The Draft Horse"), and we know from reading Frost just how seductive and destructive this fantasy can be made to seem. Poetry wants to play in this wild space, Frost says, but he manfully erects an iconographic system that mostly keeps it on the margins. When the man's voice of "West-Running Brook" bursts from its parentheses, he is driven to negate that escape in a safe melancholia that says of self, "It seriously, sadly runs away / To fill the abyss's void with emptiness." Given voice, lyricism can only dream of riding the darkness, not gaining but not losing, for to think otherwise is too dangerous.

Even as reparation to the fantasy of a noncontigent, ahistorical, seamless self is made by the lyric poem, it is undone by the lyric poem, whose already tremulous "I" must be written into a language and a form burdened with past lives, one's own and others'. "I am of deep shadow all compact like onion within onion and the savor of me is oil of tears," Frost says to Untermeyer, using an image that betrays his sense that, when you get right down to it, layers stripped away, there is nothing there but the dubious effect—onion tears aren't real tears—the lyric poem has on those who read it.[6] Frost's dark perception is right on the money: The lyric poet *must* imagine that he will be found out as a fraud or that his effect will always be cheap thrills or felt sentimentally through some misplaced identification with the so-called genuine self of the poem. His "I am," or "I promise," or "I see," predicated on a dangerous "I" that one can't (or shouldn't) get to from here, is compromised before the fact. The party who *is* present knows a mark when he sees one. And an audience that can be led like sheep will suffer their fate: "I'll dress up in sheep's clothing," says Meliboeus/Frost in "Build Soil," "and eat sheep."

This perpetually delayed consummation with the core self must be one reason why poets write poems—sometimes the same ones, sometimes new ones—over and over again, why Frost, though he may have felt that he was writing the same poem for the rest of his life after about 1906, nonetheless kept on writing and writing for another fifty-some years ("It is a very damaging secret . . . ," he says in 1916, "The poet in me died nearly ten years ago. Fortunately, he had run through several phases, four to be exact, all well defined, before he went. The calf I was in the nineties I merely take to market. I am become my own salesman").[7] This sense of himself as a kind of pimp or mountebank may be why he kept on piling lyric on lyric, keeping the poetry in eternal play, with always-new personae to speak the lines. "Seek not in me the big I capital," he warns, "Nor yet the little dotted in me seek. / If I have in me any at all, / 'Tis the iota subscript of the Greek" ("Iota Subscript"). Lyric poetry comes to seem an almost compulsive effort to pluck a self out of a river of time spending to nothingness and then to display that self, impossibly enough, as both uniquely individualistic and (by the terms of the Oedipal rules) as an homologous extension of the past. Not surprisingly, these irreconcilable imperatives ensure that lyric poetry must suffer itself gladly as, at best, nine parts genuine and one part fraud.

The lyric anxiety that results disports itself variably within the permeable layers of a poem, but it is a chronic presence that has, ironically, manifested itself over time in a series of conventions that hardly need elaborating. We see it in all of lyricism's many gestures of self-reflexiveness—in, for example, the poem's cry that language will not come or is insufficient to the task of capturing this ineffable self, and in the obligatory image of a bird whose flights must always end in a return to the ground dense with history and history's sticky, inescapable connectedness to self. These conventions have instated themselves as the codes through which lyricism

6. **Untermeyer,** 59.
7. Ibid, 29.

claims itself even as it bemoans its inevitable lapses back into history; they are, in other words, epiphenomena of a process whose end is contained in its beginning (down that road again). One could even say that poets have embraced these traditional motifs as a way to claim kinship while also, on the face of it, repudiating the notion that the lyric self is genealogically stable, reproducible, predictable before the fact. The Oedipal paradox, the one that says that a man must both kill and revere his father whose history he will rewrite in bolder terms through himself, is most piquant here: the very poetic gestures that mourn the inexpressible self also bring the poem and the poet into line with history and god. It is the lyric poet heeding his own warning—"Beware of coming too much to the surface / And using for apparel what was meant / To be the Curtain of the inmost soul" ("The Fear of God")—by instantiating history and homology at the heart of the poem itself. In other words, only a madman or perhaps a woman could strip the curtain off the inmost soul and use it for raiment, a tissue still carrying the scent of the mystery it once covered: it is against the rules to surrender so completely because the absolute core is intuited to be utterly anarchic, a place of complete and total individuation. And in love, in poetry, in politics, in religion—indeed, in *any* system of order—complete individuation is a sublime danger. These conventions necessarily mark "A fundamental similarity due to community of descent," with "descent" the shared fall into history, and thus with a "difference" made comprehensible by virtue of the sameness that is its medium. But if the poet's habits of self-reflexiveness are conventional, they are nonetheless poignant reminders that he apprehends (and this is an apprehension that his vocation enforces) that only madness or immense courage can take one beyond an alienated sameness to full lyric freedom.

Frost's poetry, relentlessly ironic, typically holds itself back from all but understated forms of lyric self-reflexiveness, because, of course, all such mirroring of lyricism's fear of aphasia or, as bad, of glossolalia must also be a mirroring of the poet himself (an apprehension that, I think, pervades "For Once, Then, Something"). Frost resolutely refuses to make his poetry "worlds-end-whimper" stuff, which is to say "modernist," inasmuch as he saw in his contemporaries a lyricism not only haunted by but directly and self-indulgently reflective upon the missing middle between being and Being.[8] Indeed, he celebrates the crudity and rawness of unformed language as an erotic challenge to which he is equal. "A real artist delights in roughness for what he can do to it," he said to Robert Coffin in 1937.

8. **Later Years,** 89.

"He's the brute who can knock the corners off the marble block and drag the unbedded beauty out of bed. . . . The poet's material is words that for all we may say and feel against them are more manageable than men. Get a few words alone in a study and with plenty of time on your hands you can make them say any thing you please."[9] One could, of course, say that Frost's extremism in this passage (the poet as rapist/seducer) protests too much. In any event, because of his reluctance to feminize the poet's relationship to language, Frost more often than not gives it to speakers who absorb it into their situations (as in "Home Burial") or transforms it into fairy tale (as in "Paul's Wife").

"The Subverted Flower" is interesting in this regard, as it clearly shows how overweening passion chokes off the speech that might otherwise be so lyrically pure as to be irresistible (the seduction poem is a pale shadow of this phantasmatic potency). The poem might almost be one of Ovid's stories of metamorphoses by the sound of it, with language breaking down as humans are turned to beasts (like Ovid's, Frost's agenda is complex, his focus on the loss of language layered with meanings, and his own poetic mastery of the mother tongue a simultaneous recovery of the masculinity forfeited within the poem); that the poem is situational is well documented. The man, possessed by desire, speaks, "Though with every word he spoke / His lips were sucked and blown / And the effort made him choke / Like a tiger at a bone." The woman, possessed by anger, speaks, though "The bitter words she spit / [were] Like some tenacious bit / That will not leave the tongue." As with Ovid, overwhelming emotion (lust, pride, fear) pushes human form toward the bestial, a transformation always marked in Ovid by the disappearance of a speaking voice that can be understood as once-human utterances come forth in animal sounds. And perhaps unlike Ovid, whose subtext may well have been more political than aesthetic, Frost also makes an oblique comment on the paradox of lyricism: that when emotion is at its purest, language fails; only when emotion can be recollected in tranquility—which is to say when it no longer metonymizes a transcendently concentrated self and so can again perform in the service of moderation—can it be spoken.[10] He performs this truth in "Beyond Words," which sputters off into silence: "That row of icicles along the

---

9. Edward Connery Lathem and Lawrance Thompson, eds., *Robert Frost: Poetry and Prose* (New York: Henry Holt, 1972), 359.

10. "Emotion must be dammed back and harnessed by discipline to the wit mill. . . . Emotion has been known to ooze off," Frost writes (**Untermeyer**, 29). This is yet another Frostian image of dissolution, with emotion "oozing off" instead of inseminating the poem.

gutter / Feels like my armory of hate; / And you, . . . you, you utter. . . . / You wait!"

His poetry, in abjuring grand statements about the chronic failure of language to capture the ineffable self, rides on undercurrents of anxiety that his sentence sounds cannot quite smooth over; there are too many ways in his poetry that nature/human nature may swallow up voices and destroy even the tincture of language one gets from listening behind a closed door. The deep snow, with its eerie muffling of sound, sometimes seems to blanket the poetry with "a blanker whiteness of benighted snow / With no expression, nothing to express" ("Desert Places"). And this silencing snow, in Frost's agrarian fantasies of cultivated wildness, is itself sterile: "A plow, they say, to plow the snow, /" the speaker says in "Plowmen," "They cannot mean to plant it, no— / Unless in bitterness to mock / At having cultivated rock." Frost, in a 1917 letter to Untermeyer, describes a strangely disassociative, almost psychotic relationship to sound that rewrites the poet as Aeolian harp: "I have heard laughter by daylight when I thought it was my own because at that moment when it broke I had parted my lips to take food. Just so I have been afraid of myself and caught at my throat when I thought I was making some terrible din of a mill whistle that happened to come on the same instant with the opening of my mouth to yawn. I have neighed at night in the woods behind a house like vampires. But there are no vampires, there are no ghouls, there [are] no demons, there is nothing but me."[11] "I have been afraid of myself," and thus this phantasmatically Ovidian vision of pouring out as inhuman sounds what once has been masked as speech. These nightmare images are a far cry from "The Aim Was Song," where man comes along to blow the whistling, rough wind right. Here is the poet as revenant, as ventriloquist's dummy, the poet who fears that his open mouth will spill out laughter and screams, the poet as everything (his open mouth the mouth of the world), and the poet as nothing (his open mouth empty of all volitional sound, and some silent scream manifested only by an external correlative beyond his control).

Lyricism most famously allegorizes its anxious self in the endlessly reiterated images of always foreshortened flight, with flying things—most usually birds—burdened with the gravity of selves felt as historical beings caught in a downdraft. In keeping with his habit of disguising or ironizing the lyric conventions, Frost creates the oven bird as the most memorable of his own aviary; it is as if he means to say (and, given his love of wordplay, probably did mean to say) that this poetic bird is in the oven, the goose

11. **Untermeyer,** 59.

is cooked. He laughs at a friend for, in effect, refusing to go behind his father's sayings: "His father objected to the word crow in a poem. The bird had to be a raven to be poetical. Then to my surprise he defended his father: whose reason he claimed was a good reason namely that poetry had to show loftiness."[12] While Frost clearly accepts the bird as a metonymy for lyric poetry, he also, quite clearly, chooses to go the Heckle and Jeckle way with the trope. He has timid birds ("Come In"), mynah birds ("A Minor Bird"), birds like cattle in the mud ("Our Singing Strength"), birds who weep ("The Need of Being Versed in Country Things"). He even offers birdy creatures who are not birds but who, by virtue of the tunes they sing are clearly closely akin—not a woodcock but a Drumlin woodchuck much concerned about the security of his barrow, for example. But if each one of these thumbs its nose at lyricism's tacit demand for the real article, the genuine, soaring, authentic self that rides the turbulence of all the history below, each one also confesses to the poet's sense of a flawed and always partial and always compromised (poetic) self that loses altitude by the hour. "The growth of a poet is through flashes," he says. "Sight and insight makes poetry, and that belongs to the beginning poet. . . . I suppose poets die into philosophy as they grow older—if they don't die the other way. They die into wisdom. Maybe it is a good way to die."[13] In Frost's oven-bird world, it is out of the frying pan into the fire; poets die out like struck matches: "So at a knock /" the poet-bird says, "I emptied my cage / To hide in the world / And alter with age" ("The Lockless Door").

It would seem that to announce itself to a community of its brethren as lyricism, the lyric poem has to give off a whiff of "Self" in crisis (and to rely on a not-so-implicit humanism). It is this utterly communicable, pheremonic cue that allows the lyric transaction to occur: within the circular logic of an essentially unverifiable claim for the transmission of genuineness, "lyricism" functions as an idea, but our recognition of genuineness is predicated on the paradox of its necessary component of fraud. To revise Frost's lines in "Build Soil," "There's no such thing as [lyricism] / Except as an abstraction of the mind." Frost's intuition of himself as already emptied, his genuinely odd combination of self-acknowledged showman-/salesmanship, formalist precision, and near-hallucinatory extensiveness into the natural world, his repeated efforts to write himself away (all those speakers, all that irony), his resolute refusal to yield to what sometimes seems his grave anxiety: these suggest an almost

12. *Poetry and Prose*, 315.
13. *Poetry and Prose*, 374.

obsessive awareness of the eternally threatened lyric self. In his poetry, objective correlatives for that self are either sucked down, suckèd dry, and collapsing into flaccidity or inflated, blown up too tight, too near the bursting rapture of appetitive release. Self, spilling beyond even its projection into women, floods into its surroundings—into houses and hillsides and animals and trees—making the whole world a contiguous extension of the body. "I'm in favor of a skin and fences and tariff walls," Frost says, "I'm in favor of reserves and withholding," yet in this body-world what doesn't surge into a tidal wave or an atomic explosion ("The Flood," "Bursting Rapture") sinks instead into the grave (houses collapsing in on themselves, cellar-holes filling themselves in).[14] This "pastoral" poet, this avuncular, crusty figure, this New England sage, creates a lyricism whose dread of itself seeps into the bones.

Perhaps love poetry has become lyricism's most predictable and suffi-cient metonymy because love poetry takes the heat off the self by bringing in another part and diminishes the fantasized risk of lyricism's releasing some potently autonomous, anarchic energy. Love, after all, epitomizes the condition of failed promises, of always imminent detachment from the self who loves and of always imminent return to an alternative and very different self that can only see the other (the once-loved other and the once-loving other) as mistaken, alien, dispossessed. "Love" is, after all, encoded with the first fall and its schismatic separation from one into two ("Therefore a man leaves his father and his mother and cleaves to his wife, and they become one flesh," *Genesis* 2.24), a reversion to incompleteness that can be, at best, only patched into the momentary wholeness of carnal acts, themselves defined, at best, in dualisms. Being "in love," the essence of vulnerable empowerment and the epitome of that condition where one feels the most and the least like a single, authentic self, seems the necessary and sufficient condition by which lyricism speaks itself as fragmented selves. And the language of love—what could be more performative than "I love you," what more impeachable promise than "I will always love you"?: what better state to sum up the intuition that, speaking in any way the world knows how to speak, there can be no inalienable "Self" from which lyricism flows? Frost's equation—the poem, the same as for love, its beginning, "a lump in the throat, a sense of wrong, a homesickness, a lovesickness"—is sheer genius, and that he understood and meant what he said is proven in the poetry itself.[15] Here, then, is the paradox (which would seem cruel if

14. **Letters,** 387.
15. **Untermeyer,** 22.

it weren't a burden equally shared) of lyricism: the one who confesses will always know his language as the product of a compromised self; only the one who reads, and who would suffer the same knowledge at the moment of confession, can afford to take the lyric poem as transcendent.

This intuition of a failure of the heroically unified "Self" may be the universal truth that lyricism tells: poetry may be received as salvational precisely because the lyric contract demands genuineness, and genuineness cannot exist without an apprehension of its own fallen condition. (Without this knowledge of the fall, there could only be an "I" of such monstrous proportions that it would override the "I" that reads the poem.) A genuine catch-22: if it is real lyricism then it cannot be felt as such by the one who produces it; its power—Heidegger would give it the true salvational force of homecoming—can only be a gift, made by the always partially impaired poet, for the equally impaired receiver (is this why Frost's world is filled with deserted homeplaces?).[16] Think of it as like saints feeding each other in heaven: hell, and sinners with elbows locked and arms straight at a table laden with delicious food, food flying everywhere and every mouth empty; heaven, and saints with elbows locked and arms straight at a table laden with delicious food, each being fed by his neighbor's hand.

HOMOLOGY, TYPOLOGY, AND LYRICISM

At the millennium, it seems appropriate to evoke the very old with the (relatively speaking) very new. Homology: "a fundamental similarity due to community of descent." Typology: "the doctrine or study of types or prefigurative symbols, esp. in scriptural literature." Homology follows typology as night follows day. Typology, forever the authoritative business of the patriarchs, looks backward to find prefigurations of present and future events; it is bound up with canon formation and dependent upon a linearity that can argue sameness with a difference because there is a God whose plan will by definition make itself manifest over time and whose covenants cannot be broken. The typologically significant events themselves will never be exactly the same, and only the critical and symbolic consciousness of the exegete can expose the infallible logic behind certain selected progressive events. Only authority can form and close a canon, and each repetition of canon formation is itself typologically

16. Martin Heidegger, *Poetry, Language, Thought*, trans. Albert Hofstadter (New York: Harper and Row, Publishers, 1971), 91–142.

prefigured, first in the establishment of the Pentateuch (sometime before the middle of the third century BCE) and again of the Septuagint (which became standardized at the time of the council of Jamnia, about BCE 90–100), where what would count as the definitive Word also took the Apocrypha as epiphenomena in the developmental process of becoming the Hebrew Bible), and then yet again in the closing of the New Testament around CE 367.[17]

As is fitting for science, homology seems to go typology, its own first cause, one step better. Homology may declare sameness over time where none seems to have been prefigured: the symbolic is no longer a functional category (or so it seems), and genealogical connectedness can endure without proving itself as either figuratively similar or as practically alike. Authority, though, remains the unifying concept, for in either case only true initiates may claim possession of the causal truth, which is in some fundamental way a claim to knowledge, of God. Extending from this intimate relationship to deity, both homology and typology determine what counts as autonomously existent, not epiphenomenal but ontologically stable. We don't need Derrida to tell us that patristic authority is the original ontotheology, a borrowing of God's sightedness to organize, classify, and delimit being (it is interesting for lyricism to note that, though the Old Testament did not stabilize into a *textus receptus* until the first century AD, the criterion for acceptance was temporal, based on the belief that prophetic revelation was supposed to have ceased about the time of Ezra. Inspiration, then as now, marks the dividing line between truth and invention). But so too is homology an ontotheology. Based on the assumption that meaning verifies itself retroactively through the developmental history of the organism and is able, thus, to determine what counts as being, homology is faith in disguise. Between the idea and the reality, between the motion and the act, between the conception and the creation, there is no shadow.

Lyricism is a concept bracketed by the compatible systems of typology and homology sharing the word *true* and privileging history as the only legitimate means by which truth may be seen to test itself. Yet as a concept (or a dream) lyricism stands for something entirely other, which is why, of course, it is so often felt as "femaleness"; it stands for the claim that being is most definitively itself only when freed from the obligations and imperatives of the fathers. "I'm all for abruption," Frost says in 1916, "I

17. See Herbert G. May and Bruce M. Metzger, eds., *New Oxford Annotated Bible with the Apocrypha* (New York: Oxford University Press, 1977).

like a young fellow as says, 'My father's generation thought that, did they? Well that was the Hell of a way to think, wasn't it? Let's think something else for a change.' A disconnected young fellow with a plenty of extrication in his makeup. You bet your sweet life."[18] "Poetry is the renewal of words forever and ever. Poetry is that by which we live forever and ever unjaded. Poetry is that by which the world is never old." Poetry, Frost says, "plays perilously between truth and make-believe." "Poetry is a young thing, as we all know."[19] Lyricism is heroic, which is to say that it embodies the demand that some passionate thing rises for a time above history, to do and say things that, if sustainable, would be seen by an Oedipally bound, history-driven world as madness.

"Robert Frost" is a most complex package in this regard. The poet commodified himself, as he confessed more than once ("I tell you, Louis, it's all over at thirty. People expect us to keep right on and it is well to have something to show for our time on earth. . . . And I took measures accordingly . . . I have myself all in a strong box where I can unfold as a personality at discretion").[20] As with many modern poets, he believed that poetry can only arise within the young; the unmistakable correlative to this often repeated assertion must be that he felt himself to be ever afterward writing something like history, not the unmediated stuff that is lyric poetry but a secondhand account of the same (not poetry as in not philosophy, a radical, severe, and compelling newness of thought, but the history of philosophy; it is the distinction between the writer and the typewriter salesman). Clearly, too, he held poetry, the real stuff, in mind as something perfectly transcendent, something beyond emotion, beyond wit, and beyond all artifice, even beyond (or perhaps especially beyond) the virtuoso manifestations of formal constraints for which "The Silken Tent" may metonymously stand.[21]

And yet he says of himself in 1917, "I discovered that do or say my damndest I can't be other than orthodox in politics love and religion: I can't escape salvation: I can't burn if I was born into this world to shine without heat."[22] (The overhead projector school of poetic inspiration.) All this he said of himself, and even leaving room for irony, even obeying him when his Tityrus self says in "Build Soil," "Don't let the things I

18. **Untermeyer,** 32.
19. *Poetry and Prose,* 358, 360–61, 375.
20. **Untermeyer,** 29.
21. *Poetry and Prose,* 413.
22. **Untermeyer,** 59.

say against myself / Betray you into taking sides against me," one cannot escape feeling, after immersion in his poetry, that Frost was a man most haunted by his sense that his lyricism was somehow fraudulent: not poetry but history.

And, reading the poetry, one also learns that Frost was right about himself, that he was telling the truth when he claimed a congenital predisposition to trinitarian orthodoxy, with "politics love and religion" destined to keep him always, really, out of the wild places where he claimed that poetry must perilously play.[23] In declaring, and accurately I think, his allegiance to these three cornerstones that define the Oedipal contract with history and the fathers, he might just as well have proclaimed himself Oedipally bound and gagged. His habits are typological: he uses the past to define the present in order to legitimate the mean-making of poetry, and his homage extends backward into long distant time; and he uses the typological present, with its natural cycles of regress and return, to allegorize the larger truths of the theological and paternal system within which these very truths are made. His deepest, most compulsively repeated suspicions are homological: How, exactly, does the generative process unfold, where does it begin, where does it end, who counts as being, and what interloper has snuck out the back door in the dead of night? One is hard-pressed to know whether the sexual motif that permeates his poetry is a projection of his poetic anxiety about the generation of poetry or whether his poetic anxiety is a sublimated sexual preoccupation; but about both love and poetry, which are the same, he teaches us that all fundamental samenesses due to community of descent may be the wishful thinking of the genealogically impaired.

So why does the poetry work, for it quite clearly does work? Precisely for the reasons above, I think. Lyricism can never be pure, if one takes lyricism to be a genuine manifestation of self, because such a self, if there is one, can only exist outside of language (and it doesn't matter whether there is "one" or not since all positions on this subject make equally unverifiable claims; it is enough to say that the fantasy of such a thing persists). The instant an "I" begins its performance it makes a promise that it knows cannot be kept, a promise that has taken as its earthly form (and earth's the right place for it), love poetry, which has become the shorthand for "lyric." "I will always. . . ." Brought to the exigency of saying this, one already knows that the "I" in question has, as Frost would put it, extrication in its makeup. Self seriously, sadly, madly, gladly runs away and leaves behind only an eternal

23. *Poetry and Prose*, 360.

play in eternal progress. Other poets say this stuff out loud and, at their best (Wallace Stevens on a good day), suffuse their paradoxes with poetry; Frost resists himself, and who knows why. Maybe stubbornness, maybe anti-intellectualism, maybe neurosis, maybe something like heroism, maybe because he wants to live up to being a New Englander (and certainly, whatever Frost was, it was something so compelling as to push Lawrance Thompson to the edge of obsession). In any event, only one who thinks himself a fraud would push so very hard to get from delight to wisdom by writing a lifetime of poetry, right up to the very end, after having professed to have died as a poet around 1906. The poetry that escapes from Frost is quite remarkably mundane and quite remarkably powerful because it is born of necessity. Frost probably would have laughed at all this fuss and declared in a carnival barker's voice that he was the gen-u-wine article. And the thing is, he would have been right.

BIOGRAPHY
AND
CULTURAL
STUDIES

Frost and the Cold War

A Look at the Later Poetry

Mark Richardson

ON OCTOBER 15, 1962, United States intelligence discovered that Nikita Khrushchev, at the invitation of Fidel Castro, had built ballistic missile sites in Cuba. It was a fact the Soviet premier had somehow neglected to mention to Robert Frost some six weeks earlier when they met for a ninety-minute conference in Gagra, Georgia, a Russian resort on the Black Sea. Their conversation was to have been on the theme—or so Frost had hoped beforehand—of a new and "magnanimous" rivalry between the two superpowers. The eighty-eight-year-old poet had traveled to the USSR under the auspices of the U.S. Department of State as part of a program of cultural exchange, and, as his talk about "magnanimous rivalry" suggested, he apparently had high ambitions that the New Frontier/Khrushchev era might be one characterized by what, in his inaugural poem for John F. Kennedy, he had called a "golden age of poetry and power" (437). Kennedy had himself issued the invitation to his literary friend and political booster to go to Russia. But he was considerably more than chagrined at the results when the aging Frost addressed reporters sent to greet him on his return at New York's Idlewild Airport. Khrushchev, Frost announced, had claimed Americans "were too liberal to fight." So much for magnanimity. Some weeks later, in October, Frost spoke at the Library of Congress. This was during the crucible days of the missile crisis itself, and under the circumstances, he had the good grace, if that is what it was, to concede that Khrushchev had said nothing about liberals and fighting; the sentiment and the words had been Frost's all along (as any careful reader of him might have suspected). But the concession came too late. Frost was never invited to the Kennedy White House again. It was a lesson about the limits of an analogy Frost once drew between poetry and warfare. Many years earlier, in 1923, he had said that a poet's words were nothing "unless they amount[ed] to deeds, as in ultimatums or battle cries" (701). But his kind of play never met that standard, nor should it have. And when things

55

really did come to ultimatums and battle cries in October 1962 Frost duly stepped aside. William Pritchard understands the meaning of the episode: "The final lesson appeared to be that poetry and power went together only in poems, and that to prophesy—as Frost had done—a golden age, and then try to help bring it about, was a course fraught with peril."[1]

Frost's brief moment on the stage with Khrushchev and Kennedy didn't mark an aberration of the role he set himself as commentator on the Cold War so much as it marked an exaggeration of it. And, as I will be suggesting in this paper, the episode points up a kind of paradox both in Frost's general literary personality and in his response to the new dynamics of the Cold War. Let us say that there is, on the one hand, the publically approved Robert Frost, the one who participates in the official culture of the Cold War as Kennedy's supporter, as a speaker at Kennedy's inaugural, and as cultural emissary to the USSR. Then there is the other Frost, the one much harder to hold captive to the purposes of tact and sound policy; this one is mischievous, at times a little cynical and bleak, and almost always quite uncontainable. This is the Robert Frost who appeared so much to Kennedy's embarrassment at Idlewild Airport. And he is, in other moods, attuned to certain countercultural energies at play in the early years of the Cold War that would later more forcefully emerge in writers like Norman Mailer and Thomas Pynchon. His later poetry is at odds with itself, at least with regard to the Cold War. And this makes Frost particularly interesting, I should think, to scholars of American culture in the postwar years. The paradox in Frost's literary personality to which I allude, familiar to students of his work, often presents, on the surface, a very reassuring aspect, but under scrutiny, it may come to seem very strange and insubordinate—rather like the years of the 1950s themselves, which are, after all, the period in question here. Frost, it is true, participated in the Cold War arena in a quasi-official capacity, and he often sounded the notes of national piety required by an occasion such as the inauguration of a president. But his example had all along suggested that the place of the poet and of poetry was much more properly *outside* institutional politics and constitutional piety. That example was soon enough to be taken to new extremes by a younger generation of writers. And it ultimately made Frost himself much less useful to Kennedy's purposes than Kennedy had apparently hoped.

1. **Pritchard,** 255.

Kennedy's inaugural address, delivered as Frost sat nearby on the po-
dium, issued a challenge familiar to Americans in those days. Speaking of
the military rivalry between the USSR and the United States, he says:
"Let both sides seem to invoke the wonders of science instead of its
terrors. Together let us explore the stars, conquer the deserts, eradicate
disease, tap the ocean depths and encourage the arts and commerce."
Notwithstanding his inadvertently candid phrasing—"Let both nations
seem to invoke the wonders of science"—Kennedy's call is the familiar
biblical one to beat swords into ploughshares. Americans often heard that
call made in the 1950s and early 1960s in support of continued high-level
funding for military research and development. The hope was that the
new technologies, particular nuclear technologies, would "spin off" into
civilian and benevolent channels. Michael Sherry, a historian of the period,
points out that such promises were offered first in the advertising of the
World War II era, which insisted that "war-born ingenuity would yield
wondrous civilian devices." One might view this sort of claim cynically—
many have—as a ruse to ensure the continued growth of what Dwight
Eisenhower famously called the "military-industrial complex": "Let both
sides *seem* to invoke the wonders of science" indeed. Such claims were,
in any case, an indication that American culture was becoming, for the
first time, more or less permanently militarized. In the 1940s and 1950s,
Americans, Sherry suggests, were constantly reminded of the connection
between militarization and national prosperity and affluence "in adver-
tising, government pronouncements, paeans to science, magazines, and
science fiction. No youngster reading *Popular Mechanics* could miss it, and
it suffuses material culture—in cars with rocketlike grills and space-age fins
or bicycles resembling jet fighters in miniature." Americans were invited to
look forward to an earthly paradise achieved through the miracle of nuclear
energy. "Atoms for Peace" was the slogan. The purposes of peace and of
war-making, we were assured, could be served simultaneously without
contradiction. Robert Hutchins, president of the University of Chicago,
promised that nuclear energy would "'usher in a new day of peace and
plenty' and develop 'the most backward places of the earth.'" The *Nation*
(perhaps wryly) proposed that atomic bombs be used to dig canals and
"generally to tidy up the awkward parts of the world." Among statements
like these, Kennedy's remarks in the inaugural about the "wonders of
science" are hardly striking; they are very much the official line. The effect
of all this propaganda, as Sherry suggests, was to encourage Americans
"not only to tolerate the militarized state but to embrace it as the source

of wonders in their daily lives, focussing only 'incidentally' on its military dimensions. The swords, if not beaten into ploughshares, would at least generate them."[2]

Frost was fond of troubling the distinction many Cold War liberals wanted to draw between peaceful and martial technologies and fond of satirizing the idea that science might be harnessed to serve merely "national" aims by its political overseers. He says in a 1959 essay on "The Future of Man" that "the challenge of science to government takes the form of asking What will you do with our latest? Will you use it as a weapon or a tool or both? If you ignore it, we shall go elsewhere with it and try it on your rivals. If you suppress it, we will do the same" (869). The implication, inevitably, is that science is, in certain respects, its own nation whose loyalty is always to be doubted. It is a disturbing idea. Anyway, it must have been disturbing to Americans who felt somehow reassured when Julius and Ethel Rosenberg were put to death in 1953 for having passed along atomic secrets to the Soviets. Of course, Frost is not indifferent to the question of *personal* loyalty. In "The Future of Man" he is talking not about the disloyalty of particular scientists, or of those involved in espionage; he is talking about the dubious loyalty of the institution of science itself—a much more problematical thing. His remarks, I suspect, evoke something of the ambivalence with which many Americans regarded the scientific establishment that had grown up among them so impressively from the seeds first planted in the deserts of New Mexico during the Manhattan Project, which had pioneered the new alliance, characteristic of postwar American life, of government, the military, and major research universities. Frost's unsettling claim is that the scientific enterprise is itself naturally insubordinate. "We become an organized society," he says in "The Future of Man," "only as we tell off some of our number to be law-givers and law-enforcers, a blend of general and lawyer, to hold fast the line and turn the rest of us loose for scientists, philosophers, and poets to make the break-through, the revolution, if we can for refreshment. Science is the most formidable in challenge but philosophy has been formidable too. Philosophers have had to be given hemlock and burned at the stake" (869). Socrates notwithstanding, then, scientists have always made the most dangerous heretics. So, why shouldn't science itself be regarded as

2. John F. Kennedy, "Inaugural Address," in *Great Issues in American History*, ed. Richard Hofstadter and Beatrice Hofstadter, vol. 3 (New York: Vintage Books, 1982), 548; Michael S. Sherry, *In the Shadow of War: the United States since the 1930s* (New Haven: Yale University Press, 1995), 143–44.

constitutionally heretical and disloyal? In the nineteenth century science had inexorably eroded religious and moral institutions. Why shouldn't it threaten civil and political institutions in the twentieth? Frost has Science mischievously say to Eisenhower's apprehensive Middle America: "It seems a shame to come on you with our new novelties when you are hardly up around after what Darwin, Spencer, and Huxley did to you last century." The point is unmistakable, at least in its unstated implications: Science is an amoral business that can't be trusted to lend itself reliably to political and civic aims. Under the circumstances, it is no surprise that some Americans felt uneasy about the optimism of those in government who encouraged them to embrace the new culture of atomic science, and to stake their security and prosperity on it. "Atoms for Peace" indeed. Frost knew that any such program was treacherous, not because of the Rosenbergs, but because of the Promethean nature of the scientific enterprise itself. Science often represents itself as a preeminently rational enterprise. But what if, especially when militarized, science proves to contain within itself tendencies of the most irrational and volatile sort? What sort of "national security" could be founded on a basis like that? These are the questions Frost implicitly asks in his more countercultural moods.

Consider a sonnet Frost wrote about the atomic bomb titled "Bursting Rapture," collected first in his 1947 volume *Steeple Bush*. This book appeared early in the Cold War, one year after Winston Churchill had delivered his "iron curtain" speech with Harry Truman in the audience, two years before the USSR detonated its first atomic bomb. The United States had renewed testing of atomic weapons in the summer of 1946, detonating two bombs in July at Bikini Atoll. The threat of what Frost called "a new Holocaust" (362) was lively, even if it had not yet taken sharp focus in the context of the Cold War between the United States and the USSR. Already at this date the newly constituted United Nations had created the U.N. Atomic Energy Commission to study and, it was hoped, control the proliferation of nuclear technologies. These developments, then, provide the background for "Bursting Rapture."

> I went to a physician to complain,
> The time had been when anyone could turn
> To farming for a simple way to earn;
> But now 'twas there as elsewhere, any gain
> Was made by getting science on the brain;
> There was so much more every day to learn,
> The discipline of farming was so stern,

It seemed as if I couldn't stand the strain.
But the physician's answer was "There, there,
What you complain of all the nations share.
Their effort is a mounting ecstasy
That when it gets too exquisite to bear
Will find relief in one burst. You shall see.
That's what a certain bomb was sent to be." (362)

The sonnet lacks the argumentative focus one expects from Frost. William Pritchard, for one, complains that in its "untroubled move from a trumped-up personal complaint to the assertion that it is one shared by all nations, and that relief is just a burst away as . . . that 'certain bomb' fulfills its mission, there is a failure of taste and of scale." I will take up the question of taste presently. As for the failure of scale, the confusion of the personal and the national is certainly what characterizes this poem, what makes it difficult to read with assurance. When the physician replies that what the speaker complains of "all the nations share," it is not clear whether we are to regard the speaker as a "national" rather than a merely "personal" spokesman. Is he speaking for America, even speaking *as* America, in, let us say, a befuddled agrarian guise? True, it might be that we are meant to understand by the physician's remark simply that "people of all nations" share the speaker's complaint. But the idea seems rather to be that the nations themselves, as nations, are involved in the "mounting ecstasy" of science represented by the drive to develop an atomic bomb—in other words, by the nuclear arms race, then in its initial stage. This drive has put an end to the pastoral isolation presumably available in an earlier period, the sort of thing Jeffersonians like Frost had all along hoped to achieve in the United States—a nostalgic theme echoed in other poems of this period from Frost's life, as we shall presently see. There are no more "simple ways to earn." Ploughshares and swords are impossible to distinguish from one another: farming itself had somehow been militarized by being (somehow) made scientific. This vague confederacy of science with militarization is something that Frost's Cold War sonnet can simply take for granted. The disgruntled farmer in "Bursting Rapture" hardly understands how it all happened, but, as American farmers always do, he knows he resents it. This peculiarly agrarian sort of resentment is, after all, hardly unfamiliar in American history and culture. And it is apparently what was sending Americans to the physician complaining about "the strain" of the new world order in 1947, at least as Frost seemed to believe. The nation was having to invent a way of thinking about itself that included both the bomb and the vast military and industrial bureaucracy required to maintain, develop, and manage it. Our self-satisfied, autonomous idyll "down on the farm" was clearly at an end. Something like this idea seems to be involved in the allegory of the perplexed and beleaguered farmer. He is, of course, an American type, and one with which Frost often identified himself in public performances.[3]

But the troubling thing about the sonnet is what it implies about the nature of the newly militarized scientific establishment with its "mounting ecstasy" toward a "bursting rapture." The metaphor is, of course, sexual. The drive to achieve and use The Bomb is imagined to be a kind of frenzy, an orgy apparently unamenable to reason. This seems to be a way of saying that science is a passionate, irrational endeavor, no matter what the reassuring propagandists of the Atomic Energy Commission would have us believe: *they*, in their naive ecstasy, simply don't know what they are up to. In "Kitty Hawk," another poem deeply invested in the Cold War, Frost suggestively speaks of science as the "penetration" of matter by mind. His figure is at once sexual and agricultural: "Spirit enters flesh / And for what it's worth / Charges into earth / In birth after birth" (447). This is the master-figure of "Kitty Hawk," and it binds together several ideas: "God's own descent into flesh," as when He conceived a son (446); the Wright brothers' great experiment, which is an epitome of what Frost suggestively calls "the science zest / To materialize / By on-penetration / Into earth and skies" (447); and the entire masculine project—as Frost puts it—to "*master* Nature" (449, emphasis mine). It is the latter two ideas, about science and masculinity, that concern me here. Later in the poem, Frost admonishes any skeptical readers of "Kitty Hawk": "Don't discount our powers," he says, "We have made a pass / At the infinite, / Made it, as it were, / Rationally ours" (450). The metaphor is of amorous conquest: that's what the phrase "making a pass" means in colloquial American speech. The sexualized language in which "Kitty Hawk" is written constantly (and approvingly) insists that men, American men, are now involved in a kind of happy rape of the material world. They are out to possess it, to dominate it, to bring it under cultivation, to know its most secret recesses "by on-penetration into earth and skies." This sexualized enterprise of scientific inquiry is a variety of what psychoanalysts call "epistemophilia," which Freud recognized, in his famous case study of the "Rat-Man," as a displacement of erotic energy into the love of knowledge. Freud regarded this displacement as an essentially healthy sublimation, and "Kitty Hawk"

3. **Pritchard**, 243.

apparently takes much the same view. It invokes the "wonders of science" of which Kennedy would speak in his inaugural address, not the "terrors." "Kitty Hawk" is, in fact, very much in the Kennedy style of a vigorously masculine national optimism.[4]

"Bursting Rapture" is another thing altogether, which is what sets it apart from "Kitty Hawk" as a poem about the American postwar cult of science. It suggests that a climax will be achieved, that the arc of "ecstasy" will be consummated, only when science, through the instrument of warring nations, releases itself in an orgy of destructive energy, having "penetrated" nature even to the heart of the atom itself. We might as well spell it out, since this is what Frost is talking about in "Bursting Rapture": the lust for nuclear fission and what Americans call "screwing" are near of kin. (Inevitably one thinks of Thomas Pynchon's 1973 novel *Gravity's Rainbow*, with its elaborate allegory about rocketry and male erections.) Perhaps this is what William Pritchard has in mind when he speaks of the poem's "failure of taste." No doubt he speaks for many readers. In any case, so much for the West's healthy sublimation of erotic energies in the pursuit of knowledge. The citadel of Reason on which the nuclear Cold War state must rely for its security—Science—is, in fact, deeply irrational in its motives and ambitions. The "little death" of the Elizabethans becomes a catastrophically satisfying holocaust: "That's what a certain bomb was sent to be." Frost is already working the idea Terry Southern would develop so unforgettably in his screenplay for Stanley Kubrick's Cold War farce *Dr. Strangelove*. This is hardly the way Truman and the generals talked about The Bomb in 1947, hardly what the Atomic Energy Commission wanted to convey. And it is hardly what sensible Americans wanted to think of themselves as involved in bringing about. No wonder if they went to their physicians to complain about "the strain" that was startling them out of their pastoral slumber. In "Bursting Rapture," Frost made the diagnosis long before Norman Mailer did in an essay on the 1964 Republican National Convention, collected in his 1966 volume *Cannibals and Christians*. "Yes," Mailer writes, "our country was fearful, half-mad, inauthentic. It needed a purge. It had a liberal Establishment obeisant to committees, foundations, and science—the liberal did not understand that the center of science was as nihilistic as a psychopath's sense of God." Without, it is true, Mailer's brooding intensity, Frost is nonetheless

---

4. I have in mind such characteristic passages from "Kitty Hawk" as the one beginning: "Westerners inherit / A design for living / Deeper into matter . . ." (446–48).

working toward the same repudiation of the Cold War liberal's bland, unquestioning faith in the new scientific "Establishment."[5]

In view of this, there is peculiar irony in the citation inscribed on the honorary degree conferred on Frost by Oxford University in 1957. He had traveled to Great Britain under the auspices of the U.S. Department of State as a kind of cultural ambassador. The immediate occasion was an exhibition of his works at the U.S. Embassy in London. But the whole affair was a part of the State Department's effort to ease the strain in relations with Britain that had arisen when the U.K., with France, invaded Egypt the previous fall to secure the Suez Canal. The invasion collapsed when the Soviet Union threatened to intervene. In fact, the United States and the United Nations had opposed the invasion precisely because they feared it would augment Soviet prestige in the Near East. In accepting the State Department's invitation to play his small part in making repairs, Frost wrote: "If my country believes I can be of any use in reminding the British people of our own warm affection and strong friendship, why, of course I'll go." Then, taking up a ready Cold War metaphor to show he understood, Frost concluded: "I don't want to be an unguided missile, however; don't spare me. Tell me where you want me to go and when." The Oxford degree itself formed no official part of the mission. But the authors of the citation—the original is in Latin—seemed to understand the meaning of Frost's visit: "Amid the clash of arms and the mounting terror of our new instruments of war, his poetry, with its echoes of Virgilian serenity, has brought, and will continue to bring, unfailing consolation to a suffering world." "Bursting Rapture" more or less explodes the idea of "Virgilian serenity" in a nuclear age. Frost wasn't in the atomic "consolation" business, State Department portfolio notwithstanding. The physician's "There, there" in "Bursting Rapture" is hardly bracing.[6]

Frost would continue to trouble our Virgilian serenity for some time to come, as in "The Objection to Being Stepped On," collected first in *In the Clearing* (1962), his last volume:

> At the end of the row
> I stepped on the toe
> Of an unemployed hoe.

5. Norman Mailer, *Cannibals and Christians* (New York: Dell, 1966), 43.

6. Frost's remarks about the trip to Great Britain are quoted in Jay Parini, *Robert Frost: A Life* (New York: Henry Holt, 1999), 397, 399.

It rose in offence
And struck me a blow
In the seat of my sense.
It wasn't to blame
But I called it a name.
And I must say it dealt
Me a blow that I felt
Like malice prepense.
You may call me a fool,
But *was* there a rule
The weapon should be
Turned into a tool?
And what do we see?
The first tool I step on
Turned into a weapon. (460)

The agricultural metaphor spoofs (again) the biblical injunction to turn swords into ploughshares. But there is more to the poem than that. The farmer who speaks in the poem—I assume the speaker is a farmer—expresses the bewilderment of an agrarian-minded people as yet unused to the challenges of the troubling technoscientific establishment that had arisen in the first decade of the Cold War. To them it apparently seemed a protean, dangerously unpredictable force, represented here in the person of a hoe—that most familiar, ancient, and trustworthy of implements—actually capable of "malice prepense." The vexing thing is that the only way to control this force is to "employ" it, since, as Frost says in "The Future of Man," it will neither be ignored nor suppressed. But employ it to what end, and how, given that its loyalties seem so inevitably and naturally divided between Mars and Ceres? So much for talk about harnessing the atom. So much for newspaper cartoons depicting a benevolent goddess opening a locked chest marked "ATOMIC ENERGY." So much for consolation. The leaders of the military-industrial establishment, in their scientific boosterism, simply protested too much. It is salutary to find Frost treating their claims with skepticism. All the same, the Oxford degree cited above wasn't altogether off the mark in its congratulation. It was simply partial, attending, as it did, only to Frost's official profile in the Cold War years. Nobody is given a degree for being mischievous about the bomb. And Frost's mischief was easy enough to ignore, at least until he met the reporters at Idlewild Airport in 1962 fresh from a chat with Krushchev. The fact remains that Frost had always been an "unguided missile," or in any case a loose cannon on the ship of the Cold War state, which may explain why he once declined an invitation, originating with President Eisenhower, to write an essay on "American life" for the U.S. Information Agency.[7]

And as for "American life" in the Cold War, Frost was aware of, and at times indulged, a nostalgia for an America untouched by the entangling alliances, the political and diplomatic intrigue—not to mention the espionage, lies, and rancor—of the Cold War era, with its Red scares, its hydrogen bombs, its Cuban fiascoes, all of which had carried us so far away from the ideal agrarian America imagined in George Washington's farewell address. I am thinking of a poem collected in *In the Clearing* called "Does No One at All Ever Feel This Way in the Least?" The poem speaks to the anxieties excited by military and political leaders who, throughout the postwar years, warned that America was no longer invulnerable, that the blessing of geographical isolation we had long enjoyed, owing to the Atlantic and Pacific oceans, was extinct in an age of thermonuclear war, long-range bombers, Sputnik, ICBM's, and baffling geopolitics.

> And now, O sea, you're lost by aeroplane.
> Our sailors ride a bullet for a boat.
> Our coverage of distance is so facile
> It makes us to have had a sea in vain.
> Our moat around us is no more a moat,
> Our continent no more a moated castle.

The imagery of the poem makes clear that the passing away of no merely *cultural* integrity and independence—such as Emerson and Whitman had called for—is here lamented. We had lost much more: the military invulnerability that American geography used to provide. We had lost what the poet William Cullen Bryant spoke of in an 1821 poem about America called "The Ages." Bryant, of course, was addressing his countrymen in the so-called "Era of Good Feelings" that followed the successful conclusion of the War of 1812. He is exhilarated with a sense of American possibilities. "These are thy fetters," he said to America, "seas and stormy air / Are the wide barrier of thy borders, where / Among thy gallant sons that guard thee well, / Thou laugh'st at enemies." Well, no one in America was

---

7. For the cartoon, see Sherry, *In the Shadow of War*, 143. For the proposed article on "American life," see Parini, *Robert Frost*, 396.

laughing at our enemies in 1962. And it certainly is a new age when, as Frost's confusing metaphor implies, airplanes and missiles, civil technology and martial technology—not to mention the navy and the air force—can hardly be told apart: "Our sailors ride a bullet for a boat," he says. The poem is not without resentment at America's having been thrust—or having thrust itself—onto the world stage that the European nations had trod for centuries, acting out their tragedies. The promise of American exceptionalism to this European contagion, which indeed dates from James Monroe's Era of Good Feelings, had somehow been foreclosed. NATO, established in 1949, had declared that an attack against any nation in the treaty organization would be an attack against them all. The New World was the Old World yet. In short, sometime in the late 1940s Americans apparently woke up into the nightmare of history that had always made Europe seem to them so unwholesome, as it had seemed, certainly, to William Cullen Bryant in 1821. Frost continues in "Does No One at All Ever Feel This Way in the Least?"

> O ocean sea for all your seeming vast,
> Your separation of us from the Old
> That should have made the New World newly great
> Would only disappoint us at the last
> If it should not do anything foretold
> To make us different in a single trait.

Many Americans didn't like these insidious developments at all and were grateful when, in 1951, former president Hoover denounced the "rash involvement" of the Truman administration in "hopeless" European campaigns. He demanded that no further troops, and no further aid, be sent to the continent until its nations showed the ability and the will to defend themselves. The speaker of Frost's poem pretty clearly stands with the Hooverite isolationists. A little sadly, perhaps even a little pathetically, this embattled speaker imagines a retreat back into the dreamy heartland of Hoover's America, where, it seems, the only real America remains, if, in fact, any remains to be had at all.

> The ocean had been spoken to before.
> But if it had no thought of paying heed
> To taunt of mine I knew a place to go
> Where I need listen to its rote no more,
> Nor taste its salt, nor smell its fish and weed,
> Nor be reminded of them in a blow—

So far inland the very name of ocean
Goes mentionless except in baby-school
When teacher's own experiences fail her
And she can only give the class a notion
Of what it is by calling it a pool
And telling them how Sinbad was a sailor.

Of course, these stanzas suggest a psychological retreat into the inno-
cence of childhood as much as a geographical retreat into—where *would*
it be?—Iowa, Kansas, or Nebraska. Sad indeed to arrive all the way out
there only to stumble upon an installation of the Strategic Air Command.
It must be admitted that the heartland spoken of in the poem would soon
become, in President Eisenhower's new era of "massive nuclear retaliation,"
essentially a condition of mind, a certain state of naiveté and boyish grace
that had long made up a part of America's self-image. With the advent of
the Cold War, we decisively lost this particular sort of innocence. There was
nothing innocent about Korea, nothing innocent about the Bay of Pigs,
nothing innocent about Whittaker Chambers and Richard Nixon, nothing
innocent about the hydrogen bomb. The sentiments expressed in "Does
No One at All Ever Feel This Way in the Least?" belong to an American
tradition of nativism and isolationism that, Frost seems well aware, was
untenable, bankrupt. We are not asked to adopt these sentiments, only to
see them for the quaint anachronism they amount to in the new period of
the Cold War. Certain residual sympathies for Hoover notwithstanding,
Frost would become, in his most readily available public profile at least,
essentially a poet of Kennedy's New Frontier, ready to "play any game
the nations want to play," as he says in the poem he wrote for Kennedy's
inaugural (437). And yet there is much of him in "Does No One at All But
Me Ever Feel This Way in the Least?", as the unwieldy, slightly longer title
under which the poem was first published in 1952 makes clear. Frost was of
two minds in the 1950s, as was America itself. His writing in the postwar
years is therefore in perfect harmony, I should think, with the discord of a
nation characterized at once by the sunny optimism of the Golden Age of
Television and by troubling and turbulent developments as varied in their
meaning and origin as McCarthyism, the Beat rebellion, film noir, and
the struggle for civil rights.

Frost's late poetry is perhaps most challenging when it turns to the
problem of how the Cold War changed Americans' sense of their identity
as a nation. An impressive poem on this theme is "A Cabin in the Clearing,"
eventually collected in *In the Clearing* and surely among the best short

poems presented in Frost's last two volumes.[8] Like "Does No One at All Ever Feel This Way in the Least?" and "Bursting Rapture," it concerns our national awakening from a pastoral dream of cabins in clearings—always a self-image that appealed to Americans—into something much more troubling and confusing. As I have implied, the poem anticipates what the Kennedy people would soon be calling—the poem appeared first in 1951— the New Frontier. The metaphor of homesteading, on which Frost relies in the poem, neatly marks out the cultural continuities linking the old frontier of the American "errand into the wilderness" with the new frontiers of the Cold War. The poem takes the form of a blank verse dialogue between Mist and Smoke.

> MIST
> I don't believe the sleepers in this house
> Know where they are.
>
> SMOKE
> They've been here long enough
> To push the woods back from around the house
> And part them in the middle with a path.
>
> MIST
> And still I doubt if they know where they are.
> And I begin to fear they never will.
> All they maintain the path for is the comfort
> Of visiting with the equally bewildered.
> Nearer in plight their neighbors are than distance.
>
> SMOKE
> I am the guardian wraith of starlit smoke
> That leans out this and that way from their chimney.
> I will not have their happiness despaired of.
>
> MIST
> No one—not I—would give them up for lost
> Simply because they don't know where they are.
> I am the damper counterpart of smoke
> That gives off from a garden ground at night
> But lifts no higher than a garden grows.

8. Other poems on this theme include "America Is Hard to See," "Our Doom to Bloom," "For John F. Kennedy His Inauguration," and, in a great many passages, the long poem "Kitty Hawk." All of these poems appear in *In the Clearing*.

I cotton to their landscape. That's who I am.
I am no further from their fate than you are.

SMOKE
They must by now have learned the native tongue.
Why don't they ask the Red Man where they are?

MIST
They often do, and none the wiser for it.
So do they also ask philosophers
Who come to look in on them from the pulpit.
They will ask anyone there is to ask—
In the fond faith accumulated fact
Will of itself take fire and light the world up.
Learning has been a part of their religion.

SMOKE
If the day ever comes when they know who
They are, they may know better where they are.
But who they are is too much to believe—
Either for them or the onlooking world.
They are too sudden to be credible.

MIST
Listen, they murmur talking in the dark
On what should be their daylong theme continued.
Putting the lamp out has not put their thought out.
Let us pretend the dewdrops from the eaves
Are you and I eavesdropping on their unrest—
A mist and smoke eavesdropping on a haze—
And see if we can tell the bass from the soprano.

Than smoke and mist who better could appraise
The kindred spirit of an inner haze.

This poem, whose title echoes that of the volume in which it appears,
lends a specifically national focus to *In the Clearing.* Before us here is the
old American parable of pioneering, which has contributed so much to our
way of imagining ourselves. It is a poem about national identity, about, as
I suggested, what the Puritans called our "errand into the wilderness." The
mood of the poem is wry, amused, a shade ironical, though not without a
certain gravity communicated in the cadence of Frost's iambic pentameter
lines, as well as in the tendency of certain phrases to take on, it may be, a

touch of quiet gloom: "*Than smoke and mist who better could appraise / The kindred spirit of an inner haze.*" In other words, the tone of the poem is finely poised just this side of anything like real anxiety about our national purpose. That is what keeps it well within what might be called the official Cold War culture that Kennedy thought he could trust Robert Frost to respect when he sent him to the Soviet Union. But this is not to say that "A Cabin in the Clearing" evades the new complexities that attended our errand into the wilderness of the Cold War, haunted, as it always was, by The Bomb, by a thing of our own devising. Frost knew that the American frontier had always been haunted by violence: our "deed of gift" to it, as he says in the poem he ultimately recited at the 1961 inauguration, "was many deeds of war" (437).

At the time "A Cabin in the Clearing" was first published, U.S. troops were fighting the Chinese Communists in Korea. Truman had conceded in a press conference in December 1950 that the administration was "actively considering" the use of atomic weapons: "The military commander in the field," Truman said, "will have charge of the use of weapons, as he always has." The remarks startled American allies in Europe. British Prime Minister Clement Attlee went so far as to fly to Washington for private talks with Truman, who soon clarified his position by acknowledging that he, and not commanders in the field, would decide whether atomic weapons were to be deployed. I mention this well-known episode the better to bring out the specific resonance, not without its tone of apprehension, of these lines late in "A Cabin in the Clearing":

> If the day ever comes when they know who
> They are, they may know better where they are.
> But who they are is too much to believe—
> Either for them or the onlooking world.
> They are too sudden to be credible.

There *was* something a little incredible, to the onlooking world, about the Americans in 1950–1951: the world's greatest military power was risking an expanded war in Korea with, it seemed, no especially clear sense of its mission, nor, apparently, of its chain of command with regard to the use of nuclear weapons. It wasn't even clear, until Truman fired MacArthur, that the military was duly subject to civilian authority. Truman did nothing to check the air of panic when, on December 15, 1950, he called for the mobilization of a 3.5 million–man army. "Our homes, our nation, all the things we believe in are in great danger," he told the nation. No wonder

Frost has Mist say, in "A Cabin in the Clearing," "I don't believe the sleepers in this house / Know where they are." The winter of 1950–1951 certainly was perplexing, a kind of watershed of the early Cold War period by which Frost's poem is so much marked. And yet, in "A Cabin in the Clearing," neither Mist nor Smoke—nor Frost himself for that matter—will have the "happiness" of the nation "despaired of": the poem retains the essential optimism, if not the millenialism, of the old American sense of errand. Its domestic idyll is relatively unperturbed, as Smoke and Mist well know, for the one issues from the hearth and the other from the garden: the great American homestead is, after all, maintaining its stays against confusion—against the cold of the outer night with its hearth-fires, and against the wilderness itself with its gardens. "A Cabin in the Clearing" suggests just how resilient, just how adaptable, the story about our domestic tranquility had always been, for here it all is again: a man and wife, a "bass" and a "soprano," making their wholesome mark upon the land and pushing back the woods. No matter that this time the American advance was into a New Frontier of geopolitics and Cold War and that the "bass" and "soprano" inhabiting this "cabin" might well be Ozzie and Harriet. The ideological equipment that Americans had always carried with them would serve just as well here as it had in Ohio in 1830.[9]

Frost seems sure enough, in poems like "A Cabin in the Clearing," about the basic soundness of the American enterprise, notwithstanding the apprehensions of the "onlooking world." No wonder Kennedy liked him. But the question to be asked is this: How harmoniously does the essential complacency of "A Cabin in the Clearing" settle in with the very weird mood of "Bursting Rapture"? How are the "mounting" technosexual energies imagined in the latter poem, with their carnival urge toward Thanatos, to be "contained"—since that was the going term—in the domestic idyll imagined in "A Cabin in the Clearing"? In short: Can America have The Bomb and still remain America? That is a question raised, implicitly but inevitably, by Frost's late poetry about American national identity and the American "errand." There were those, already in 1950, who believed that The Bomb had brought into our midst something uncontrollable, something irrational, something absurdly "un-American." Critics of what Eisenhower (a little darkly) called "the military-industrial complex" rose up to issue jeremiads about the state of the union in the Cold War. It would certainly be going too far to rank Frost among such critics,

9. Truman is quoted in Jim Patterson, *Grand Expectations: the United States 1945–1974* (New York: Oxford University Press, 1996), 223–24, 225.

even if he did, as in "Bursting Rapture," seem to understand something of the potentially grim logic of nuclear weapons research and the oncoming international arms race. But his late poetry, taken as a whole, does register a fairly wide range of possible responses to the new American situation. And not all of them are sunny. If "A Cabin in the Clearing" is a poem of Kennedy's up-going New Frontier, "Bursting Rapture," for its part, looks forward to criticisms of the culture of The Bomb made by writers like Mailer, Pynchon, and Ginsberg, not to mention filmmakers like Kubrick in *Dr. Strangelove* (already alluded to above). And it involves the sort of Cold War mischief of which Frost was often capable, and which, I am suggesting, made him ultimately unreliable to the Kennedy administration.

Frost's remarks about The Bomb were often provocatively whimsical, and they struck some readers as exhibiting very poor taste. It is as if Frost's chief aim were to escape the gravity of most public debate on the subject, whose tone had for many been set by J. Robert Oppenheimer's much-quoted remark on witnessing the first detonation at the Trinity site at Alamagordo in the summer of 1945. He, of course, had quoted the *Bhagavad Gita:* "If the radiance of thousand suns were to burst into the sky, that would be like the splendor of the Mighty One. I am become Death, destroyer of worlds." At about the time Oppenheimer made his remarks Frost wrote a little poem called "It Bids Pretty Fair" on much the same theme. It was collected in his 1947 volume, *Steeple Bush.*

> The play seems out for an almost infinite run.
> Don't mind a little thing like the actors fighting.
> The only thing I worry about is the sun.
> We'll be all right if nothing goes wrong with the lighting.
>
> (356)

The allegory is the Macbethian one of life as a play and the world as a stage. But in "It Bids Pretty Fair" we find none of the nihilism of Macbeth's great speech about "a tale told by an idiot" or about "sound and fury signifying nothing." Instead there is the wicked Yankee understatement of the title: "It bids *pretty* fair." Macbeth simply couldn't afford that kind of modesty. We are apparently meant to be solaced by the last two lines of Frost's poem: if there's to be an apocalypse, the bursting of a thousand suns in the sky, it will probably be a natural and not a "man-made" apocalypse. Again, as he says, "it bids pretty fair." The human comedy is out for "an almost infinite run." God, or whoever the Producer is, must be delighted. We will outlast even *Cats.* It is hard to imagine Oppenheimer—

not to mention more conventional Cold War liberals—taking this sort of fable with good grace. But then again, Oppenheimer would later oppose development of the H-bomb. He may have been—as Frost irresponsibly said of American policymakers in general—"too liberal to fight."[10]

"Bursting Rapture" and "It Bids Pretty Fair" date from the earliest years of the Cold War, when the USSR had not yet tested its bomb, and when the number of nuclear weapons the United States possessed could be counted on the fingers of two hands. But Frost's way of thinking about The Bomb and what it portended did not essentially change as the Cold War deepened and as the megatonnage of the weapons mounted absurdly toward, it seemed at the time, "a bursting rapture." "Pod of the Milkweed," which opens Frost's last book, *In the Clearing* (1962), is fascinating in this regard.

> Calling all butterflies of every race
> From source unknown but from no special place
> They ever will return to all their lives,
> Because unlike the bees they have no hives,
> The milkweed brings up to my very door
> The theme of wanton waste in peace and war
> As it has never been to me before.
> And so it seems a flower's coming out
> That should if not be talked then sung about. (425)

"*Wanton* waste in peace and war," Frost says, and the adjective is crucial: it establishes the sexual coordinates of the poem, which is, after all, about pollination. The milkweed flower is a kind of debutante, and this is its "coming out," its debut. The theme of "wanton waste" was one to which Frost often recurred, as in a poem he never collected called, simply, "Wanton Waste." There, looking out on the universe, he speaks of the incredible "expense of seed" it apparently took to "bring to birth the puny human race": all that matter, all that space, and for what? (558). "Pod of the Milkweed," as we shall see, gives this idea a disturbing twist by implicitly asking if humans are not waste. If so, then what might we spawn? What will be the end of our end? The question is leant urgency by the context of the Cold War and, more immediately, by those poems in Frost's last two books that take up the theme of nuclear holocaust. This is evident enough in "Pod of the Milkweed" itself, which is, after all, about wanton waste in peace *and war*, as Frost is careful to point out.

10. For Oppenheimer's remarks, see Patterson, *Grand Expectations*, 6.

"Bursting Rapture," as we have seen, already introduces the idea that there is something orgiastic, something intensely sexual, about the martial end to which, in those days, we seemed wedded. There, you will recall, Frost imagines the lust for science in the nuclear age to be "a mounting ecstasy / That when it gets too exquisite to bear / Will find relief in one burst. You shall see. / That's what a certain bomb was sent to be." "Pod of the Milkweed," too, brings together martial and sexual metaphors to contemplate a prospect of waste. "Countless wings," arising as if from "the infinite," harass the flower (and one another) for knowledge of what it holds—just for a taste of its "distilled honey." They riot and war among themselves with "thirst on hunger to the point of lust." But the meaning of this orgiastic battle is hardly clear.

> In being sweet to these ephemerals
> The sober weed has managed to contrive
> In our three hundred days and sixty five
> One day too sweet for beings to survive.
> Many shall come away as struggle worn
> And spent and dusted off of their regalia
> To which at daybreak they were freshly born
> As after one-of-them's proverbial failure
> From having beaten all day long in vain
> Against the wrong side of a window pane.

The sober weed is said to have "contrived" a day "too sweet for beings to survive." The observation seems to involve the concept of natural selection, as if to say that the weed had arrived at some cunning stratagem for putting to its own use the corporate energies of countless butterflies who extinguish their lives to perpetuate his. Of course, Frost understood that nothing can be said to "contrive" to meet an end like this. Natural selection doesn't work that way. There is nothing deliberate, nothing premeditated about its processes—nothing at all "meditative," in fact. And with this recognition we arrive at the bleaker horizon of the poem, which is, I believe, profoundly Darwinian in its thinking. The world imagined in this poem is without point and purpose, certainly without a narrowly "human" purpose. In fact, it is without a "scheme" of any sort, unless "waste" itself may be said to constitute one. "Waste" is, in any case, the "*essence* of the scheme," we are told (426). And the meaning even of that remains cryptic, as well it might. As for the butterflies:

And all the good they did for man or god
To all those flowers they passionately trod
Was leave as their posterity one pod
With an inheritance of restless dream.
He hangs on upside down with talon feet
In an inquisitive position odd
As any Guatemalan parakeet.
Something eludes him. Is it food to eat?
Or some dim secret of the good of waste?
He almost has it in his talon clutch.
Where have those flowers and butterflies all gone
That science may have staked the future on?
He seems to say the reason why so much
Should come to nothing must be fairly faced. (426)

The last lines point to the moral. The flower and the lovely butterflies may seem to us to lie at the very heart of the matter, to be its most significant features, its *purpose,* in fact. Surely such beauty, and not "waste," is the "essence of the scheme"; surely the world, as we know it, is meant somehow to bring these things out, to allow them to flourish. But the poem says waste, not grace, is the essence of the scheme. All that color, all that vitality, which seems to us so important, may only be an instrument, a device to be discarded by a god who doesn't exist. The lesson, if we take the liberty of extrapolation, is grim: Why *should* we call it a waste, really, if we should destroy ourselves, and the planet with us, in some such martial orgy of intemperate lust as "Bursting Rapture" imagines? Why should it be regretted, after all, if "so much should come to nothing"? The question must be "fairly faced" whether or not *we* are, in fact, "of the essence of the scheme," whether or not we know what the scheme is, whether or not we are, like Frost's butterflies, lovely ephemerals being made use of by some sober weed—a brilliant illumination on a green planet, and then nothing. A note Frost appended to these lines in *In the Clearing* suggests, somewhat ominously and cryptically, that this overwhelming question "shall," in fact, be faced "in due course" (426). But faced by whom, and when? Exactly what occasion will force that question on us? We can't answer these questions about the poem precisely. But a hint of an answer is most certainly— and subversively—provided by the poem itself. "Pod of the Milkweed" approaches—and this is certainly a provocative maneuver at the height of the Cold War—some "dim secret of the good of waste," and not only of waste in peace, but of "*wanton* waste" in *war,* as Frost says. That is the kind of waste that "Bursting Rapture" seems to anticipate. Science may have been all along betting on the wrong horse—humanity, a lovely ephemeral. In "staking the future" on our own success—whether as a nation or as a species—the rest of us laymen may only do the same. The point is insidiously antihumanist. That is no surprise, given what the poem owes to Darwin. But it is precisely its antihumanism that makes "Pod of the Milkweed" remarkable, both as a literary document of the Cold War and as a poem in a volume as touched by the Cold War as *In the Clearing*.

"Pod of the Milkweed" tends toward resignation at the thought that the great world might vanish and leave not a rack behind, as Prospero says in *The Tempest*. "It's a wonderful world," Frost said in concluding his last public lecture in Boston on December 2, 1962: "to hell with it." William Pritchard reports that Frost's audience was uncertain whether or not to laugh at that remark. And for good reason: the great extravagance of Frost's later poetry, insofar as it engages the Cold War, is precisely that it asks us to take ideas like that one seriously. As he says in a 1947 poem called "The Planners":

> No burst of nuclear phenomenon
> That put an end to what was going on
> Could make much difference to the dead and gone.
> Only a few of those even in whose day
> It happened would have very much to say.

It is possible that such talk appealed to Frost for personal reasons, perhaps because it seems to offer such good equipment for contemplating one's own end in peace, however ironically. Frost was, in those days, a very old man. On December 3, the morning after he consigned the world to hell in Boston, he entered Peter Bent Brigham Hospital, never again to leave. Maybe in 1962 he had all along been learning how "to go with the drift of things," how, at last, to "bow and accept the end" of a season, as he put it in an early poem (38). He certainly seemed to know "the end was in sight," as Pritchard says, when he concluded another December 1962 lecture by reading "The Night Light," collected first in his 1947 volume, *Steeple Bush*. Talking about bad dreams, broken sleep, and gloom, the speaker of this nocturne supposes that he has ahead of him "the darkest of it still to dread" (346). "Suppose I end on that dark note," Frost said. "Good night." Perhaps—to take another poem he recited at that late lecture— Frost was thinking of a day when everything, for him, would be "Closed for Good":

And so on into winter
Till even I have ceased
To come as a foot printer,
And only some slight beast
So mousy or so foxy
Shall print there as my proxy. (429)

Nevertheless, I hesitate to limit the reference even of this poem, with its vision of winter waste, to merely personal or vocational concerns. In *In the Clearing*, it is neatly framed by two Cold War parables about the identity and fate of America, "A Cabin in the Clearing" and "America Is Hard to See." And the poems of *In the Clearing*, together with certain poems on Cold War themes collected in *Steeple Bush*, amount to a pretty serious effort on Frost's part, humor notwithstanding, to think through the "nuclear phenomenon" that Americans and the onlooking world had alike brought to birth; and a pretty serious effort as well to think through even the possibility of an apocalyptic "bursting rapture" itself, though what he had in mind was hardly the "rapture" good Christians imagine.

There is always in these late books at least the prospect of a wasteland. And that wasteland is seldom contemplated with pious gravity, or even, at times, with any note of concern at all. To repeat: "It is a wonderful world," Frost said twelve days after Kennedy announced the resolution of the Cuban missile crisis: "to hell with it." He had certainly faced fairly the reason why, as he puts it in "Pod of the Milkweed," "so much should come to nothing." And he was facing it, as was only typical of him, in a way that the official culture of the Cold War simply couldn't properly "contain." By 1962 it had been years since Robert Frost had Learned to Stop Worrying and Love The Bomb—years since he had learned how to "fool" with it, as he himself might have said. That was the lesson about his very literary unpredictability that John F. Kennedy had to learn the hard way.[11]

11. **Pritchard**, 260, 256.

Robert Frost's Philosophy of Education
The Poet as Teacher

Peter J. Stanlis

I. FROST'S PHILOSOPHY OF EDUCATION

NO FROST SCHOLAR or literary critic has explored the close affinity, at times amounting to identity, between his theory of language and his philosophy of education; between his method as a poet and his practice as a classroom teacher. Since his sole ambition was to be a poet, he never seriously considered teaching as a vocation. Yet, having failed as a farmer, and having earned very little by his verse, he found it expedient to teach school. It provided a sufficient means to support his family while often affording some time to write poetry.

The public image of Frost is so completely centered on his role as a poet that it requires a strong shift in perspective to perceive him primarily as a teacher, with a uniquely original philosophy of education and pedagogical method. The poet himself once noted that "the three strands of my life" were "writing, teaching, and farming."[1] All three strands were intimately interrelated, and in time Frost himself became aware that a special identity little short of absolute existed between his poetry and his teaching: "It slowly dawned on me that my poetry and my teaching were one, and if you know my poetry at all well, you'd see that."[2] If Frost's poems are perceived as parables in metaphorical language and structured form, and as intimate dialogues between the poet as speaker and his readers, they can indeed be regarded as instrumental means to a pedagogical end.

In his essay "Education by Poetry" (1931), Frost made it clear that the essence of both poetry and education is to teach readers and students how

---

1. **Lathem**, 242.
2. Horace W. Hewlett, *In Other Words: Amherst in Prose and Verse* (Amherst: Amherst College, 1964), 176. For an account of Frost as poet-teacher, see Robert Pack, "Robert Frost's 'Enigmatical Reserve': The Poet as Teacher and Preacher," *Robert Frost: Lectures on the Centennial of His Birth* (Washington, D.C.: Library of Congress, 1975), 43–55.

to think validly in metaphor and to acquire a sense of form, regarding structured physical and spiritual reality: "Unless you are at home in the metaphor, unless you have had your proper poetical education in the metaphor, you are not safe anywhere. Because you are not at ease with figurative values: you don't know the metaphor in its strength and its weakness. You don't know how far you may expect to ride it and where it may break down. . . . You are not safe in science; you are not safe in history."[3] As he increasingly came to believe that all sound thinking was essentially metaphorical, that "all things still pair in metaphor," involving comparisons, contrasts, parallels, conflicts, contradictions, ambiguities, and so on, within the vast range of interactions between matter and spirit, the great ends of poetry and education became identical means for knowledge, revelation, insight, and understanding. Both Frost's theory of poetry and his philosophy of education were based upon his dualistic view of reality, and this provided the inexorable bond of unity between his poetry and his teaching.

To understand Frost's philosophy of education, it is essential to take fully into account the historical and philosophical origins of the cultural traditions of Western civilization as embodied in the humanities and liberal arts. Although he believed "there's no such thing as progress," he did contend that there were golden eras in the westward historical course of empire:

> There are flowering times—Greece, Rome, Byzantium, Spain, France, England, and so on. . . . Rome wasn't so good as Greece, by general consent . . . and before that, too, of course, Babylon, Assyria, Phoenicia, Egypt. . . . But for a little golden time—the Periclean Age—a great flowering with philosophers and artists, and the general color and glow. Washington was one of ours. He made his form with people and large social forces. That was our flowering time.[4]

In 1937, Lawrance Thompson enlarged upon Frost's belief regarding the course of Western civilization:

> The Western approach, Frost held, had been an attempt to blend materialism and spirituality to the greatest possible extent. The "run" of civilization, for Frost, had been west-northwest, from the Tigris and

3. **Prose**, 39.
4. **Cox**, 121–22.

Euphrates valleys, from Israel and Asia Minor, up and across the corner of the Mediterranean to Greece and Rome, up across Europe and England to the United States: west-northwest all the time. He saw America as the high point of civilization.[5]

According to Frost, American democracy also had its ultimate origins in the ancient political traditions of the Greek polis: "Ours is a very ancient political growth, beginning at one end of the Mediterranean Sea and coming westward—tried in Athens, tried in Italy, tried in England, tried in France, coming westward all the way to us."[6] The westward course of civilization included the extension and refinement of the philosophy, art, literature, religion, government, laws, and science of the ancient classical world, combined with and embodied in the world order of Christianity during the Middle Ages, and transmitted after the discoveries of Columbus to the Western Hemisphere. Frost was well aware of how science evolved out of the rationalism of scholastic thought late in the Middle Ages and during the Renaissance, and how it became increasingly important in providing the worldview of Europeans and Americans regarding the place of mankind in the universe. Science, he held, was not limited to physical nature; its methods came more and more to be applied to every branch of knowledge. Yet to Frost science always remained a part of the humanities. He contrasted the dynamic duality and interactions between matter and spirit so characteristic in Western civilization and culture with Oriental civilization, which he thought was too rooted in a spiritual passivity, without much science.

To Frost, a person was well educated to the extent that he possessed knowledge and insightful understanding of the essential facts and principles that gave substance and spirit to all of the enormously complex historical and philosophical elements that had formed Western civilization. Both his positive principles and methods in education, and his harsh negative strictures on all that he perceived to be wrong with modern American education, from high school through college and graduate studies, reflected his belief that Western culture provided the norms for a valid system of education. At the heart of Western culture were the humanities, which Frost on several occasions called "the book of the worthies."

The classical Christian-oriented system of education had remained virtually intact throughout Europe and America up to modern times.

5. **Later Years,** 226.
6. **Lathem,** 240.

In June 1939, in conversation with students at the Bread Loaf School of English, Frost indicated his awareness that a revolutionary change in education had occurred during the Victorian era. This was the very period in which Frost matured as a student and teacher. The Victorian conflict was precipitated by Thomas Henry Huxley, among others, who advocated that science and technology, as independent and self-sufficient subjects, should displace the ancient classical curriculum in British education. His chief opponents were Matthew Arnold and John Henry Cardinal Newman, who defended the long-established humanities tradition of education. Frost was highly emphatic in making it clear that his sympathies were entirely with Arnold and Newman, particularly because Huxley's educational program in an accelerated form slowly but surely was becoming dominant in the twentieth century.

Matthew Arnold was himself the product of his father's philosophy of education, as summarized by Gordon A. Craig:

> In the first half of the nineteenth century, the curriculum of Rugby School in England was dominated, as was true of other public schools, by instruction in Greek and Latin. In addition . . . all students from the first to the sixth grade read history, both ancient and modern, which was interlarded with generous portions of Herodotus, Thuseydides, Xenophon, and Livy. Dr. Thomas Arnold, the famous headmaster of Rugby, once gave the rationale for this by saying, "The history of Greece and Rome is not an idle inquiry about remote ages and forgotten institutions but a living picture of things present, fitted not so much for the curiosity of the scholar, as for the instruction of the statesman and citizen."[7]

Matthew Arnold strongly rejected Huxley's crusade to replace the ancient Greek and Latin languages and classics, taught at Cambridge and Oxford, with modern science and technology, centered in a utilitarian curriculum and pragmatic courses in mechanics, industry, business, and commerce. In "Literature and Science," he had disapproved of Huxley's criticism of the liberal arts as too remote from life and therefore useless, or at best an ornamental appendage in human nature. Frost told the students at Bread Loaf that Arnold's line from "Dover Beach," *where ignorant armies clash by night,* inspired much of his negative view on modern education. His

7. Gordon A. Craig, "The Good, the Bad and the Bourgeois," in *New York Review of Books,* 45, no. 13 (August 13, 1998), p. 8. For a brief account of the conflict between Arnold and Huxley, see Lionel Trilling, *Matthew Arnold* (New York: Harcourt, Brace and Jovanovich, 1954), 371–72.

awareness of the whole course of modern education was a refinement of Arnold's thesis against Huxley, but it was reinforced by his own experience of American education. He feared that the blend of matter and spirit that had characterized Western culture for centuries would increasingly be subordinated to a monistic materialism based upon science. Both in high school and college, Frost had studied Greek and Latin languages and literature, so that when he stated to the Bread Loaf students that the degeneration and corruption of modern American education began when Greek and Latin were dropped from the high school curriculum, he meant far more than the loss of a knowledge of these ancient languages.[8] He meant that the literature, art, philosophy, and culture of the ancient classical world was largely abandoned, with the result that students were rendered incognizant of a great deal of what had made Western civilization the greatest achievement of mankind.

Frost found much to admire in Newman's educational philosophy in *The Idea of a University* (1852). Like Frost, Newman was a philosophical dualist, and neither found any contradiction between science and religion.[9] The two also shared an essentially Aristotelian rather than a Platonic view of reality and the arts. Despite all of their differences in time, place, and religion, the broad premises and the view of human nature that they held in common eventuated in their having remarkably similar conceptions of education. Their most important difference was between Newman's belief that theology was central in higher education and Frost's that the power of artistic creativity and originality in ideas was most crucial in the educational process.[10] Yet even in this vital difference they had something in common: Frost's four "beliefs," culminating in belief in God, are very similar to Newman's "Discourse III, on the bearing of theology on other knowledge." Also, Newman's argument that studies which "exercise the faculty of judgment . . . are the true basis of education for the active and

---

8. On two other occasions Frost stated his conviction that the loss of Latin from the high school curriculum was the beginning of the serious decline of American education. In 1916 to Morris P. Tilley he lamented the replacement of the classics by vocational studies. After a visit to Frost at Bread Loaf on June 3, 1962, Robert Cotner wrote: "He felt the decline in American education began when Latin was made an option and finally removed entirely from the curriculum" (Robert Cotner to Peter Stanlis, June 26, 1998).

9. See John Henry Cardinal Newman, *The Idea of a University* (New York: Longmans, Green, 1923), 227. All references are to this edition of Newman's book.

10. As Louis Untermeyer observed: "Frost was almost as preoccupied with teaching as he was with creating. As a teacher he dwelt almost entirely upon the creative impulse." *Robert Frost: A Backward Look* (Washington, D.C.: Reference Department, The Library of Congress, 1964), 22.

inventive powers" close to Frost's emphasis on aesthetic creativity as basic in education.[11]

Both Newman and Frost believed that the humanities went far beyond Bacon's scientific dictum that "knowledge is power"; they held that moral and aesthetic wisdom were greater traits of human character. Frost agreed with Newman's belief that the chief object of education was to develop the total nature of a student by acquiring the essential principles of universal knowledge through a cultivation of the intellectual virtues. As Newman put it: "general culture of mind is the best aid to professional and scientific study; and educated men can do what illiterate cannot."[12] Both held that good judgment and a cultivated taste were among the great values of liberal education, because the humanities form a habit of mind that endures for a lifetime.

Frost found many of Newman's particular points very close to his own beliefs. He certainly agreed with Newman's criticism of John Locke's attack upon the learning of Latin, which the philosopher held to be a useless language.[13] Then too, his attitude toward formal instruction coincided with Newman's, whose unqualified endorsement of independent studies echoed Frost's frequent advice to students to abandon their university studies to pursue their own genius: "Self-education in any shape . . . is preferable to a system of teaching which, professing so much really does so little for the mind. . . . How much better . . . is it for the active and thoughtful intellect . . . to eschew the college and university altogether, than to submit to a drudgery so ignoble."[14] Newman's belief that "knowledge is its own end," his opposition to narrow specialization in education, and several other important points, were close in substance and spirit to Frost's philosophy of education.

In an interview with Janet Mabie, published in *The Christian Science Monitor* (December 24, 1925), Frost stated what was probably his most important positive conviction about education. It was based upon his entire previous experience as a student and teacher, but more directly upon what he underwent as a member of the faculty and poet-in-residence at Amherst College and the University of Michigan. He called his basic method "education by presence." It was his alternative to the standardized academic

---

11. Newman, *The Idea of a University*, 175.
12. Ibid., 165, see also, 166–67.
13. Ibid., 158–63.
14. Ibid., 148–49, see also, 150. Newman praised George Crabbe's "Tales of the Hall," which celebrates the self-education of a farm boy, a work that Frost admired.

assumptions and methods in American colleges. In essence, "education by presence" was Frost's adoption and original refinement of the tutorial method of instruction practiced in Oxford and Cambridge universities, as he applied it broadly in the more democratic and informal conditions of American colleges. He noted that "students get most from professors who have marked wide horizons," because they pay close attention to teachers with a reputation beyond the local campus.

Education by presence led Frost to state that "the business of the teacher is . . . to challenge the student's purpose" beyond any occupational objectives. The most effective method in challenging a student's purpose was not through formal contact in the classroom, that is, through a structured course of lectures, and the routine of a fixed curriculum for majors, which includes tests, keeping notebooks, research assignments, prescribed papers, busy-work, and the whole formulated apparatus of colleges, through subjects divided into specialized departments—all aimed at a final grade. Even academic committees were pure anathema to Frost. He once remarked that if he were president of a college he would abolish all committees, except one—a committee to abolish all committees. He did not believe that the primary objective of a college was to stock the student's mind with all sorts of detailed knowledge, much of it beyond his capability to utilize in any purposeful and creative activity. He held that instructors evoked the best response from students not by "putting the screws" on them, but by placing them in "an atmosphere of expectations." He acknowledged that his greatest inspiration as a student at Harvard was from William James, "a man whose classes I have never attended," and that "the book that influenced me most was *Piers the Plowman*, yet I never read it." In both of these instances Frost's creative imagination was released in ways that inspired him to pursue his own life's work in thought and poetry. Although education by presence was the most essential element in Frost's philosophy of education, it assumed the necessity of acquiring a set of prerequisites that included the ancient classics and an understanding of the history, philosophy, literature, religion, and science of Western civilization.

Of the three basic ways of teaching—by formal contact through lectures in the classroom, by informal social contact, and by virtually no contact between teacher and student—Frost ranked the last first in importance. Even in "formal classroom teaching," he contended, "it is the essence of symposium I'm after. Heaps of ideas and the subject matter of books purely incidental." The give-and-take of good talk between two individuals came the closest to "the wild free ways of wit and art" which led to superior "prowess and performance" in studies, in art and in life. A conversation between a teacher and student was to Frost a "seminar of the elect," which allowed talent and genius to develop ambitions without the restraints of system.[15] Informal contacts between independent and original teachers could draw out the best in students by creating "an atmosphere of expectations." In 1924, at Amherst, he urged the administration to bring a famous painter to campus, so that students could have the experience of a studio apprenticeship. He believed that the presence of great artists, scientists, and scholars would benefit everyone on campus, and that the whole cultural life of the community would be enhanced, thus minimizing the materialism that threatened to subordinate or even to destroy the humanities in education.[16]

At the New School of Social Research in New York City, Harry Hansen recorded in 1930 how Alvin Johnson practiced Frost's concept of education by presence in a small seminar: "Alvin Johnson used to place Frost in a circle of students and give him free rein to do as he would. It wasn't long, he says, before the room was surcharged with a spirit—a feeling of common understanding superinduced by the elemental and profound wisdom of the teacher."[17] Clearly, Frost's breadth and depth of knowledge in many fields, and his brilliance as a conversationalist, were the key ingredients for success through education by presence. In such a seminar, a run-of-the-mill teacher could easily be a disaster. Yet Frost advocated that "every teacher should have his time arranged to permit freer informal contacts with students. Art, the various sciences, research, lend themselves to this treatment. . . . Courses should be a means of introduction, to give students a claim on me, so that they may come to me at any time, outside of class periods." Such an informal system of education required students who were genuinely interested in learning and in developing their talents. Frost called such students "self-starters" and said of them: "I favor the student who will convert my claim on him into his claim on me. . . . Give me the high-spirited kind that hate an order to do what they were about to do of their own accord." Like Matthew Arnold's "saving remnant," such students were what Frost called "the free-born," who wished to develop their intellectual, moral, aesthetic, social, and physical nature as an end in itself, apart from any regard for professional objectives.

15. **Cox,** 49.
16. See *Robert Frost at Bread Loaf* (Middlebury, Vt.: Middlebury College Press, 1964), 4.
17. Louis Mertins, *Robert Frost: Life and Talks-Walking* (Norman: University of Oklahoma Press, 1965), 213.

It would be a mistake to conclude that Frost's education by presence made his philosophy of education too elitist for American society. In contrast to the "free-born" students were "the slaves," those who accepted uncritically the whole conventional system of structured institutional training. Frost stated his preference unequivocally, but he made it clear that he would also provide for the slaves: "I am for the wide-open educational system for the free-born. The slaves are another question. I will not refuse to treat them as slaves wherever found. 'Those who will, may,' would be my first motto: but a close second, 'Those who won't must.' That is to say, I shouldn't disdain to provide for the slaves, if slaves they insisted on being. I shouldn't anyway unless I were too busy with the free-born."[18] He was well aware that in American democratic society it was necessary and good to accept and support the general compulsory system of free public education which prevailed from kindergarten through high school.

In an interview in South Shaftesbury, Vermont (August 18, 1936), he acknowledged that in American education "we have generally made it possible for most anyone to go as far in any direction as he seemed willing and capable." He agreed that students should "get as much general education over as wide a field as possible," without regard to distinctions based upon special ability and interests. He would "let the sheep and the goats run together for a good long while," confident that because of the range in ability and cultural interests students "eventually . . . separate themselves." On this occasion the one caution he adopted was to advocate "the extension of general education and the postponement of specialization until later years." To Louis Untermeyer, he confided that he was for people learning as well as learned people: "I'm for educated humanity all the time—except in any undiscriminating way."[19] Although Frost's philosophy of education laid great stress on superior intellectual and creative ability and the possession of cultural interests, it did not preclude instruction for the less qualified members of the general public.

II. FROST AS CRITIC OF MODERN EDUCATION

Although Frost called himself a "radical" in education, he also insisted that he was not a "rebel." In his defense of the ancient classical tradition in education, centered as it was in the humanities and liberal arts, he

18. **Lathem,** 67–71.
19. Louis Untermeyer, *Robert Frost: A Backward Look*, 22.

was in fact a traditionalist; his radicalism consisted of an attack on the leaders in American education, those who had betrayed that tradition and had established a science-oriented and materialist system of instruction. Frost believed that the great failure in American education was in the high schools. In 1958, while he was Consultant in Poetry at the Library of Congress, he answered questions by teachers, students, and would-be writers and delivered himself on the state of education in high schools, on which, half spoofingly, he declared himself to be "the greatest living expert":

> I have long thought that our high schools should be improved. Nobody should come into our high schools without examination—not aptitude tests, but on reading, 'riting, and 'rithmetic. And that goes for black or white. . . . A lot of people are being scared by the Russian Sputnik into wanting to harden up our education or speed it up. I am interested in toning it up, at the high school level. . . . If they want to Spartanize the country, let them. I would rather perish as Athens than prevail as Sparta. The tone is Athens.[20]

By toning up high school education as Athens, Frost meant two things: disciplining the students and retaining the highest possible standards in a curriculum centered in the classics and humanities. During an interview on December 1, 1961, he made his meaning clear: "I'm at large, and I'm a civilized man, but school is for discipline. A student is an orange pip between my fingers: if I pinch him he'll go far. I'm not violent, but I'm going for the whole damn system. Discipline. Tightness, Firmness. Crispness. Sternness, and sternness in our lives. Life is tons of discipline."[21] A high-minded puritan element was clearly part of Frost's libertarian philosophy of education.

Probably the greatest error ever made regarding Frost's views on education was committed by Jeffrey Meyers when he claimed that the poet was an "advocate" of and a "strong believer in progressive education."[22] Nothing could have been further from the truth. Meyers committed the common fallacy of the false single alternative. He assumed that, because Frost and John Dewey's disciples were both highly critical of the established system of schools, their views must be identical. In fact, Frost regarded the reforms initiated and popularized by Dewey at Columbia University as

20. **Later Years,** 263–64.
21. **Lathem,** 270.
22. **Meyers,** 212, 262.

the worst possible solution for what was wrong with American secondary education. To Sidney Cox, who knew Frost well for almost forty years, who regarded him as his mentor, and who modeled his teaching style on that of the poet, he wrote: "Something in school should save us from the fatal credulity of progress prophets."[23] He reminded Cox that in America "progress is our chief native simile."[24] As Cox noted, Frost's antithetical philosophy of education was formed independently, years before Dewey's theory became public:

> Before anyone had heard of John Dewey outside the University of Chicago and Columbia, Robert Frost was mocking at the rigidities and unrealities of formal education, turning his back on them, and then, as teacher, inconspicuously sabotaging them in academy and normal school. But by the time that all the quick catchers-on were practicing the new progressive stereotypes, Robert Frost was saying school was a place for drill, rote learning, the three R's; literature and experience were too delicate and too much alive for school. Let school deal with numbers and letters. Let it not mechanically meddle with imagination, insight, taste.[25]

Cox observed that one of the most important differences between Frost and "progressive" educators was in their conceptions of freedom: "He was no early Dewey. Freedom from rote learning was not his point; there was need for that. It was not freedom from direction. . . . It was not freedom from lecturing. . . . It wasn't freedom to say 'No, no, no' to the teacher's 'Yes, yes, yes.'"[26] Whereas Frost wished to tighten student discipline, progressive theorists loosened the reins of control, and introduced the child-centered school.

But the differences between Frost's views and those of Dewey went far beyond their respective conceptions of freedom. Even as a high school student, Frost defended tradition and social custom. He wrote that he would "follow custom—not without question, but where it does not conflict with the broader habits of life gained by wanderers among ideas." This, he added, was in sharp contrast with the "radical enemies of custom," who would establish "an inquisition to compel liberality."[27] To Frost, progressive education was a closed system that would "compel liberality."

23. **Cox,** 46.
24. Ibid., 264.
25. Ibid., 40–41.
26. Ibid., 52–53.
27. **Early Years,** 119.

Like Rousseau, it would force students to be free, not merely from self-discipline, but from social traditions and normative beliefs. As Louis Mertins has recorded, the qualities of disciplined character that Frost cherished were the opposite of those fostered by progressive education:

> In a world trembling toward progressive education—he is stressing rules of hard learning. . . . Frost wanted, always, for himself and for his students, complete freedom of thinking and acting. . . . He wanted the student to be a free agent, untrammeled by the teaching system. But he went against the "new" theories that 'readin,' 'writin,' and 'rithmetic' were expendable and unimportant. How many times he has excoriated some lazy pupil for handing in a dirty school "project" full of slovenly spelling and impossible grammar! . . . For the slovenly teacher who said case didn't matter, he had many scornful words.[28]

To Frost, the progressive theory of the child-centered school was false. Its worst feature was to encourage immature and uneducated students to have a decisive voice in determining the curriculum. Frost's response was to declare "There is such a thing as not being old enough to understand."[29] He always insisted that youth must go to school in the humanities. His views had ample room for "self-starters," students who were "daft on education," like the college boy in "The Death of the Hired Man," who "studied Latin, like the violin, because he liked it." Such a boy was truly a wanderer among ideas, destined to live "the broader habits of life," regardless of his professional objectives.

Two things in progressive educators provoked Frost's particular rage—their abandonment of the ancient Greek and Roman classics and their attempts to apply the scientific method in teaching. The latter separated form or technique from genuine content. On February 8, 1917, he wrote to Untermeyer on "the latest thing in the schools"; "Damn these separations of the form from the substance. I don't know how long I could stand them." Twenty years later, on January 5, 1937, he again wrote to Untermeyer on the same theme, noting that in his view the president of the University of Chicago advocated the progressive theory in studying languages:

> I see where President Hutchins doesn't believe in learning languages ancient or modern. Only grammar (from the Chinese glamour) logic mathematics and rhetoric. Of all the god dam— . . . Some more of this

28. Mertins, *Robert Frost: Life and Talks-Walking,* 317, see also, 318.
29. **Later Years,** 443.

form-without-content guff. Ain't we had almost enough of it pro tem? Kick me under the table if I'm out of order. The best way to learn to swim is out of water, pivoted on a skewer. I was taught all the motions of a screw driver before I saw my first screw. Very expensive Montessori education at Madam Zitsker's in San Francisco circa 1880.[30]

To Frost, teaching technique without reference to the content in subjects resulted in ignorance, and avoided the complex experience of creativity— "the breathless swing between matter and form," which only the free and creative mind could experience.[31] In his view, teaching was an art, not a science, and the scientific method was out of place in classroom teaching.

The teacher-training methods of John Dewey's theory came in for some of Frost's harshest criticism, yet his censure was qualified by an awareness that some teachers do need help:

> The beautiful bare text for me. Teachers who don't know what to do with it, let them perish and lose their jobs. I don't allow for the existence of teachers who depend on "teachers' helps". But I dunnow! There are more people on earth than are provided for in my philosophy—latitudinarien though I try to be. . . . If there are teachers in quantity who need your help you must help them. Only do it as little as you can and withdrawingly so as to throw them finally on their own resources.[32]

When Frost accepted a one-year appointment in 1911–1912 to teach at the Plymouth Normal School in New Hampshire, the first thing he did was to discard the textbook, Monroe's *History of Education.* He replaced it with William James's *Talk to Teachers on Psychology* and *Psychology: The Briefer Course* and such primary fictional works of literature as Mark Twain's "The Celebrated Jumping Frog of Calaveras County." In teaching the James texts, he deliberately sabotaged the assumption of progressive educators that psychology is a science and that it could provide the key to better teaching: "I went up there to disabuse the Teacher's College of the idea that there is any immediate connection between any psychology and their classroom work, disabuse them of the notion that they could mesmerize a class if they knew enough psychology. That's what they thought."[33]

30. **Untermeyer,** 287–88.
31. **Cox,** 26.
32. **Untermeyer,** 183, 194.
33. "Robert Frost," *Writers at Work: The Paris Review Interviews,* Second Series, introduced by Van Wyck Brooks (Viking Press: New York, 1960), 24.

Frost also rejected the social objective of progressive education—to indoctrinate students in favor of egalitarian democracy. He always favored education that would allow "the cream to rise to the top." He believed that in secondary education the progressive theory stressed emotion too much, whereas graduate studies were too centered in abstract reasons: "I know there is a crowd of 'emotionalists' who threw all to the winds except emotion. I think they're perhaps worse than the 'intellectualists,' who are the other extreme. But a happy mixture, that's it."[34] To Frost, sound education involved all of human nature.

Frost was very fond of Mark Twain's short story "The Celebrated Jumping Frog of Calaveras County," both for its lyrical qualities as a prose narrative and for its essential theme. He interpreted the story as "a great parable in education."[35] When the frog was trained and sensitized to jump with only a featherlike prod in his rear, he outjumped all rival frogs set against him. But when the city slicker, who bet against his owner, secretly slipped a handful of buckshot pellets into the champion frog, even strong and persistent prods could not budge him, and very ordinary frogs were able to outjump him. Frost explained that before the frog was filled with buckshot he was "like a poet . . . a free spirit" who had assimilated only as much knowledge as was needed to give him strength to jump far. But after swallowing the buckshot pellets the frog "became a scholar . . . weighted down and ponderous with useless knowledge, and unable to jump." Frost's own prototype of a ponderous professor was Dr. Magoon, in "A Hundred Collars," a satirical portrait of a deadly introverted nervous academic who was rather too fond of calling himself "Doctor." When he is forced to share a hotel room with a half-literate French Canadian bill collector named "Lafe," who mistakes him for a medical doctor, Magoon corrects him by saying, "Well, a teacher." Frost was favorably oriented to sound scholarship, but he despised academic affectation.

Perhaps nothing reveals more about Frost's philosophy of education than his conflict over first principles with Alexander Meiklejohn, president of Amherst College from 1912 to 1923. In 1916, Meiklejohn began his program to build an unusual faculty by appointing Frost to teach at Amherst, beginning in January 1917, even though the poet had no degree. Frost approved of Meiklejohn's opposition to the elective system, which had been propounded by President Eliot at Harvard, and also his apparent

34. **Lathem,** 13.
35. Ibid., 98. In 1940 Frost discussed Twain's jumping frog story with Peter Stanlis: "Robert Frost at Bread Loaf—1939–1941," in **Tharpe III,** 237–38.

endorsement of the core curriculum centered in the ancient classics and humanities, called "The Amherst Idea," so that initially he and the president got along well.

But when Meiklejohn hired and gave preferential promotions to young faculty members in courses in sociology and economics, many of whom were ideological theorists and believers in the idea of progress, Frost became skeptical of his leadership. His skepticism was confirmed when the president invited radical visiting lecturers to Amherst, such as the Marxist-anarchist Emma Goldman. Sidney Cox recorded Frost's response to the new faculty who assumed that science and religion were incompatible, and therefore thought it their right and duty to disabuse students of their traditional religious beliefs in favor of science and radical partisan politics: "Robert Frost indignantly denounced college teaching that 'frisks freshmen of their principles,' because 'a boy with all of his beliefs drawn out of him is in no condition to learn.'"[36] Meiklejohn's special interest was logic, and unlike Frost he believed that it was possible to translate logic through speculative discursive reasoning and argument into life's practical problems and to find solutions to them.

To Frost, Meiklejohn's conception of academic freedom was merely a collegiate adaptation of Dewey's progressive education in the form of doctrinaire compulsory liberalism, centered in social problems rather than in psychology. Meiklejohn's educational reforms were in the spirit of what Frost called "the guild of social planners," men who assumed that abstract reason and logic were sufficient to solve the world's great perennial problems. After meeting with some of Meiklejohn's young faculty appointees, Dwight Morrow, an Amherst trustee, described them to a friend as "bumptious young men . . . who insisted that nobody thought or studied at Amherst until they came."[37] Frost's similar criticism of the whole experimental method introduced by Meiklejohn was centered in its effect upon the students, giving them the happy illusion that, despite their ignorance of the humanities, they were profound thinkers:

> The boys had been made uncommonly interesting to themselves by Meiklejohn. They fancied themselves thinkers. At Amherst you *thought*, while at other colleges you merely *learned*. . . . I found that by thinking

36. **Cox,** 45. In 1939 Frost said the same thing in conversation with Peter Stanlis: **Tharpe III,** 207. These conversations are filled with a great variety of Frost's comments on education.

37. "The Story in the Meiklejohn Files," Amherst College Archives: (fall, 1982; spring, 1983), part 2, p. 57.

they meant stocking up with radical ideas. By learning they meant stocking up with conservative ideas—a harmless distinction, bless their simple hearts. I really liked them. It got so I called them the young intelligences—without offense. We got on like a set of cogwheels in a clock. They had picked up the idea somewhere that the time was now past for the teacher to teach the pupil. From now on it was the thing for the pupil to teach himself using, as he saw fit, the teacher as an instrument. The understanding was that my leg was always on the table for anyone to seize by that thought he could swing me as an instrument to teach himself with. So we had an amusing year. . . . I sat there patiently waiting, waiting for the youth to take education into their own hands and start the new world. Sometimes I laughed and sometimes I cried a little internally. I gave one course in reading and one course in philosophy, but they both came to the same thing. I was determined to have it out with my youngers and betters as to what thinking really was. We reached an agreement that most of what they had regarded as thinking, their own and other peoples, was nothing but voting—taking sides on an issue they had nothing to do with laying down.[38]

Frost then made it clear that unless students had original ideas based upon essential knowledge in the humanities, ideas that they could put forth in terms of metaphors, analogies, comparisons, and so on, they could not rightly claim to be "thinkers":

Many were ready to give up beaten and own themselves no thinkers in my sense of the word. They never set up to be original. They never pretended to put this and that together for themselves. Never had a metaphor, never made an analogy. But they had. I knew. So I put them on the operating table and proceeded to take ideas they didn't know they had out of them as a prestidigitator takes rabbits and pigeons you have declared yourself innocent of out of your pockets, trouserlegs and even mouth. Only a few resented being thus shown up and caught with the goods on them.[39]

As Frost saw the matter, the Meiklejohn program merely converted faculty and students alike into social meddlers: "Shakespeare says it is the right virtue of the meddler to be rotten before it is ripe. Overdevelop the social conscience and make us all meddlers."[40] In general, Frost disliked reformers and considered many of them to be mindless activists.

38. Ibid., 55. See also, **Untermeyer,** 170.
39. "The Story in the Meiklejohn Files," 55.
40. Robert Frost, "Maturity No Object," in **Prose,** 49.

The hubris of their young teachers deluded egotistical students into imagining that through their rational discussions they could find easy and valid solutions to the complex problems of society. Frost's poem, "An Empty Threat," (1923), concludes in a satire aimed at this type of rationalism: " . . . life's victories of doubt / That need endless talk-talk / To make them out." If Meiklejohn's rationalism would come to prevail in American education, Frost believed it was only a matter of time before the so-called "social sciences" would replace literature; psychology would replace philosophy, and modern languages would replace Greek and Latin, and, in turn, be replaced by philology.

In pursuit of his educational objectives, Meiklejohn perceived himself as an avant-garde pioneer preparing the way for an enlightened future America. In his inaugural address, he said he hoped to give students "that zest, that delight in things intellectual" that would make them "men of intellectual culture." His course in logic created disciples among his students, who regarded him as a brilliant, witty, socially charming, and eloquent teacher and man of ideas. His charismatic talks in chapel inspired his devoted students with an enthusiasm to go out and conquer the world. Years after he was forced to resign, largely for financial mismanagement, Phyllis Bottome defended him in the *New Republic:* "President Meiklejohn was adored by the undergraduates, and the attention of America was sympathetically focused upon his great experiment."[41]

Although Meiklejohn's progressive ideas provoked strong opposition among the faculty, his difficulties at Amherst were more the result of his administrative decisions and policies. He dismissed faculty members who failed to meet his requirements and forced retirement at age sixty-five. Above the objections of the faculty committee on promotions, he advanced one instructor to associate professor. He dismissed five associate professors whom he regarded as "deadwood," and when the faculty objected to their bad treatment, he confronted them with charges of disloyalty. Among the long-established faculty, Professor George Bosworth Churchill in the department of English became Meiklejohn's chief adversary. By 1920 the Amherst faculty was divided into two strongly opposed factions, pro- or anti-Meiklejohn, and Frost was clearly on the side of the traditionalists in

41. Phillis Bottome, *New Republic* (April 15, 1936): 280. For a version of the Frost-Meiklejohn conflict more sympathetic to the president, see **Triumph,** 97–122, 550–57. In defense of Frost, see Louis Mertins, *Robert Frost: Life and Talks-Walking,* 154–59, 161.

education.[42] To the poet, the system of education introduced by Meiklejohn was simply the American version of Julien Benda's *trahison des clercs*, teachers who abandoned the quest for philosophical truths based upon the Western tradition of humanities and instead engaged in political squabbles. Frost was aware that Meiklejohn held him in contempt as an "anti-intellectual." In his view, the president was a Pied Piper of Hamelin, luring innocent students to their destruction. The differences between the two men became so unbearable to Frost that he resigned from Amherst in 1920 and returned to his farm in Franconia, New Hampshire. In declining to speak before an Amherst alumni group who had invited him, Frost wrote that he had resigned because he was "too much out of sympathy with what the present administration seems bent on doing with this old New England College."

In retrospect it appeared to Frost that Meiklejohn had subverted his own original "Amherst Idea" that had first attracted the poet to Amherst in favor of the illusions of the idea of progress. On May 15, 1920, he wrote to Wilbur L. Cross at Yale on why he had left his first academic teaching post:

> I discovered what the Amherst Idea was that is so much talked of, and I got amicably out. The Amherst Idea as I had it in so many words from the high custodian is this: "Freedom for taste and intellect." Freedom from what? Freedom from every prejudice in favor of state, home, church, morality, etc. I am too much a creature of prejudice to stay and listen to such stuff. Not only in favor of morality am I prejudiced, but in favor of an immorality I could name as against other immoralities. I'd no more set out in pursuit of the truth than I would in pursuit of a living unless mounted on my prejudices.[43]

It is clear that, like Edmund Burke, whom the poet greatly admired, by "prejudice" he simply meant moral habit beyond reflection built into human nature from infancy in favor of home, church, and state. Frost was convinced that Meiklejohn's "freedom for taste and intellect" was destructive of the norms in the basic institutions of civil society, and involved a drastic separation of the intellectual virtues from the moral virtues.

In 1924, Frost accepted President George Olds's invitation to return to Amherst College as poet-in-residence and stated that he was eager to "help show the world the difference between the right kind of liberal

42. See Elizabeth S. Sergeant, *Robert Frost: The Trial by Existence* (Holt, Rinehart and Winston: New York, 1960), 258.
43. **Letters**, 250.

college and the wrong kind."[44] His connection with Amherst continued with occasional interruptions for several decades, and in the long run his influence on the college was far greater than that of Meiklejohn. An ironical conclusion to this complex story was made in 1954 by Charles Cole as president of Amherst: "Alexander Meiklejohn's great contribution to Amherst was Robert Frost."[45] The poet's "education by presence" had become a legend, not only at Amherst, but in the collegiate institutions of the surrounding region: Mount Holyoke, Smith, and the University of Massachusetts.

III. THE POET AS TEACHER

One of the supreme ironies in Frost's life, particularly as a teacher, was the common charge by educators such as Meiklejohn that he was an "anti-intellectual." This charge often resulted from the poet's skepticism of certain ideas propounded by academic specialists, whose affectation, vanity, or pride led them to parade their erudition. He once responded to the charge by asking, "Does anyone go around calling himself 'pro-intellectual.'?" Frost's favorite phrase for self-styled "intellectuals," not only in academia but in the arts and poetry, was "pseudo-intellectual." He applied the phrase to the esoteric style and poetry of allusion characteristic of works by Ezra Pound and T. S. Eliot and warned against their partisan literary critics, who loved to explicate their methods and symbolism to uninitiated students: "You want to watch for those people who seem to enjoy what they don't understand."[46] Frost distinguished between obscurity and profundity and held that it was arrogant to equate specialized knowledge with intellectual superiority and to treat with condescension the nonacademic world or the general reader as stupid or ignorant.

Frost's own range and depth of knowledge and understanding, so evident in his teaching, was far greater than that of many of his critics. Sidney Cox recorded of the poet's intelligence: "I . . . think him the wisest man, and one of the two deepest and most honest thinkers I know."[47] According to G. A. Craig, Frost's colleague at Amherst, the poet's knowledge "was astonishingly ample and exact . . ." with "an almost photographic

---

44. **Triumph,** 229.
45. Mertins, *Robert Frost: Life and Talks-Walking,* 324.
46. **Lathem,** 186.
47. **Cox,** 9.

knowledge of a great many poetic, philosophic, and historic texts."[48] Rabbi Victor Reichert, himself a highly educated and intellectually sophisticated scholar, recorded: "Frost with . . . not too much experience in the scientific literature connected with the Bible, would grasp things—deeply too— with greater penetration than many of the so-called great scholars who were committed to that kind of work."[49] Reichert also noted: "Robert Frost was probably the most formidable intellect I'd ever encountered in my life."[50] He was also frequently amazed at the unexpected depths of knowledge Frost revealed in many fields: "More than once he absolutely astonished me by the treasures it [Frost's mind] contained and upon which he could draw as from a bottomless well with effortless ease. . . . Frost could amazingly sit on top of endless facts. He held in his grasp a university of learning in all branches of literature, philosophy and science."[51] Frost's astonishing memory made him a walking encyclopedia of knowledge in literature, history, and philosophy. Professor Hewette Joyce of Dartmouth College once asked Frost to teach his class impromptu for an hour in Milton's "Lycidas" and discovered that he knew the whole poem by heart. His brilliant and loving comments on the poem electrified the teacher and left the students awestruck. In my eight summers of conversations with Frost at Bread Loaf (1939–1944 and 1961–1962), I discovered that he knew by memory thousands of lines of poetry, not only from the whole tradition of English and American poetry, but also Greek and Latin poets, especially Homer, Virgil, Lucretius, and Horace. Frost took the whole history and culture of Western civilization as his field of knowledge as a teacher, but he wore his learning without ostentation and without claiming to be an intellectual.

Frost's career as a teacher extended from the spring of 1893 almost to his death in 1963. It included teaching in a one-room country school in New England to the most complex and prestigious ivy-covered gothic-structured colleges and universities. His first instruction was to "twelve barefooted children in the neck of the woods in South Salem, New Hampshire," in the rudiments of English, Latin, and algebra.[52] In an interview in 1961, Frost said: "I've taught every darn year from kinder-garten to graduate school, Latin, English, mathematics, history, algebra,

48. G. A. Craig, "Robert Frost at Amherst," 8. Amherst College Archives.

49. Andrew R. Marks, *The Rabbi and the Poet* (Alton, N.H.: Andover Green Book Publishers, 1994), 1.

50. Ibid.

51. Victor Reichert, "The Robert Frost I Knew," **Tharpe III**, 117–18.

52. **Untermeyer**, 290. See also, 352.

philosophy, and one year psychology."[53] He held a great variety of academic positions, beginning in Pinkerton Academy in Derry, New Hampshire (1905–1911); in the Normal School in Plymouth, New Hampsire (1911–1912); at Amherst College (1917–1920); at the University of Michigan (1922–1923 and 1925–1926); and again at Amherst (1923–1925 and 1926–1938 and 1949–1963). In addition to these positions, he delivered the Norton lectures at Harvard (1936), and was the Ralph Waldo Emerson Fellow in Poetry at Harvard in 1942–1943, concluding his career as the George Ticknor Fellow in the Humanities at Dartmouth College. Lawrance Thompson has noted Frost's "unusually extensive participation in the teaching activities at Bread Loaf," which included sessions with the summer school graduate students and in the poetry clinics at the Writers Conference between 1920 and 1962 at the school, and after 1926 at the conference.[54] Some schools invited Frost back time and time again, such as Wesleyan University in Middletown, Connecticut; the New York School of Social Research; Agnes Scott College in Decatur, Georgia; Kenyon College in Gambier, Ohio; Vanderbilt University; and Pierson College, Yale University. In December 1956, during a television interview on "Meet the Press," Frost said: "I think the best audience the world ever had, probably, is the little town-and-gown audience that we get in the little college towns in the U.S.A.—two thousand towns."[55] As C. P. Snow observed of Frost: "No professional writer has ever spent so much time in contact with academic life."[56]

It may seem paradoxical that Frost spent so much of his adult life as a teacher or poet-in-residence in academia yet was constantly severely critical of colleges and universities. The paradox is partly resolved by observing that while he despised the methodology, institutional requirements, and excessively structured bureaucratic hierarchy in higher education, he nevertheless thoroughly enjoyed close relationships with many faculty members and students, some of whom became lifelong friends. In a letter to Louis Untermeyer (May 9, 1936), commenting on how his series of Charles Eliot Norton lectures was well received by an enthusiastic town-and-gown audience, he revealed his doubts about the response of the Harvard administration and some faculty:

53. **Lathem,** 269.
54. **Later Years,** 51.
55. **Lathem,** 161. Frost repeated this remark in "Maturity No Object."
56. C. P. Snow, "Robert Frost," *Variety of Men* (New York: Charles Scribner's Sons, 1966), 192.

I don't feel I made too big a hit with the dignitaries and authorities. . . . There was a moment in March when I thought that perhaps they were giving me back my father's Harvard. But probably I was fooling myself. I'm imperfectly academic and no amount of association with the academic will make me perfect. It's too bad, for I like the academic in my way, and up to a certain point the academic likes me. Its patronage proves as much. I may be wrong in my suspicion that I haven't pleased Harvard as much as I have the encompassing barbarians. My whole impression may have come from the Pound-Eliot-Richards gang in Eliot House here.[57]

Time and time again, Frost spoke of being "always at it against colleges in a vain attempt to reconcile myself with them." But his severe negative strictures need to be understood as only a part of the strong ambiguity he always felt about institutional education, which was a factor in his role as a teacher: "I've been a teacher all my life . . . but I've been a dissatisfied teacher. I can't leave it alone. I'm like some monkeys Darwin tells about. Somebody showed them some snakes, and they screamed and ran away, but they kept coming back. I'm that way about education."[58]

C. P. Snow was probably right in holding that while Frost's "literary originality" differed sharply from "academic literary thinking," neverthe-less, "in his subtle and labile temperament, he was much more academically inclined than he pretended, or liked, to think."[59] For over four decades, Frost haunted the academic scene, partly because it provided him with a steady income and a variety of literary prestige, but also because, as a teacher, the caliber of people he knew in colleges, and their cultural concerns, were of a much higher order than what was to be found anywhere else. He loved to wage a fine scholastic contention with academically oriented and sophisticated people.

A more personal reason also continued to link him with higher ed-ucation. He admitted that his continuity with colleges was in part his gratitude for their positive response to his poetry: "What has brought me back in and partly disarmed me is the kindness the colleges have shown my

---

57. **Untermeyer,** 277. On another occasion Frost clarified what he meant by "giving me back my father's Harvard": "I was at Harvard while the old education, unaffected by Madison Avenue, was in full swing. There wasn't too much difference between the way I was taught there and the way my father was." Frost noted that his father "was permitted to offer those two books of memorized Latin of Caesar for the whole course. . . . Wouldn't that idea kill the progressives in education" (Mertins, *Robert Frost: Life and Talks-Walking,* 338–39).
58. **Lathem,** 269.
59. C. P. Snow, *Variety of Men,* 192.

poetry. I find myself even anxious to be useful to them in requital."[60] Frost was especially grateful for the many honorary degrees conferred on him by American and British colleges and universities. To Louis Mertins, he admitted how deeply he valued his many connections with the academic world: "One can't take a home, or a companion, or a college out of his heart without leaving a great void, great empty place."[61] In "Build Soil," Frost ranked colleges in his hierarchy of social values right behind friendship, the nation, and the family:

> Don't join too many gangs. Join few if any.
> Join the United States and join the family—
> But not much in between unless a college.

To Louis Untermeyer he wrote on June 26, 1939: "I wonder at myself for still hanging around education after all these years: but I suppose what keeps me is the reasonable doubt that the college belongs entirely to the scholars."[62] Frost clearly believed that the college belonged far more to the teacher and student than to the scholar, and least of all to the administration.

As much as he deplored the excessive machinery of administration, modeled upon the rigid and impersonal methods of industry and business, he also objected to the analytical methods employed by many teachers, particularly in literary criticism. Much as he despised scientific scholarship for the sake of erudition, he objected to any literary criticism which assumed that the scientific method was a valid intrument in the discussion of literature. Untermeyer recorded Frost's strong disapproval to pages and pages of detailed analytical criticism of "Stopping by Woods on a Snowy Evening":

> The trouble with this sort of criticism, he said, is that it analyzes itself—and the poem—to death. It first depersonalizes the idea, then it dehumanizes the emotion, finally it destroys whatever poetry is left in the poem. It assumes that criticism is not only an art but also a science; it acts as though poetry were written in order to be dissected and that its chief value is in offering a field-day for ambiguity-hunters. You've often heard me say . . . that poetry is what is lost in translation. It is also what is lost

60. **Later Years,** 49, see also, 396.
61. Mertins, *Robert Frost: Life and Talks-Walking,* 220.
62. **Untermeyer,** 316–17.

in interpretation. That little poem [Stopping by Woods . . .] means just what it says and it says what it means, nothing less but nothing more.[63]

Frost was aware that the great danger for the common, literal-minded, inexperienced reader of poetry is that much that is vital in the poem will be missed—its form, technique, and content; its tone and mood in the emotional, phonetic, and imaginative use of metaphorical language. But he thought that the opposite danger often seduced the professional literary critic and classroom teacher—the use of the poem as a springboard for analytical speculations, and the reading of far more into the content of a poem than is warranted. Such readers assumed that the aesthetic imagination is no more than reason and that a poem could be read the same way as a discursive prose argument in a scholarly article. But to Frost a poem was "a felt-thought thing," to be read on its own terms, and it involved the total nature of the reader, not merely abstract reason. In his Notebook 001726 in the Baker Library at Dartmouth College, Frost asked: "What can you do with a poem besides read it to yourself or someone else?" He listed forty-one things that can be done with a poem, such as memorizing it, or applying it to everyday experience, but he was adamant in rejecting analytical criticism as a valid response to literature.

In a letter to Sidney Cox (January 2, 1915), even before he became a regular teacher in academia, Frost expressed his skepticism and dislike toward academic scholarship and literary criticism and the failure to appreciate literature as an aesthetic art form:

I see you really doing something in the next few years to break into the worst system of teaching that ever endangered a nation's literature. You speak of Columbia. That reminds me of the article on American literature by a Columbian, George Woodbury [Woodberry], in the Encyclopaedia Britannica. I wish you would read it or the last part of it just to see that we are not alone in thinking that nothing literary can come from the present ways of the professionally literary in American universities. . . . Everything is research for the sake of erudition. No one is taught to value himself for nice perception and cultivated taste. Knowledge knowledge. Why literature is the next thing to religion in which as you know or believe an ounce of faith is worth all the theology ever written. Sight and insight, give us those. I like the good old English way of muddling along in these things that we can't reduce to a science anyway such as literature, love religion and friendship. People make their great strides in

63. Louis Untermeyer, *Robert Frost: A Backward Look*, 18.

understanding literature at most unexpected times. I never caught another man's emotion in it more than when someone drew his finger over some seven lines of blank verse—beginning carefully and ending carefully—and saying simply "From there to—there." He knew and I knew. We said no more. I don't see how you are going to teach the stuff except with some such light touch. And you can't afford to treat it all alike, I mean with equal German thoroughness and reverence if thoroughness is reverence. It is only a moment here and a moment there that the greatest writing has. Some cognizance of the fact must be taken in your teaching.[64]

Frost clearly agreed with William Wordsworth's dictum: "We murder to dissect," so that as a teacher he believed that nothing was more fatal to the humanities and liberal arts than the application of analytical reason and the scientific method. Things of the spirit, such as religion and the arts, could not be understood in the descriptive and quantitative terms of the physical sciences.

In an interview in February 1916, Frost was vehement in his criticism of academic education: "I hate academic ways. I fight everything academic. The time we waste in trying to learn academically—the talent we starve with academic teaching."[65] As a student, Frost had "walked out of two colleges like nothing at all," rather than put up with all that he found wrong with their academic methods and requirements.[66] At the Unterberg Poetry Center of the Ninety-second Street YMHA, in New York in 1958, Frost warned students against being drowned in a sea of irrelevant and unassimilated knowledge: "My great complaint of education is that it is so loaded with material you never move in the spirit again. You've got to get into it but no more than you can swing and sing."[67] He believed that far too many students, even at the Ivy League schools, become corrupted and overwhelmed by excessive materials required by the faculty. To Untermeyer, Frost expressed this conviction in a stark simile on August 8, 1921: "You remember that beautiful line of Wilkie Collins in *The Woman in White:* 'Her son was drowned at Oxford at the age of eighteen.' Eighteen is just about the age at which most of them get drowned at Harvard and Yale."[68]

64. **Letters,** 146.
65. **Lathem,** 12.
66. For Frost's reasons for leaving Dartmouth and Harvard, see Morris P. Tilley, "Notes from Conversations with Robert Frost," *Inlander* (February 1918); and **Untermeyer,** 353.
67. Sergeant, *Trial by Existence,* 410.
68. **Untermeyer,** 132.

Probably the most recurrent theme in Frost's criticism of "academic rigidity and myopia" was that "excessive planning deadened innovation" and creativity and depersonalized the whole process of learning. He asked: "Why did everything have to be programmed?" It was folly to institutionalize "what should remain free and adventurous" like a love affair.[69] Students and faculty who accepted "laid-on" education often lacked any sense of play, of fancy and imagination, and became deadened by scholastic methodology. Frost's lifelong ambition as a teacher was "to make school as unschoollike as possible."[70] Academia was especially fatal in developing skills in good writing: "That's the trouble with graduate studies—graduate schools. They think you command what is in your notebook. You can't command it. You've got to be so familiar with it you can throw the notes away. . . . Theses from graduate school are hard to sell."[71] For Frost, mere factual erudition not only did not help to make good writing, it could be a positive hindrance. In a letter to Untermeyer (January 9, 1947), Frost translated Scaliger's "Erudita inscitia est" as "Erudition is a form of ignorance," and added: "The learned Duns Scotus, patron saint of scholars, was so full of things not worth knowing that his name has come down to us spelled Dunce: 'Sapientaea pars est quaedam aequo animo nescire velle.' (There is a kind of wisdom in calmly choosing not to know)." To Frost, an intelligent, widely read nonacademic writer, who had assimilated knowledge over many years of interest in a subject, was often a far better and more vital writer than scholars trained in graduate schools. With some reservations, he instanced James Truslow Adams as a case in point: "Adams . . . is a better scholar because a livelier, a less deadened by school, than any of the academics. He has the freedom of the real as you never get it in the teacher-taught. He has come to learning as you come to the table, not the conference round table, but the dinner table." No one knew better than Frost how much the scientific method and the "German thoroughness" introduced into American higher education at Johns Hopkins University had reduced the humanities to mere raw materials for dead doctoral dissertations.[72]

To the end of his life, Frost believed that the arts and humanities should be at the center of education. But under the system that had

69. Reginald L. Cook, "Robert Frost in Context," **Tharpe III,** 139; see also, **Lathem,** 13.
70. **Untermeyer,** 180.
71. Mertins, *Robert Frost: Life and Talks-Walking,* 356–57. The best study of Frost as a teacher of writing is Elaine Barry, *Robert Frost* (New York: Frederick Ungar Publishing, 1973).
72. **Lathem,** 230.

come to prevail in American education, they received short shrift, and their neglect resulted in a vulgarized national culture in which values were largely materialistic. When M.I.T. added a humanities program to its scientific curriculum, Frost criticized it because it was introduced "like an ingredient" in bread; it wasn't, as it should be, the essential part of education. Through the humanities, "the past," he asserted, "is the great book of worthies," which provided the basis of Western civilization, in its history, literature, philosophy, religion, science, law and politics.[73] Frost believed that in both the personal lives of individuals and the cultural life of a nation "the denouement tells the story," and however much individuals were well trained to excess in a profession, to the extent that they were deficient in the arts and humanities, they were not truly educated.[74]

73. Reginald L. Cook, "Robert Frost in Context," **Tharpe III,** 139.

74. The history of Frost as a teacher reflects his lifelong defense of the humanities in the classroom and on the lecture platform. His outstanding qualities as a teacher derive from his mastery of the humanities. When he taught at Pinkerton Academy, Ernest Silver, principal at Pinkerton, and Henry C. Morrison, superintendent of education in New Hampshire, called Frost the best teacher in New Hampshire. John Bartlett, his best student at Pinkerton, stated that Frost was "a good measure above any other teacher he had ever known." (Margaret Bartlett Anderson, *Robert Frost and John Bartlett,* 15). For other examples of student responses to Frost as a teacher, see Marcia Pushell's unpublished essay in Lamson Library, Plymouth State College, Plymouth, New Hampshire, file 67. Letters from students at Plymouth in support of her essay are in files 68 and 69. Manuscript essays on Frost's outstanding teaching by P. N. Youts, Gardner Jackson, and G. Armour Craig are recorded in the Robert Frost Library in Amherst College. Warren Bower's essay on Frost as a teacher is in the *New York University Notebook,* vol. 7, no. 3 (February 1964). For student and faculty responses to Frost as a teacher, see Dorothy Tyler, "Frost's Last Three Visits to Michigan," **Tharpe I,** 518–34; and "Robert Frost in Michigan," **Tharpe III,** 7–69. Tyler's comments are typical of what many students wrote: that "an extraordinary richness of influence pervades that first year of Frost's presence in Ann Arbor"; "how astonishingly Frost found his way into the University life of the time"; there was an "unquestionable and lasting influence of Frost upon both faculty and students who knew him." **Tharpe III,** 14, 26, 42. For a general estimate of Frost as a teacher, see **Later Years,** 459–60.

Original Originality

Robert Frost's Talks

Lisa Seale

IN TWO TALKS GIVEN in the 1950s, Robert Frost posed a question he imagined being asked of himself and answered it in such a way as to suggest that his originality was of the ordinary kind, that is, that found among those who work within a tradition. In the last talk of a three-part series given at the YMHA's Poetry Center in New York City on November 22, 1952, Frost spoke of the prerequisites for reading poetry and of poetry as belonging to "the realm of the spirit," then said, "As for writing poetry, see, 'Why do you write poetry?'—if anyone said. Well, the reason I write it is because it's been written. Why do I teach school? Well, because school's been taught. See, I am not original enough to have started an entirely new thing, like poetry." Four years later, in a 1956 radio interview with Dr. Jonas Salk, Frost elaborated on the point, saying, "they ask me why I write poetry. I write poetry because it's been written before. I'm not original enough to originate a whole new realm of action."[1] As regards his poetry, he was right, but we may, in considering his talks—or better, the introductory remarks he made before his many readings over the years—argue that he was more originally original than his own assessment of himself suggests.

It is possible to feel some ambiguity about the worth of Frost's talks, to regard them more as a form of vaunting self-indulgence than is seemly,

---

1. The first quotation is transcribed from "Robert Frost Speaking at Y. M. H. A., New York City, November 22, 1952," Robert Frost Tape 70, Amherst College Library, audiocassette; the second from "Heritage One, Program Nine: An Intimate Conversation between Mr. Frost and Dr. Jonas Salk, WQED, Pittsburgh, Pennsylvania, 1956," Robert Frost Tape 26, Amherst College Library, audiocassette. Permission by the Estate of Robert Lee Frost to quote in this work from previously unpublished tape recordings of Robert Frost's talks in the Archives and Special Collections of Amherst College Library and from unpublished material at Dartmouth College Library is gratefully acknowledged, as is permission from Amherst College Library and Dartmouth College Library. Unless otherwise indicated, all transcriptions of previously unpublished recorded talks quoted in this essay are my own.

however good individual talks may be. The title of one of Frost's later poems "How Hard It Is to Keep from Being King When It's in You and in the Situation" might be unfavorably applied to Frost himself before an audience, according to this line of thinking. Though there is some truth to this assessment, taken as a whole, the talks are an extraordinary enterprise on Frost's part, interwoven with his life as a poet. Thus, while the attention of most readers of Robert Frost is understandably focused on the poems, attention to his talks is also rewarding. These talks can give valuable insights not only into the poems but also into how the poet's mind worked beyond the poems. Like the poems, they vary considerably one from the next. Some of Frost's talks are like meandering, conversational letters, while others are like spoken essays, still associative in their organization, still conversational, but always circling back to a central theme or metaphor. Others hold little of interest for listeners or readers today except for a phrase or two, as in this excerpt from the brief introduction to a November 4, 1959, after-dinner reading Frost gave at the Twenty-fifth Anniversary Dinner of the Academy of American Poets in New York, in which he refers to several lines by the Elizabethan Thomas Nashe, writing a defense of poetry in his 1592 pamphlet *Pierce Penilesse, His Supplication to the Divell:* "Poetry is the hunny of all flowers, the quintessence of all Sciences, the Marrowe of Witte, and the very Phrase of Angels":

> You want to hear a definition of poetry? I heard a pretty one. I don't know where I heard it. It's some years ago. It's in prose. These things follow me around like a strange dog. "Poetry"—somebody may identify it; sounds as if it came from another century—has the flavor of another century. "Poetry is the honey of all flowers." That'd be clear all the way down from clover to buckwheat, common kind, common man stuff, see? Some might try to write that kind of honey. "The honey of all flowers, the quintessence of all the sciences." "All the sciences"—that sounds like another age. We talk—"science," we say. "The quintessence of all the sciences, the marrow of wit"—that sounds as if it came from the Elizabethan time; I don't know. "The marrow of wit, and the very phrase of angels." Now, it doesn't say "phrases of angels." "The very phrase of angels." That's the most poetic thing, expression, in it all. And it's all splendid. I could make a talk out of every one of those four things.[2]

2. Thomas Nashe, *Pierce Penilesse, His Supplication to the Divell* (1592, 1924; rpt. Westport, Conn.: Greenwood Press, 1970), 60; Robert Frost, "Complete Transcription of the Dinner Speeches at the 25th Anniversary Dinner of the Academy of American Poets, Waldorf-Astoria Hotel, New York, New York, November 4, 1959," Robert Frost

Frost goes on after repeating "the very phrase of Angels" to say that the phrase—or perhaps all poetry—is "such a gentle thing, so much like a smoke ring, you know." The image of a smoke ring also appears in Frost's 1946 "Letter to *The Amherst Student*," after Frost has already laid out his belief that the world is so set up that "the evident design is a situation here in which it will always be about equally hard to save your soul . . . or if you dislike hearing your soul mentioned in open meeting, say your decency, your integrity. When in doubt there is always form for us to go on with. . . . Fortunately, too, no forms are more engrossing, gratifying, comforting, staying than those lesser ones we throw off, like vortex rings of smoke, all our individual enterprise and needing nobody's cooperation; a basket, a letter, a garden, a room, an idea, a picture, a poem" (739–40). Or, say, a talk followed by a reading. About two hundred of Frost's public talks and readings, given over a period of nearly five decades, beginning in earnest in 1915 and ending only in the final year of his life, are preserved on tape recordings, and most are still unpublished. Those that are available in published form give some idea of how valuable these others are. For example, a collection of talks Frost gave at the Bread Loaf School of English at Middlebury College is found in Reginald L. Cook's *Robert Frost: A Living Voice,* and several of the talks Frost delivered and later published in more polished form appear in the Poirier/Richardson edition of Frost's work. Others may be found in excerpted form on the CD-ROM *Robert Frost: Poems, Life, Legacy,* edited by Donald Sheehy. The bulk of Frost's talks and readings that remain unpublished, and so for the most part unheard, in the quietly faithful and patient special collections of such libraries as Amherst College and Dartmouth College implicitly raise a question. Why listen to these talks, if we have the poetry and the many studies of it, the various biographies, the ever-growing body of scholarly criticism?[3]

While not all of Frost's recorded talks are memorable, while it is seductive to hang on to every last syllable just because those syllables

---

Tape 76, Amherst College Library, audiocassette (transcribed by Krista Kropp Feakes and Brad Feakes).

3. Reginald L. Cook, *Robert Frost: A Living Voice* (Amherst: University of Massachusetts Press, 1974); Donald Sheehy, ed., *Robert Frost: Poems, Life, Legacy* (New York: Holt, 1997), CD-ROM. A few of the talks appeared as pamphlets during Frost's lifetime, such as *A Talk for Students: An Extemporaneous Talk at the Twenty-eighth Annual Commencement of Sarah Lawrence College* (Bronxville, New York: Fund for the Republic, 1956); and "Playing for Mortal Stakes," *Amherst Alumni News* 15, no. 2 (1962): 4–10. More recently, transcriptions of a few of Frost's talks have appeared in little magazines, such as George Monteiro, "Introduction to 'For Glory and for Use': Robert Frost at Brown University," *Gettysburg Review* 7, no. 1 (1994): 89–99.

are what little is left to hear of the poet's recorded voice, the taped talks are nevertheless important because they are another form in which Frost worked. In fact, he made up a form for himself, what one of his biographers William Pritchard describes as "his usual blend of talking and reading from his poetry."[4] It is true that since Sidney's time—and Nashe's, who in *Pierce Penilesse* laments Sidney's death and the loss of poetry's great apologist—we have privileged poetry, as have many cultures, as one of the highest forms of thought—indeed, "the very phrase of Angels." Yet less formal forms, such as Frost's talks, also offer us insight at many levels, from very nuanced, quiet moments of observation, to silly jokes, to serious, extended argument. The forms themselves are not comparable, one loosely informal, another decidedly not, but the content is. And while the poems may nevertheless be what we most care for, they will, with luck and privilege on their side, live as long as Sappho's have. The talks, on the other hand, may never have a larger audience than those who heard them when they were first delivered.

If we can, for the moment at least, put aside our concern over which is the more refined and important form, we will see that the talks and the poems can illuminate each other, both having, as one of their functions, the larger purpose of illuminating Frost's thinking. This is the case when we consider some of Frost's commentary found in his talks together with the first of two specifically titled groups of *In the Clearing*, "Cluster of Faith." As a demonstration of this, we can explore in some detail the first poem in this group, "Accidentally on Purpose." It may be useful to suggest that the faith in this cluster is simultaneously and paradoxically in the existence of an originating design for, or a controlling thought informing, the universe; perhaps, even, in a theistic, personal God; in humanity's collective ignorance and smallness in relation to a vast and divinely ordered physical universe; and in humanity's nevertheless significant contribution to the universe as manifestations of some divine purpose. That Frost is engaged in an experimental rather than a dogmatic enterprise in "Cluster of Faith" may be further inferred from statements he makes in the 1956 recorded interview with Dr. Salk mentioned above, in which he expresses the hope that the universe has a purpose, though he doesn't speculate on what that purpose might be. A fundamental goal of both scientists and poets has just occurred to Salk: "to understand the purpose of life." Frost's response is, "The purpose of life is not a closed thing; there's always

---

4. **Pritchard,** 257.

something still about it that can't be said, isn't there?" And Frost goes on a moment later:

> Somebody has scolded me for saying in rhyme once that "We dance round in a ring and suppose, / But the Secret sits in the middle and knows." Yet I think a scientist and anybody with an active mind lives on tentatives rather than on tenets. And that you've got to feel a certain pleasure in the tentativeness of it all. The unfinality of it. And that's what you live for . . . when I say you hang around till you catch on, that doesn't mean you hang on till you get the final answer to anything— . . . the spirit in which we live, in which this is to be taken, the tentativeness of things, the process of things, and the little certainties that we get among the uncertainties, the little phrase we make or the little formula we make . . . —there's faith in it, of course, the faith that those all some way are related and maybe tumble together somewhere, that they may make something.[5]

The suggestion present in these comments and in "Cluster of Faith," that the universe has the purpose of producing conscious, independent thought, forms an important underpinning for Frost's metaphysical assumptions about the role of humanity in the universe. This is particularly true in "Kitty Hawk," which appears later in "Cluster of Faith." This role is dynamic and though expressed playfully is at the same time serious: man is "The Mixture Mechanic," here to keep the universe all stirred up and to tell it what it is supposed to mean (453). So, we might say "Accidentally on Purpose" argues that humanity is the product of a divine design as part of Frost's larger argument that two of humanity's favorite occupations (thought and sex) are divinely sanctioned. The opening stanza of "Accidentally on Purpose" seems at first to be a parody of a scientific description of the universe, yet with the qualifications iterated in the subsequent two stanzas, it may instead be a fair description of Frost's own view of the physical universe:

> The Universe is but the Thing of things,
> The things but balls all going round in rings.
> Some of them mighty huge, some mighty tiny,
> All of them radiant and mighty shiny. (438)

Frost's opening four lines can be read as an offhand, highly condensed description of a pluralistic view of the universe's origins, to use William

---

5. Frost, "Heritage One, Program Nine: An Intimate Conversation between Mr. Frost and Dr. Jonas Salk."

James's formulation of "pluralism" as it is opposed to belief in "the absolute causal unity of the universe" in his lecture "The One and the Many," found in *Pragmatism:* "If the minor causal influences among things should converge towards one common causal origin of them in the past, one great first cause for all that is, one might then speak of the absolute causal unity of the universe. . . . Against this notion of unity of origin of all things there has always stood the pluralistic notion of an eternal self-existing many in the shape of atoms or even spiritual units of some sort." Frost's view of the universe in Jamesian terms as both unified and composed of independently acting parts is also apparent in lines from "A Never Naught Song," which follows this poem: "Matter was begun— / And in fact complete, / One and yet discrete / To conflict and pair" (439). This view also appears in a March 21, 1951, talk at the Morgan Library in New York City, when Frost mentions "the one and the many" while discussing research into the ultimate beginnings of the universe, and his own speculation on it: "The ultimate things would be just all the reality we have, in hiding. It would be like shutting our eyes to all that is, it would be making it so you couldn't see, that's all, just like putting blinders on your eyes. Out of one thing— you see we're always talking about the one, and the many—out of the one, the many. If you want to get rid of the many, want to shut your eyes to the many, get to the one—you're only shutting your eyes, because the many must be in the one."[6]

Recognizing Frost's openness to a complex origin for the universe ("the purpose of life is not a closed thing; there's always something still about it that can't be said") is important because "Accidentally on Purpose" moves in the second and third stanzas through a view of the universe as simply created by some *one* intention ("His or Hers or Its"—even here, the joking reference to bath towels undercuts the single-minded view) to a view that allows for the paradox of a universe shaped by human ends. The second and third stanzas formulate Frost's scornful dissatisfaction with the idea that the universe is merely mechanical:

> They mean to tell us all was rolling blind
> Till accidentally it hit on mind
> In an albino monkey in a jungle
> And even then it had to grope and bungle,

6. William James, *Pragmatism*, vol. 1 of *The Works of William James*, ed. Frederick H. Burkhardt et al. (Cambridge: Harvard University Press, 1975), 68; "Robert Frost Speaking at the Morgan Library, New York City, March 21, 1951," Robert Frost Tape 40, Amherst College Library, audiocassette.

> Till Darwin came to earth upon a year
> To show the evolution how to steer.
> They mean to tell us, though, the Omnibus
> Had no real purpose till it got to us.

It is interesting that, in contrast to the apparent disparagement of Darwin's evolutionary theory here, in "Kitty Hawk" Frost will nod his approval of the immodesty behind the notion that man directs evolution by having discovered it. Frost is able in "Cluster of Faith" to insist on humanity's humility and ignorance before a divinity full of an undisclosed purpose of which humanity is a part, and then in "Kitty Hawk" to insist that it is humanity which nevertheless plays the starring role in such a universe. Frost has an experimental turn of mind, and is, indeed, even at his most emphatic, relying on tentatives. Another of William James's descriptions in "The One and the Many" of the pragmatist's belief in a multifaceted, pluralistic universe is worth quoting in this regard, as it makes clearer Frost's own tightrope-walk between belief in a master-planning divinity, and true pride and delight in the meaning, for him, of humanity's capacity for conscious rational thought. James's pluralism is Frost's as well: "Provided you grant *some* separation among things, some tremor of independence, some free play of parts on one another, some real novelty or chance, however minute, she [pluralism] is amply satisfied, and will allow you any amount, however great, of real union."[7] In other words, humanity matters as much as a divine origin of the universe, because both show that mind is moving along in the universe.

The fourth and fifth stanzas of "Accidentally on Purpose" further elaborate Frost's belief that the universe has a divine, unified purpose. Mind, or consciousness, didn't suddenly appear "In an albino monkey in a jungle" but is part of a larger scheme:

> Never believe it. At the very worst
> It must have had the purpose from the first
> To produce purpose as the fitter bred:
> We were just purpose coming to a head.
>
> Whose purpose was it? His or Hers or Its?
> Let's leave that to the scientific wits.
> Grant me intention, purpose, and design—
> That's near enough for me to the Divine.

---

7. James, *Pragmatism*, 78.

In a May 19, 1961, talk at Yale University, Frost runs a similar argument by his audience—the fact that purposefulness exists at all in humans means it must also occur, on a grander scale, in the physical universe:

> Talking with some boys the other night at another college, somewhere, about a thousand miles from here, I asked them, if they thought the universe had a purpose. They all agreed that it hadn't a purpose. And then I said—or nearly all did: one or two thought . . . Bible-belt boys, you know [laughter], eh—like me—I was surprised at 'em, but I said, "Do you believe it still admits of your having purposes?" And most of them thought they could, have purposes themselves. And then I asked them if they, I asked them if they didn't think that that indicated that the universe might've had the purpose of producing them. Heh—no, they laughed at that.[8]

In his poem, Frost's suggestion paradoxically replaces the genuine haphazardness essential to evolution with a programmed haphazardness: the divine deliberately allows accidents, chance, and random selection to work independently. The wisecrack of the title (as Frost would have probably described it) thus gives an aphoristic turn to a snide old phrase. Frost at various times spoke of his early answer to the challenge evolution had posed to his belief in God. His answer was that evolution only meant that God had used prepared mud to create Adam. Frost closes the poem with a phrase meant to show the role individuals play in a larger evolutionary design:

> And yet for all this help of head and brain
> How happily instinctive we remain,
> Our best guide upward further to the light,
> Passionate preference such as love at sight.

Karl Popper, writing in his autobiography, offers an "enrichment of Darwinism," the first part of which is similar to Frost's idea of "passionate preference": "I distinguish external or environmental selection pressure from the organism itself and, I conjecture, ultimately from its *preferences* (or 'aims') though these may of course change in response to external changes." Later Popper elaborates, while discussing preference as something incorporated into gene structures of all forms of life, not just human: "But what may perhaps be identified with the higher forms of life is a

8. *Robert Frost Reading at Yale University*, rec. May 19, 1961, Carrillon Records.

behaviourally richer preference structure—one of greater scope; and if the preference structure should have (by and large) the leading role I ascribe to it, then evolution towards higher forms may become understandable."[9] Frost's phrase "passionate preference" marks a qualification of the absolute determinism of his belief in the universe as having a governing divine design. The phrase, which he used in various talks as well as in this poem, implies that humans exercise individual free will by trusting to the chanciness of their instincts. It is interesting as well to note that it takes reason, an exercise of the will, to discover and admit that the passions might probably be our best guide.

In praising passionate preference on an equal level with "head and brain," Frost is acknowledging what Martha Nussbaum calls "a rich plurality of values" in our world: here, the plurality of the often conflicting values we place on rationality and on the passions, both of which, Frost suggests, we need in order to think clearly. A look at one of Nussbaum's accounts of the proper way to respond to a text and to practical conflict (she refers specifically to texts of Greek tragedies but does not imply that this approach is limited to such texts) is worthwhile in understanding why Frost might argue—as he does implicitly in the last stanza of "Accidentally on Purpose"—for the interconnectedness of reason and emotion. Describing how the Choruses of two different plays consciously "cultivat[e] responsiveness by working through the memory of the events [of Agamemnon's sacrifice of Iphigenia in Aeschylus' *Agamemnon,* and Eteocles' passion for meeting his brother in war in *Seven against Thebes*], until 'the painful memory of pain drips, instead of sleep, before the heart' (*Ag.* 179–80)," Nussbaum writes that:

> The presentness of the Chorus before this action, and their patient work, even years later, on the story of that action reminds us that responsive attention to these complexities is a job that practical rationality can, and should, undertake to perform; and that this job of rationality claims more from the agent than the exercise of reason or intellect, narrowly conceived. We see thought and feeling working together, so that it is difficult to distinguish one from the other. . . . We see, too, a two-way interchange of illumination and cultivation working between emotions and thoughts: we see feelings prepared by memory and deliberation, [and] learning brought about by *pathos.* (At the same time,

9. Karl Popper, *Unended Quest: An Intellectual Autobiography* (La Salle, Ill.: Open Court, 1976), 15, 176–77.

if we are good spectators, we will find this complex interaction in our
own responses.)[10]

Frost himself advocates just this sort of complex interaction in guiding
oneself through life. It is clear that love (and all emotional responses to one's
immediate, personal experience of the everyday world) and thought were
highly interconnected in Frost's mind, although the degree to which either
predominates varies from poem to poem. In the early "Bond and Free," for
example, Frost votes for love over thought as the center of one's life. In "The
Silken Tent," the former opposites are given equal standing: the woman
is bound by "countless silken ties of love and thought / To everything on
earth the compass round" (302). In no poem, talk, or essay does Frost
ever confuse love and thought, but in the last stanza of "Accidentally on
Purpose" he makes it clear that one cannot think clearly without having
experienced passion, or without having the capacity to do so. Emotion is
our guide, our touchstone, along with reason, divine or human, as we strive
"upward further to the light" for excellence.

Like the Greeks he so admired, Frost values the morally insoluble
connection between thought and feeling. And while we may intuit it as
we read his poems (or understand it flat out while reading "Love and
Thought"), in the talks we can also see how much more problematically
true it could be for him. In a high school commencement address he gave
in Billings, Montana, upon the graduation of his granddaughter Robin
Fraser, Frost shows us how it is possible that the emotional beginnings
of thought can take the form of pride, as we see here in his discussion of
originality as a form of pride:

> Now one or two more things I hope you've learned. I hope—I won't call
> it learned—I hope you've been roused to a spirit of preferring to tell than
> be told, of showing, I mean preferring to show rather than be shown, to
> point out rather than have things pointed out to you. Now that's a fear,
> there's a fear I have that there's not enough of that in our education. That
> sounds like a kind of intellectual pride, mental pride, but nobody's any
> good from my point of view who hasn't some of that pride. I want to
> be humble enough to let some of the telling be done by other people,
> but I want to do some, a good deal of the telling myself. Pointing out,
> especially, mental, things in nature—somebody walking with me sees

---

10. Martha Nussbaum, *The Fragility of Goodness: Luck and Ethics in Greek Tragedy and
Philosophy* (Cambridge, Mass.: Cambridge University Press, 1986), 47.

the bird, names the bird before I do, or flower, or tree, and I'm always a little jealous. I want to be—I feel as if I'm not as sharp as I used to be, something like that comes over me. I want to be the one—in a little rhyme I made once, as short as that one, "ABC and 123"—"Let me be the one / To do what is done." Instead of letting George do it. [Laughter] I always had that pride. And the humility, too—you don't need to call it humility—the modesty to let somebody else do part of it, and think of part of it. And the greatest thing of all is to get up something. Not only do something, but get up something to do. And that oughta be in our education, and it isn't enough for my taste quite anywhere, just some of it; depends a good deal on this teacher and that, some teachers have it more than others. I said in a line of verse, shows how long I've been a teacher and thought these thoughts, in an old poem of mine, I say, "I'd rather / He said it for himself." I could tell him about why the wall falls down, but I'd rather he said it for himself, that he'd make the remark. And I've gone into class in my day, when I had a class of fifty, and sat in front of them, hoping somebody'd start talking, but I got embarrassed and started it myself. I used to think that'd be a teaching method, to make up my mind I'd never say another word in my class till somebody else said something. And not asking for it either, and I'd just sit there until somebody else, you know, spoke up, something like that. "I'd rather / He said it for himself."[11]

A question to ask about this selection is whether Frost is talking down to his audience. The answer would be yes, in the sense that he is simplifying his own experience, perhaps as much for himself as for the high school students he addresses. Careful simplification is a deliberate feature of his intellectual life: he describes why in one of his talks at the New School for Social Research in 1938:

> The effort to get around the ambiguity of things drives you in poetry to make poems of very few and simple elements. I can see that more and more I crave a poem that has a very delicate thread of logic in it and [has] nothing in it that doesn't rest on everything else in it. It doesn't stem from half a dozen things, doesn't have all sorts of hangnails on it. I don't believe that you can have great art except in very simple outline. That seems to

11. "Robert Frost Speaking at the Commencement, Billings Senior High School, Billings, Montana, June 1952, Robin Fraser Graduated," Robert Frost Tape 144, Amherst College Library, audiocassette.

you to say that I am sitting here advocating nothing but the very simple and obvious.[12]

We may feel skeptical about the chances for the obvious being much more than the obvious, but perhaps we can hear in Frost's explication of the line from "Mending Wall" ("I'd rather / He said it for himself") a novelist's interest in the emotional beginnings of thought. Degrees of pride or jealousy become not vices for Frost (as his official biographer Lawrance Thompson makes them out to be) but preconditions, even desirable states to experience, for noticing something new about the world. In the selection just quoted, then, we can find some insight into the emotional beginnings of thought in a man like Frost. We can also see that the deliberate simplicity of Frost's talk to the 1952 graduating class of Billings Senior High School represents an essential characteristic of his thinking.

We have seen two extended examples of how Frost's talks may illuminate both aspects of his poetry and of his ideas about the origins—universal and emotional—of thinking. We can also note when we listen to the tapes of Frost's talks an important quality of Frost's thinking *as* he is thinking: he has, as does any serious thinker, a willingness to discuss conflicting ideas, expressing even a leaning toward each while being still aware that they conflict. The practice suggests a flexibility of mind that could produce original work, as, naturally, Frost could. An example of this particular quality occurs in a March 29, 1941, talk at the Library of Congress, when Frost interprets "the figure on the reverse of the Seal of the United States," the familiar "truncated pyramid, a pyramid cut off halfway up into a table, and the rest of it indicated by an eye at the apex," appearing on the back of the one-dollar bill:

> All figures, all figurative things in verse or prose, can be taken probably more than one way. I jumped at once to the conclusion, that whoever put that on the Seal—Jefferson, I never looked into it—meant this: that democracy would always mean refraining from power—beyond a certain point, that we would never, in this country, have anybody at the apex but God.
>
> Now that's one way to take it. Another way to take it (very pretty, too, and I think it's been taken by some of my friends, the second way)—the Fathers who put that figure there had in mind an incompleted building,

12. Robert Frost, "Lectures delivered at the New School for Social Research, New York, January 29, 1931–March 12, 1931, as preserved by G. Taggard," Robert Frost Collection, file 931129, Dartmouth College Library, typescript.

an uncentralized government, up to a certain time, up to, say, about 1860, 1861, to be exact—"the cruel war was first begun." And they expected, they foresaw, a gradual centralizing toward the apex. And the centralizing has gone on all my lifetime to the tune of many criticisms, much fault-finding.

I was brought up a states-rights Democrat, and my parents, my grand-parents, went through the—in the North—went through the agonies of the Civil War as Southern sympathizers, as states-rights Democrats. So I've been—had this on my mind many years; met it, met sort of [a] fulfillment of it all in this figure shown me here in Washington. And I'm inclined to say that the greatest weakness in me is—whether you call it democratic or not—I stand here and say the greatest weakness in me is a willingness to see the United States of America the most powerful thing in the world, even if it costs us some democracy.[13]

Frost goes on in this talk to discuss changes in historical attitudes toward "the common man," using various examples and referring at one point to Byron's *Don Juan* (canto 8, stanza 5). He then returns to his two interpretations of the Great Seal:

Then, again, I've thought that the one thing left to go on with (I could enumerate other things that I've noticed in the drift toward the common man, toward our being considered in literature and in the world, [and] government)—one thing I'd be waiting for if I were going to live a thousand years, would be to see the common man, everywhere, refuse his own advantage, refuse to seek his advantage, as was expected only of the gentleman in the old times. The car, the automobile, seemed to set us back a little. We can't stand at a crossing with the lights going and coming, you know, and say, "After you, Alphonse." We rush in and take our advantage. We're expected to take it. There's very little courtesy about it. Someone seizes the advantage, you see him go in and take the road, and he doesn't even look to you and smile, and say, you know, "You understand? I had to." But that would be the ultimate thing, the same as in the figure on the Seal of the United States. The government itself, I would like to dream—that I would have liked to dream—was going to refuse its own advantage, refuse to centralize beyond a certain point. The old theory was, you see, that forces contending, each for its own advantage, gave a resultant that made a nation. And, of course, the logic of that is an apex of one man, over everything—force fighting force, and a resultant mounting to an absolute monarch. And I'd like to have thought

13. "Robert Frost Reading His Own Poems, March 29, 1941," Library of Congress, Washington, D.C., Robert Frost Tape 81, Amherst College Library, audiocassette.

that in, with us all that democracy meant a refusal to bow. . . . You go back to Byron talking about George Washington. I can't quote entirely, but he tells about how it goes with men who have the chance to seize power: "they that have power to hurt," how they take it, and then he says, "And such they are, and such they will be found. Not so George Washington." That's from a man living in the time. "Not so George Washington." I saw a picture hanging behind one of our well-known writers, a painting by a middle-Westerner, large oil painting, making fun of the old story about George Washington and the hatchet and the cherry tree. I'd much rather turn away from people making fun of George Washington like that to as bad a man as Byron, knowing, knowing what greatness [was] when he saw it. And greatness of that democratic kind, that refusal to go beyond.

I'm at—you see, I'm caught at a certain place there; there's a difficulty; it's a quandary for me. But I settle it this way: maybe, to use an analogy again, maybe a nation cannot refuse to go on to its logical end of power. Maybe it's like a woman trying to stay younger than she is—if we try to refuse this centralization that seems to be coming to us. There: poets, you know, live in analogies, metaphors. But that—that's where you find me.

Frost's two interpretations of the Great Seal are in conflict: in the second, government refrains from the excessive power allowed by centralization, but in the first, it accepts it. Frost seems attracted to both possibilities, for very different reasons. Clearly, he had not come to any settled conclusion about where American government is headed. In his November 22, 1952, talk at the YMHA, we see that Frost is still thinking about this subject. He approaches it in a discussion of the problem of how much wisdom is necessary in a poem. Using three of his own poems with lengthy titles to illustrate the problem (the first is "Happiness Makes Up in Height for What It Lacks in Length"), and being just on the point of introducing "Does No One at All Ever Feel This Way in the Least?" Frost says of "How Hard It Is to Keep from Being King When It's in You and in the Situation":

See, if I asked you to name a name that that [the title of the poem] put into your head, it might be George Washington. You thought I was going to say somebody else. Now this, this third one—and you see, how wise is that? How long have we had a republic? How great is the republic? How strong is the republic? How much of it—all that comes up with a title like that: "How Hard It Is to Keep From Being King When It's in You and in the Situation." You know what that is? If you want to search the doctrine—that's Nazism, isn't it: it's your duty to tyrannize over your fellow men if it's in you and in the situation, see? That's not my own doctrine at all.[14]

Frost writes in a 1938 letter to R. P. T. Coffin of the "fluidity" of his talks, noting that they are the "inner world of raw material" for his poems.[15] This fluidity is apparent in the two talks discussed above, the 1941 talk at the Library of Congress and the November 22, 1952, talk at the YMHA in New York City, offered eleven years apart. We see from this later talk that Frost quite understands that the idea he had considered earlier (that the government cannot refuse its power or eventual centralization) is morally reprehensible, having thought through the implications of his interpretation of the Great Seal. Frost's willingness to experiment with ideas he did not completely believe in, changing them over time, is an important quality of his thinking. Equally important are the qualities exhibited in the commencement address in Billings, Montana—a deliberate simplicity of expression that we recognize also in his poems, used to convey his understanding of the usefulness of pride and jealousy—and in the philosophical arguments for purpose in the universe found in his March 21, 1951, talk at the Morgan Library, New York City, as well as his May 19, 1961, talk at Yale, both of which help to clarify his point in "Accidentally on Purpose."

Frost's talks are inexhaustibly useful, and the ways laid out here are the merest fraction of what might be said about them as they reveal the poetry, the poet's processes of thinking, the inherent interest of his spoken language, and the developments in his attitudes toward political and philosophical questions over time. The talks show Frost between the poems, living his way toward them. Given Americans' individual and cultural tastes, Frost's poems will probably remain privileged, at least over his talks; they can even be counted in Elizabethan terms of extravagance as "the hunny of all flowers, the quintessence of all Sciences, the Marrowe of Witte, and the very Phrase of Angels." But we might as well pay attention to the mortal man living between the poems, too, for he is a moving image: human, that is, fallible, and, when in the midst of discovering or exploring an interesting idea—thinking—he is intensely exciting, because we see him using his creativity in a new way. The talks are another chance to

14. "Robert Frost Speaking at Y. M. H. A., New York City, November 22, 1952," Robert Frost Tape 70, Amherst College Library, audiocassette.
15. **Letters,** 461.

observe Frost *as* he is creative—or, to be more exact, to have the illusion of this chance, as we have when we read a poem. Listening to or reading either form, we feel as if we were reliving a moment of creativity. Frost knew that poems give this illusion, as we know from his description in "The Figure a Poem Makes" of a true poem as being one that "can never lose its sense of a meaning that once unfolded by surprise as it went" (778). The talks can give us this same sense of participating in creativity—and beyond this, of having, in whatever responses we have to a poem (or a talk), our own creative moments.

THE
INTERTEXT

The Echo of Frost's Woods

David Hamilton

EVERYONE KNOWS "Stopping by Woods on a Snowy Evening," and when remembering it, nearly everyone remembers right off, I should think, its repeated last line. Here is a unique moment in Robert Frost's poetry, and so a unique effect. Nor can I think of a close parallel in anything I have ever read. It is deeply satisfying, and strange, yet somehow, for all its strangeness, familiar. Hence it has monopolized our commentary, which to my knowledge has never gone far enough, for we are in the territory of Echo who is always a mystery and a provocation.

Who has not felt the return of Echo to have enlarged his or her voice? Echo is more demanding than rhyme and is, paradoxically, both quintessentially poetic and antipoetic. Exact repetition often seems a blunder, a want of grace, the way Homer nods, even though it is also one of the more profound markers of the Homeric poems. We go back and back to "wine-dark sea" and "clean-limbed Hera," and the more we repeat those words the more their suggestions expand.

For just as exact repetition can seem a defect, it can deepen the mystery so that poetry might be defined as, precisely, that which bears repetition. If so, the more repetition borne, the more poem. Consequently little seems more certainly a poem than a villanelle, a pantoum, a sestina, or a blues song, with all their demanding repetitions—so long as we are not bored. If we are bored, the work fails, for it has not borne repetition well. But when we read with deepening attraction—admittedly our less frequent situation—we have found a "maiden" all but "makeles," as another old poem that bore its repetitions well knew to put it.

For these reasons, it seems to me that the single best commentary on Frost's last lines is the anticipatory insight of Christopher Smart: "ECHO is the soul of the voice exerting itself in hollow places."[1] "Not the voice

---

1. Christopher Smart, *Selected Poems,* ed. Karina Williamson and Marcus Walsh (London: Penguin Books, 1990), 76.

of the soul," Rebecca Clouse remarked as she brought that line to my attention. The voice of the soul, that shopworn figure, now hardly gives us pause. But Echo, the soul of the voice, she who repeats exactly—with that figure, Smart prefigures Frost, who by holding to the letter of the line, for whatever reason—as if reason would explain it—makes a blues song of his lyric and breathes such spirit into it as has yet to exhaust itself.

The blues repeat a line and advance, their movement incremental. In that, they overlap with the formalities of terza rima which repeats sounds, rather than lines, while inserting a new note by which to extend itself—aba bcb and so on. Dante apparently felt such a system required rounding off, so he added a line after the final stanza of each canto: . . . xyx yzy z. That last "z" sound finds its rhyme, which allows for closure. I mention this because Frost's quatrains employ the same principle of incremental extension: aaba bbcb. . . . The lonely "b" sound, "here," in the first stanza, becomes the dominant rhyme of the next: "queer," "near," "year" and so on. This is a top-heavy or off-balance terza rima. Moreover, Frost's concluding repetition of "And miles to go before I sleep" would seem a parallel way of bringing his "canto" to closure. His solution alludes, we might say, to Dante's underlying principle of incremental advance with no potential rhyme left dangling. We hear an echo of Dante in the formal matter of Frost's poem, and our reading seems very much a matter of attending to Echo.

My own awareness of this particular reverberation was sparked by a lecture in Spain, when Professor Viorica Patea suggested that the "owner" of those woods might have a providential aspect and that Frost's lingering by them was passing strange. Mediterranean language was in my ear, and Dante's *"selva oscura"* leapt to mind. It probably helped that Patea was from the University of Salamanca, from which Fray Luis de Leon had been taken to prison during the Inquisition for translating the *Song of Songs,* and where after five years, according to legend, he returned to his lecture hall, with its crude wooden benches, and greeted his students that first morning back with, *"Dicebamus hesterna die. . . ."* [*"Decíamos ayer"*; "We were saying yesterday. . . ."] It was as if his last day in class had been echoing in him all those years to come through finally, and then ring over and over again as the tale has been repeated.

Not that I had stumbled onto anything new by catching Dante from Patea's remarks. John Pollock's note of 1979 reminds us that "Frost . . . knew Dante thoroughly."

> Thus when the speaker of "Stopping By Woods" states that he has paused
> in his journey "Between the woods and frozen lake" . . . it is difficult not
> to think of Dante's experience in the first book of *The Divine Comedy* . . .
> which begins in a dark wood and progresses to a frozen lake at the center
> of hell.

George Monteiro also draws Dante into a discussion of this passage, though he discusses only the "woods," not the lake, and hurries on to a comparison with "The Draft Horse" and its "pitch-dark limitless grove."[2]

Wherever we find Dante, we may find Eliot, and that is the echo that I would draw out further. *The Waste Land* appeared only one year before "Stopping by Woods," and I suspect in the latter an oblique reply. Responses to *The Waste Land,* after all, are not in short supply. In his provocative anthology, *Top 500 Poems,* William Harmon singles out "Directive" and "Spring and All" as poems that replied to Eliot.[3] As Harmon notes, the word *waste* appears in "Spring and All," and "Directive" includes lilacs, a rock-water contrast, and reference to the Holy Grail, to which I may add that Williams's poem begins as a long series of "sentence fragments" that we could say are "shored against" the mid-poem arrival of spring. We wait that long for a complete sentence which, by offering grammatical shape, puts winter "waste" to order. "Spring and All" also appeared in 1923. Harmon suggests that Eliot challenged poets to portray their own ideas of "the good place," just as "The Deserted Village" had helped evoke *The Waste Land.* In that case, "New Hampshire" may be yet another reply to Eliot, a half-ironic tribute to a good place, it being "restful," Frost observes, "just to think about New Hampshire," even though, as he no doubt enjoyed adding, he was "living in Vermont."

Eliot drew on Dante repeatedly, for the epigraph for "Prufrock," for *"il miglior fabbro," The Waste Land's* dedication to Pound, and in "Tradition and the Individual Talent," to mention several instances. In "Tradition," he describes artistry as a "pressure" that transmutes the materials of memory and emotion. "It is not the 'greatness', the intensity of the emotions, the components, but the intensity of the artistic process, the pressure, so to speak, under which the fusion takes place, that counts," is the way Eliot

2. Pollock, "Dante and Frost's 'Stopping by Woods.'" *Notes on Contemporary Literature* 9 (March 1979): 5; Monteiro, *Robert Frost and the New England Renaissance* (Lexington: University Press of Kentucky, 1988), 50–52.

3. *The Top 500 Poems,* ed. William Harmon (New York: Columbia University Press, 1992) in headnotes to the respective poems.

put it in 1919, and his examples are from Dante.[4] Allusions to Dante became a kind of signature, and several passages in *The Waste Land* become such pastiches of the *Commedia* that "After Dante" could have served as their title.

It seems to me that Frost turns on all this and works his own will on remembrances of Dante but in a style that makes any sense of pressure, as such, only lightly felt. His is a poem with a light touch even if its implications are weighty. "Stopping by Woods" has been much loved as a Christmas card scene, though being alone in woods filling up with snow could prove unlucky. Indeed quite a bit of dread adds up quietly but quickly. The lack of a farmhouse could suggest something to the horse, and to us, that the speaker minimizes. The darkest evening may not specify the coldest or the most forlorn, but it implies as much. No skating party and bonfire glitter on that frozen lake. As Thompson's biography makes evident, Frost had enough experience of death, silence, and suicidal thinking to make his famous last line anything but restful, and "death wish"—as Ciardi suggested, and suffered for suggesting—seems not at all far-fetched.[5] How can we define "lovely" as "dark and deep" without entertaining its equation to heart-stopping desire? Our general rejection of Lathem's ameliorating emendation ("lovely, dark, and deep") has been, perhaps, one more way of leaning toward Ciardi's reading.

For all these reasons, we may say that Frost writes a North American wasteland in sixteen lines. He alters and extends the terza rima stanza, providing a short string of them rounded off as a canto, not precisely as Dante does it, but with an allusion to Dante's method of closure. Whose woods these are we can guess. The darkest evening of the year suggests cosmic matters. The frozen lake is where the woods lead, and where the downward journey ends. As in Dante, there is no rest; the speaker must keep on and on. Even the "easy wind," one of the more Currier and Ives touches, is in keeping with how easily one slides into the *Inferno* by way of Paolo and Francesca, whose restless, erotic play sets them whirling on a ceaseless wind.

Once I heard Frost read this poem. Actually he "said" it. He would "say" his poems, he told us, differentiating himself from those who did not wholly know theirs. So he said "Stopping by Woods" all the way

---

4. *Selected Essays* (New York: Harcourt, Brace and World, 1964), 3–11.
5. "Robert Frost: The Way to the Poem" in *Dialogue with an Audience*, ed. John Ciardi (New York: J. B. Lippincott Company, 1963), 147–68.

through and then raised the question of the repeated last line. His tone was bantering, mocking commentators who would give it "meaning," readers like Ciardi and perhaps Ciardi in particular. He said nothing about solving the problem of bringing his off-balance terza rima to closure. He insisted on an "easier" explanation, more in the nature of Ockham's razor. He wanted to go to bed; that was all—that was all?—and repeating the last line was his quickest way of getting there. At the time, I took his explanation as an invitation to share in a small joke, but it is a joke that bears repetition.

There are, of course, other explanations of this lyric, and among them we might privilege two credited to Frost himself. One comes from an anecdote told by N. Arthur Bleau. Bleau recounts having attended a Frost reading at Bowdoin in 1947 and of having asked, from the audience, what was his favorite poem. At first Frost ignored the question, saying they were all his favorites and ended the session. Then he invited Bleau to the podium and spoke with him privately. "Stopping by Woods" was his favorite poem because it arose from a particularly bleak Christmas and the "darkest evening of the year" just before it. Having no money, Frost loaded a wagon with farm produce and went to town, but he found no buyers and returned empty-handed, without even small gifts for the children. He felt he had failed his family, and rounding a bend in the road, by woods, and quite near his house, the horse, who seemed to understand his mood, and who had already been given the reins, slowed and stopped, letting Frost have a good cry. "I just sat there and bawled like a baby," Bleau reports Frost as having said.[6] In a following note, Frost's daughter, Lesley, confirms the story, saying her father gave her that same explanation "sometime in the forties," that she assumed he had told no one else except her mother, and that Bleau's telling was particularly persuasive for his use of the word *bawl*. "Oh, come now, quit bawling," her father would say. She adds another few words of her father's that she remembers: "A man has as much right as a woman to a good cry now and again. The snow gave me shelter; the horse understood and gave me the time." She even remembers the name of the horse, Eunice.

This is a remarkable anecdote. For one thing, it shows Frost as readier to let poetry arise from his emotions than Eliot would seem to be. Not "the intensity of the emotions," Eliot had said, "but the intensity [and pressure] of the artistic process." For Frost, the emotions had to be strong, and he applied his pressure, but it is the pressure of astonishing restraint, a

6. "Robert Frost's Favorite Poem" in **Tharpe III,** 174–76; Lesley Frost's "Note," 177.

pressure that hardly shows. No "bawling" enters the poem. The surprising phrase by which the woods "fill up with snow" could be read as a correlative for it, the abundance of snow being imaginatively commensurate with an abundance of tears. Had we had tears, no one would have seen this as a winter wonderland scene. That such a reading remains possible, however, is further tribute to Frost's restraint, for the "little horse," "harness bells," "easy wind," and "downy flake" are all details that a speaker, wishing to emphasize his sorrow, would be likely to suppress. Without them we would be more directed to the evocation of a personal wasteland. With them, Frost maintains a balance, or a "suspension" as Jarrell suggested, between despairing and regenerative tones.[7]

To put it differently, those phrases suggest an apparent ease, rather than pressure working upon the materials of memory and emotion, which no doubt has had much to do with the poem's staying power. The real pressure Frost felt appears to have been to deflect the feeling that was there, from the speaker to his horse, to the woods themselves, and to the snow. Lesley Frost remarks that her father withheld this story because he did not want "pity" from the reader; "pity, he said, was the *last* thing he wanted or needed." Once the reader is relieved of investing in the speaker's need, other aspects of the poem surge forward, and these tend to obscure the darker reading that I, too, favor.

Bleau's anecdote was apparently unknown to Thompson, who died five years before its printing, and who only records Lesley Frost's comment that a woodside pond near their Derry, New Hampshire, farm was the "frozen lake" in question. The Frosts lived there between 1900 and 1909, when the family was at its poorest. That was the period, too, when they had a horse named Eunice. The story about the poem that Thompson records is a summer story set several years later.

Thompson reminds us that Frost was something of a mythmaker about himself, one favorite being his writing poems of miraculous inspiration. "Stopping by Woods" was an example, which was, in turn, a reason for his favoring it. In June 1922, after Frost's first year at Michigan, when he was no longer quite so plagued by poverty, he was working on "New Hampshire." After working all one June night, he was surprised and pleased by dawn. Standing at the window, stretching, looking at the sun, he was overtaken

---

7. "Two Essays on Robert Frost," *Poetry and the Age* (New York: Vintage Books, 1955), 39.

by a thought and returned to a fresh page and quickly, "without too much trouble" drafted the complete poem.[8]

Ciardi took this story at face value, without knowing what poem Frost had spent the night working on and with the confident assertion that were it known, "it would be found to contain the germinal stuff of 'Stopping by Woods'" (Ciardi, 156–57). Thompson took offense at Ciardi's certainty. "There is no connection between either the themes or the subject matter of 'New Hampshire' and 'Stopping by Woods,'" he asserted (I, 597). That Frost finished it at one sitting seems a bit of a stretch since drafts exist that indicate his revisions. For example the key Dantean line was "Between a forest and a lake" before Frost found his more fortunate second thought.[9] When informed of all this, Ciardi tempered his view and thanked his former teacher John Holmes for the information and for "his understanding from Mr. Frost that the long poem in question is 'New Hampshire.'" Then he added that if all that be so, his guess about its containing the "germinal stuff" of the new poem "becomes questionable" (Ciardi, 158).

So Frost had two good stories to tell about his poem. We know that it was first published on March 7, 1923, in the *New Republic* (on the same page as "Moon Rider" by William Rose Benét and under the common title, "Two Winter Poems"), then in *New Hampshire* later that year, making likely its composition the summer before. His Christmas story need not rule out its composition early one June morning. Frost did not say what more than early sun had inspired him. Judith Oster finds a connection between the two poems in that both balance notions of responsibility and wildness.[10] And I suspect that Eliot, along with the prior night's work, played a part.

Thompson believes that the composition of "New Hampshire" was influenced by an intellectual current of the early twenties with which Frost, characteristically, was at odds. The *Nation* ran a series of articles, state by state, about capitalistic corruption in the United States with Edmund Wilson, among others, contributing. Wilson wrote of New Jersey. Having sold "The Pauper Witch of Grafton" to the *Nation*, Frost was asked to add to the series. So he composed "New Hampshire." Amy Lowell and

---

8. **Early Years** and **Triumph.** See **Triumph,** 236–37 and the extended notes, **Early Years,** 595ff. and **Triumph,** 596ff.

9. Charles W. Cooper and John Holmes, *Prefaces to Poetry* (New York: Harcourt, Brace, 1943), 604.

10. **Oster,** 151–52.

Emerson were targets, because of their dismissive attitudes toward upper New England (Thompson, II, 233). Even unnamed, Eliot could be in the background of all this, for the common denominator seems to be fashionable denigration from which Frost stood apart.

One could, in fact, consider "Stopping by Woods" a radical revision of "New Hampshire," the long work of the night before, which is what Ciardi seems to have imagined. He speaks of "what was a-simmer . . . all night without finding its proper form" (Ciardi, 157). Sometimes the best revision comes not from tinkering but from starting over, making a new cut through the material from an entirely different point of view. We can only conjecture, but suppose on that early morning, standing in the sun, after one of the shortest nights of the year, Frost remembered its opposite. Derry became his starting point and that moment "between a forest and a lake" on a night still poignant to him. His lengthy, detailed, often tongue-in-cheek discussion of New Hampshire gives way to a moment that could stand as the emblem for it all. Such a background would add to the reasons why Frost once remarked "that 'Stopping by Woods on a Snowy Evening' was the kind of poem he'd like to print on one page, to be followed with 'forty pages of footnotes.' "[11] And that, with a touch of irony, brings us around again to Eliot.

If recent criticism has taught us anything, it is that no writer's explanation is to be trusted, and readers have their own claims in these matters. But in that respect, too, Frost anticipated us. Frost never closes off our own restless and doomed way of seeking meanings in what he wrote. That night in May 1961 when he invited the audience I was part of to share his joke about his final line, he teased but did not repudiate our will to make a riddle of it. "I'll take credit for anything you find," he said while walking off the stage.

It is an admonition I have long heard echoing. In a way it is silly to think of Frost devising this poem as an "answer" to Eliot. Eliot publishes *The Waste Land* the year before. Frost reads it, frets, and devises a reply. Our better poems don't usually get written and published quite that quickly or with such singular motives. But whether or not Frost had Eliot in mind, his lines evoke a pattern of thinking from which we can construct such a reading. Writing much more quietly than Eliot, with exquisite subtlety,

---

11. Reginald L. Cook, "Frost's Asides in His Poetry," in *On Frost: The Best from American Literature,* ed. Edwin H. Cady and Louis J. Budd (Durham: Duke University Press, 1991), 34.

and with numerous echoes, Frost offers a most ambiguous poem. Is this a Christmas card or a more serious scene of threat? Is his speaker only a short distance from the barn, or must he endure longer, colder travel? Could "Stopping by Woods" be a negative Twenty-third Psalm? Ideas such as these may not be necessary to our reading, but as they come to us, they are not easily displaced. And I for one would like to think they lean toward an interpretation for which Frost would have been pleased "to take credit."

A Tale of Two Cottages

Frost and Wordsworth

Jonathan N. Barron

I

EVER SINCE HE PUBLISHED his first book, critics have read Robert Frost's poetry in light of Wordsworth's. But nearly a hundred years later the connection between the two poets still lacks a sustained, extended critical examination. In part, this absence results from a lack of critical attention to Frost's own intellectual, cultural, and literary allusions. Unlike allusions in the poetry of Pound, Eliot, Moore, and H.D., Frost's are subtle, even disguised. As a result of such canniness surprisingly little work has been done on the intertextuality of Frost's poetry. In hopes of changing this situation, I want to tease out more fully the impact of Frost's Wordsworthian allusions in order to call attention to an allusive and an *elusive* Frost—a poet who refuses to fit either of the two major literary categories so often associated with his work: modernism and romanticism. By looking at Frost's allusions to Wordsworth, one discovers a poet who manipulated the work of his predecessor not because he rejected its poetics but rather because he wanted to free that poetics from a false interpretation. Rather than condemn the muddiness and naiveté of Wordsworth's poetic turn to nature and posit, in its place, the fixity of Pound's history and economics, the faith of Eliot's religion, or the scientific naturalism of Moore's animals and plants, Frost's poetry, instead, destabilizes the critical assumption that Wordsworth's poetry itself ever endorsed an idealized nature or the truth claims such idealism invokes. Rather than read Wordsworth as an idealist nature poet, Frost instead reads the more social aspects of Wordsworth's poetry. Frost's Wordsworth, in other words, is not the poet of what M. H. Abrams called "natural supernaturalism" but rather a far more social poet of men and women, common speech, "flesh and blood."[1] Two recent books on Frost, one on his interest in the social and one on his interest in nature, agree that Frost's poetry attributes to neither the natural world nor the social a divine power that one can somehow know, discern, or understand. Both books convincingly argue that Frost's poetry, whether its focus be on nature or on the social milieu, is resolutely antiteleological, anti-idealist, even potentially diabolical in its skeptical attitude toward ethical and moral certainty. Without saying so, both books refuse to read Frost as a latter-day idealist in the tradition now associated with Wordsworth's poetry. In his discussion of nature in Frost's poetry, for example, Robert Faggen argues that in Frost's natural world one does not find Arcadia. Instead, Frost's nature "creates hierarchies and stability only for a moment before its relentless warfare cancels and levels inequalities insect and human alike."[2]

Meanwhile, in his discussion of Frost's attention to the social world, Mark Richardson argues that in Frost's poetry there is a striking lack of any desire to overcome the "ordeal" of social situations. Rather than find new ways of eradicating and resolving the "fear of man" upon which so much social organization depends, Frost, says Richardson, invoked, even welcomed, that very fear.

What neither Richardson nor Faggen have any reason to say but which, nonetheless, ought to be said, is that this attitude does not run counter to Wordsworth's poetry so much as to an interpretation of that poetry. In effect, Frost's antiteleological natural world and his radically skeptical social environment share more with Wordsworth's poetry than many might have suspected, a connection that is particularly evident when one reads Frost's "The Black Cottage" as a response to Wordsworth's "The Ruined Cottage."

With apologies to Mick Jagger, Frost, in his poem, sees a cottage, and he wants to paint it black. Just as the Rolling Stones in *Let It Bleed* felt compelled to erase the all-too-easy and optimistic sounds of the Beatles in *Let It Be*, Frost in "The Black Cottage" means to go behind the false front of the wanderer's optimism in Wordsworth's "The Ruined Cottage." Frost's

---

1. M. H. Abrams, *Natural Supernaturalism* (New York: Norton, 1971). Wordsworth's declaration, "I wish to keep my reader in the company of flesh and blood" is from his "Preface to *Lyrical Ballads*" (1800) reprinted in *Lyrical Ballads 1798*, ed. W. J. B. Owen (Oxford: Oxford University Press, 1969), 161.

2. **Richardson** and **Faggen**. Ironically, while Richardson makes a strong case for Frost's antiteleological social vision, he nonetheless assumes that when Frost turns his attention to the natural world he finds the very teleology Faggen says cannot be found (at least not found in Frost).

poem, in other words, reminds readers that the association of morality with nature in that poem is only a strong opinion held by one man and told to another. The association is made in conversation; it is spoken only as a tenuous attempt at certitude after an emotional crisis. In other words, Frost's poem reminds readers that if the turn to nature at the end of "The Ruined Cottage" does make the poet-narrator feel better, then at least one reader, Robert Frost, thought such newly awakened optimism had very little to do with "natural supernatural" immanence. Rather than a blessing from the spirit of nature, Frost's poetic response to Wordsworth's poem argues that the optimism which arises from tragedy has far more to do with the psychological needs of individuals than with the powerful influence of nature. From Frost's perspective in "The Black Cottage," the turn to nature in Wordsworth's "The Ruined Cottage" is a psychological need born of a newly awakened fear that in both the social and natural worlds one meets mostly with indifference.

When Frost returned to "The Ruined Cottage," it so happened that he also returned to one of the first major poems Wordsworth ever wrote. He returned, whether or not he knew it, to the very origins of what is now known as "the romantic ideology," a closed system where absolute truth—faith—always returns to give comfort to the faithful.[3] Before examining the connection between the two poems, however, I want to pause briefly and consider an interesting textual problem raised by this connection: To which poem did Frost respond?

In the early twentieth century Frost would only have known this poem as Book One of *The Excursion* (1814). Frost would not have known that a complicated textual history lay behind the "The Ruined Cottage," a poem that did exist as an independent poem ready for publication in 1798. By 1799, however, it had been substantially revised, yet neither the original nor the revision with the title "Ruined Cottage" would be made public until 1969 (when Jonathan Wordsworth brought both manuscripts into the light of day in *The Music of Humanity*, which was published by Harper and Row).[4]

So what is the substantial difference? In both versions of Wordsworth's "Ruined Cottage" the poem focuses only on the conversation between

3. **Faggen,** 288. Jerome McGann, *The Romantic Ideology* (Chicago: Chicago University Press, 1983).

4. Since Jonathan Wordsworth's revival of the poem, it has been known in its second version (manuscript "d"), a version that closely resembles Book One of *The Excursion*. This version continues to be privileged by scholars; it is the version one finds in virtually every anthology of British literature currently on the market.

the peddler and the poet. Only the second version includes the turn to nature at the end. Why the change? One answer is that, in the first version (manuscript "b"), the unmitigated despair of the ending proved intolerable to Wordsworth. It had a powerful but distressing ending: "She died / Last tenant of these ruined walls." Finding this despair too intense, Wordsworth later added what scholars now refer to as the "reconciling addendum," the turn to nature where spear-grass on the cottage wall offers a kind of comfort and blessing to the two men who have been broken down by the tale.

To add still further to the textual complexity, there are also two versions of Frost's poem: one that was almost certainly written before Frost arrived in England, and another almost certainly written between 1912 and 1914, when he was there.[5] Without going into any more textual history of either poem, it is worth noting that Frost's revisions occur only *after* he returned more seriously to Wordsworth's poetry. Amazingly, Frost, as if by some weird affiliation with his predecessor, revised his own cottage poem in such a way that it would resemble Wordsworth's poem in its original first stage, a version that Frost is unlikely to have known.

A few other details are also worth noting. In *The Excursion*, the peddler is given a name, Armytage, and a complete biography, neither of which occur in either form of "The Ruined Cottage." Given such textual complications, my own sense is that Frost first read this poem seriously when he was working with his Georgian friends. And the only version he would have known well and studied in 1914 would have been Book One of *The Excursion*. Thus, it seems appropriate to discuss Frost's "Black Cottage" only in terms of Wordsworth's *Excursion*—its most exact analogue.

With this textual history in mind, it is all the more remarkable that Frost's poem should remove, or strip away, the very romantic ideology that "The Ruined Cottage" has come to represent. For if we read Frost's poem as a kind of commentary on, a reworking of, Wordsworth's earlier poem, then Frost asks readers to see "The Ruined Cottage" not as an idealistic nature poem, not as a representative of the romantic ideology, but rather as a poem critical of that very ideology: a poem that tells its readers that nature

---

5. For more on the textual variants of the poem, see James Butler, *The Ruined Cottage and the Pedlar* (Ithaca: Cornell University Press, 1979). See **Early Years,** 592–93, for a printed version of the first "Black Cottage." For discussion of the two "Black Cottages," see John Evangelist Walsh, *Into My Own: The English Years of Robert Frost* (New York: Grove Press, 1988), 47–48, 78–79 n. 263; John Kemp, *Robert Frost and New England* (Princeton: Princeton University Press, 1979), 119–20; and **Pritchard,** 93–99. Pritchard notes, "In rewriting the poem, he thoroughly re-imagined it, dispensing with the all-seeing, all-wise, poet-narrator" (94). Also, the minister only appears in the second version.

offers nothing but fuel for their own desires and illusions. For me to say that Frost reads "The Ruined Cottage" in this way is also to say that Frost goes against the grain of at least one hundred years of critical responses to the first publication of the poem as Book One of *The Excursion* (1814). How is it possible, then, for Frost to "misread" the poem so completely?

To answer that question I offer a brief summary of "The Ruined Cottage"'s story as it is told in *The Excursion,* Book One.[6] In so doing, I will show that Frost's "Black Cottage" moves to the foreground a few fundamental structural elements of the poem that have long been ignored.[7] By foregrounding those elements in his own poem, he questions the too easy association readers make between morality and nature. To summarize: "The Ruined Cottage" begins with a young poet resting idly in what he thinks is just a picturesque tranquil ruin. He then encounters a wanderer who proceeds to tell him the story of the cottage and the family who once lived there. He is particularly focused on the woman, Margaret, who had lived there with her two children and her husband, a weaver. The wanderer explains that times grew increasingly hard, and to make some money, the husband eventually enlisted in the British army to fight in the American War of Independence. It turns out that, in fact, the husband had snuck away, leaving behind the money he had received for enlisting, never to return. Driven to despair over this turn of events, Margaret herself becomes a wanderer and begins neglecting her children (one dies), her house (it crumbles), and her health (she dies), all in the hope of finding her husband. Her faith and resolute commitment to her husband are both inspiring and deeply disturbing. Hearing the tale, the poet is overwhelmed with grief. The wanderer then points to the natural environment around them and says that deep communion with it will alleviate despair. "[A]nd here she died," says the wanderer, "Last human tenant of these ruined walls" (914–15). What could be more inexpressibly awful? How, finally, can one explain or understand her behavior? The tale, as told by the wanderer, succeeds in breaking the optimistic idealistic spirit of the poet-listener even before he learns of Margaret's fate. So powerful is the tale that the poet "begged of the old man that, for my sake, / He would resume the story" (624–25). The wanderer, however, offers a glimpse of his own romantic ideology before he proceeds: "We have known that there is often found

6. "The Excursion" in *William Wordsworth: The Poems,* vol. 2. ed. W. J. B. Owen (New Haven: Yale University Press, 1981), 52–64.

7. Only recently have these elements begun to receive serious critical attention. See Paul Alpers, *What Is Pastoral?* (Chicago: University of Chicago Press, 1996), 260–85.

/ In mournful thoughts, and always might be found, / A power to virtue friendly; were't not so, / I am a dreamer among men, indeed / An idle dreamer!" (632–36). In other words, according to the wanderer, even in times of deepest helpless despair, "a power to virtue friendly" will assert itself. He has to believe that this "power exists," otherwise he is "an idle dreamer." Because "idle dreams" can refer to any frivolous document that, at best, entertains us and, at worst, demeans real events for the purely vulgar purpose of producing an emotive response, the wanderer warns the poet against such a reading of this tale. After he finishes the story, he returns to his own creed and declares that this tale is meant only for "the enlightened spirit / Whose meditative sympathies repose / Upon the breast of Faith" (953–55).[8] When the poet breaks down and cries after hearing the tale, the wanderer can rest assured that he has told it to the right person, a person of faith, of moral convictions. But the poet's grief also suggests that the story of Margaret, as he will soon record it in poetry, will be one of unmitigated grief. This will not do. To correct such a misinterpretation and to validate his own faith in natural immanence the wanderer points to some spear-grass nearby and declares that the "high spear-grass on that wall, / By mist and silent rain-drops silvered o'er" (943–44) is a sight so beautiful that virtue must exist as a real presence. This natural proof does have a salvific effect on the poet, who is suddenly convinced that "virtue" must exist where nature's beauty can be found. With a newly found cheerfulness the two men go off to a nearby pub.

According to Frost's "Black Cottage," however, Wordsworth himself is not as convinced as his characters. To make that point, Frost's poem focuses on the fact that Wordsworth's poem is fundamentally a conversation between two men. In other words, Frost focuses his attention on the psychological needs of both the wanderer and the poet; he shows that both men need the blessing of nature in order to feel better, but that need is not necessarily indicative of the actual presence of benevolence in nature. If, says Frost's poem, there is a need for nature's blessing after hearing Margaret's tale, it is the wanderer's need, the poet's need, but not necessarily Wordsworth's. More crucially, says Frost's poem,

8. As if the textual history were not complex enough, still further complications arise here. For, as it turns out, these particular lines about faith are not to be found in either "The Ruined Cottage" or the 1814 edition of *The Excursion*. Instead, they were added in 1842, according to Stephen Gill, *William Wordsworth: A Life* (Oxford: Oxford University Press, 1990), 416–17. Even though these lines do not appear in the 1814 edition, I assume it was unlikely that Frost read that early out-of-print version of the poem.

Wordsworth does not validate the "truth" that where beauty exists, there faith resides.[9]

Intriguingly, although recent scholarship does reveal more skepticism, irony, and materialism in Wordsworth's poetry than previous romanticists and modernists would ever have wanted to admit, discussion of "The Ruined Cottage" is still mostly confined to critiques of the poem as an example of Wordsworth's blindness to social and ethical problems. When New Historicists like Alan Liu, James Chandler, and Marjorie Levenson examine the natural facts of Wordsworth's poetry they discover a destabilizing artifice, a historical dimension, that, they argue, unravels the claims made on behalf of nature.[10] In Frost's "Black Cottage," by contrast, one finds a similar critique made, as it were, from inside the poem itself. Frost's poem does not confuse the poet with his characters; rather, it reveals a second story latent in "The Ruined Cottage"—a story that depicts an anti-idealistic social and natural world that particular individuals attempt to face. Not blindness, then, but insight.

II

I have argued that Frost's poetic return to the "Ruined Cottage" isolates that poem's conversational elements. By that I mean that Frost's "Black Cottage" takes its structure, and even much of its diction, from Wordsworth's "Ruined Cottage" as it appeared in *The Excursion,* Book One (see appendix). These allusions, moreover, allow Frost to engage Wordsworth's poem on three levels. First, they make of Wordsworth's poem a poetic predecessor. In so doing, they establish for Frost a tradition for what was, in the 1910s, still a very new kind of poetry: an antiteleological conversation poem. Second, they foreground the idealism latent in Wordsworth's natural world and so better prepare readers for the

9. Alan Liu, *Wordsworth: The Sense of History* (Stanford: Stanford University Press, 1989), 314–49, still offers the most trenchant contemporary scholarly critique of the social and ethical implications of this poem. He is particularly critical of the "reconciling addendum," the spear-grass episode, arguing that it manifests Wordsworth's own obtuseness to the claim of his poem. My own view is that Frost did not conflate Wordsworth with his character as does Liu.

10. New Historicist scholarship on Wordsworth has been particularly critical of this poem. In particular see, Liu, *Wordsworth;* Marjorie Levinson, *Wordsworth's Great Period Poems* (New York: Cambridge University Press, 1986); and James Chandler *Wordsworth's Second Nature* (Chicago: University of Chicago Press, 1984).

destruction of that idealism.[11] Third, by foregrounding the conversational elements of the poem, these allusions present a far more skeptical, far more social Wordsworth than is often recognized.

Given the nuances of Frost's allusions to Wordsworth, why, one wonders, did he bother to return to that poet at all? I believe the primary motivation for his return to "The Ruined Cottage" was his desire to engage the problems of patriotism and nationalism current in the 1910s when he revised his poem. These issues were far more important to him than any more scholarly need to reinterpret Wordsworth's poetry. I would even go so far as to suggest that Frost did not think he was reinterpreting Wordsworth at all. Rather, he probably felt he was the first poet to understand just how socially dependent, how unnatural, how constructed the ideals of patriotism and nationalism so often are.

This is particularly likely given the fact that between 1913 and 1914 Frost was a close associate of the Georgian poets. Like them, no doubt because of them, Frost made it his business to revitalize and reexamine the English pastoral tradition. Frost, in other words, found himself among poets who were obsessed with Wordsworth and who read his work not for its idealism but rather for its hard, bitter, "alien" truths. Whether his Georgian friends trained Frost to see a more social Wordsworth, or whether he took it upon himself to show the Georgians that Wordsworth's poetry had a long way to go before it came to the kind of anguished, bitter sincerity they wanted to achieve, one must leave to the biographers to decide. What matters is that between 1913 and 1914, when Frost composed and revised for publication the poems of *North of Boston,* his friends were unusually interested in, even steeped in, Wordsworth's poetry as a kind of precursor, or predecessor, to their own.[12] And it was in these years that Frost looked to Wordsworth as a guide to writing about his own social, political world—a world he describes most forcefully in "The Black Cottage," published on May 14, 1914, as part of the collection *North of Boston.*

11. In a wonderful study of Robert Frost and Walter Benjamin, Andrew Lakritz notes that the "destructive" man, as outlined by Benjamin, also defines Frost's poetics. See *Modernism and the Other in Stevens, Frost and Moore* (Gainesville: University of Florida Press, 1996), see esp. 69–121.

12. The Georgian milieu explains why Frost would want to return to the social milieu of New England while living across the Atlantic in England. For the Georgian poets were particularly interested in the loco-specific details that Wordsworth's poetry had authorized as necessary to the English lyric tradition. As an American, Frost was literally excluded from the Georgian anthologies on national grounds, but, as an "honorary" Georgian, he applied their poetic strategies and theories to an American context. See Walsh, *Into My Own.*

Specifically, "The Black Cottage" tells the story of a woman whose religious faith and convictions ground her sense of radical democracy and equality. Told as a dramatic monologue, it is spoken by a minister, but it is also presented as if it had been recorded by his auditor, a poet. The poem takes place beside a now-empty, nearly ruined cottage deep in the woods made black by a recent rain. Standing beside its window, the minister tells the poet the story of the woman, now dead, who used to live there. As it turns out, the men had been talking about the issues raised by this cottage in town. Excited enough to want to go to the place itself, the minister leads the poet into the woods in order to tell the story with more exactitude. Once there, he explains that the woman was the most principled person he ever knew. She was as committed to her Protestant faith as to the ideals of the American republic. Her husband died fighting in the Civil War, her children left as part of the American expansion westward, and she died alone. As far as she was concerned, the principles of freedom and equality outweighed any personal loss she might have felt. Furthermore, she connected her own patriotism specifically to her religion and so made the political dependent on the theological. Just as Wordsworth's wanderer links nature and ethics in his tale of Margaret, so the minister, in his story of this woman, links the ethics implied both by the Civil War and the Declaration of Independence to theology. In both poems, idealism is brought down to earth—whether in spear-grass or in political wars.

In Frost's poem, political principles depend on theology. But this association does not sit well with the minister. As a result, his entire monologue becomes a means by which he tries to work through his own problems with that association. As his monologue progresses, it becomes increasingly clear that he is far more of a materialist than his own parishioner; he cannot believe she ever took such principles as freedom and equality seriously.

As he tells her tale, in other words, he becomes more and more skeptical about the woman's own faith, her certitude. Eventually, he lapses into his own idealistic vision, but, in a typically Frostian maneuver, the idealistic vision is about a materialist dream. The minister wishes he could have been at the birth of Jesus because, if he had been there, he would now be able to believe in his own creed. At this point, when the narrator is most detached from the woman's tale and engaged in his own private fantasy, the poem turns to nature in the form of bees, who suddenly spring into action and zip out en masse ready to sting the human intruders. The image is a paradoxical wonder. From the naturalist's perspective, the bees are merely doing what bees do. From the literary perspective, the perspective of an interpretive reader, however, the bees tell us that nature will offer no solace.[13] When, in the last lines of the poem, the bees awaken, they send the two men back to the human world of the town where their jobs as minister and poet most need doing. Nature, in the form of these bees, sends the two men packing. The bees refuse to let the men drift into idealism: the minister who is daydreaming and the poet who is recording that dream in his own poetic dream-space are both sent running. Stung into wakefulness, the two men are forced out of the forest, out of nature, where false affinities between ideals and their material expression are only too easy to discover. In Frost's woods, nature has grown sick of the human determination to idealize its hard truths away. The bee's harsh truth, however, does not so much deny the benevolence of Wordsworth's spear-grass as deny the implication that nature as such is the location for benevolent ideals.

In Frost's day, as in our own, to lapse for a moment into platitudes, political principles were grounded in theological truth. But this obvious point bears repeating because it is precisely this association between the political and the theological that Frost's poem critiques. His use of Wordsworth establishes a poetic precedent for such critiques. "The Black Cottage" was written against the political background of the gathering political squabbles and breakdowns in policy that would lead to World War I. As the global pressures increased in the months before the Guns of August, the rise of nationalism and the cynicism it provoked would have made the contemporary association between theology and politics all the more obvious to Frost.

Frost's "Black Cottage," therefore, takes as its occasion a dispute between two men over the results of the Civil War. The minister takes the poet to the cottage in order "[t]o measure how far fifty years have brought us" (46). The minister, in other words, assumes that politics and theology define one another. But in trying to make his case, he finds that the theological principles that gave rise to the Civil War, freedom and equality, are not really believable. More troubling still, the theology itself is hard

---

13. Also from a literary perspective, the bees allude to the ancient pastoral genre, and to Virgil's bees in particular. One may, in fact, choose to read this scene as an echo of Virgil and Darwin, both of whom emphasize the social fact of the life of bees. From this perspective, then, nature tells the two men to go to *their* social world; to stop their solipsistic nonsense. My own sense is that even this pastoral and Darwinian echo must remain nearly silent because it comes too close to naturalizing "the social." As I read "The Black Cottage," Frost is doing his best to avoid naturalizing any ethical principle. Any hint that the social is better than the state of solitude because to be social is in fact to be natural runs counter to the poem's basic view that social principles should not be naturalized.

to believe—can God really have a son? Was there a virgin birth? The minister's skepticism is not tempered, erased, or denied by nature. If anything, nature in "The Black Cottage" further proves the existence of a chasm separating the social facts of political wars from theological ideals.

Just as the poem's focus on politics is not surprising given the context of 1914, so, too, the absence of immanence in nature ought not to surprise us. In the technological age of the early twentieth century, Frost's experience in both New England and rural England taught him to have no truck with either the association of industrialization with progress or the false association of rural life with tempering benevolence.

If Frost's poem makes a case against a theological ground for politics, it also makes a case against an idealism located in nature. This twofold purpose is accomplished when Frost transforms the wanderer of Wordsworth's poem into a New England minister. The change from wanderer to minister is fitting. In Wordsworth's poem, the poet gives us the wanderer's history, and we learn that the poet looks to him as a type of minister: "sometimes his religion seemed to me Self-taught, as of a dreamer in the woods" (409–10). By the conclusion to Wordsworth's poem, the poet *has* been ministered to and so learns to find solace from nature, even if such solace is not "really" there.

By contrast, in Frost's poem, neither character assumes that nature is a benign, salvific balm. It has little but the most pragmatic meaning—it is the place where the town is not. Walking through the woods, the two men eventually arrive at the cottage. Once there, they muse on the problems of politics and nationalism. First, the minister tells the poet to look through the window. They both see "a crayon portrait on the wall, / Done sadly from an old daguerreotype" (23–24)—a portrait of the woman's husband. The minister then reports:

> He fell at Gettysburg or Fredericksburg,
> I ought to know—it makes a difference which:
> Fredericksburg wasn't Gettysburg, of course.
> But what I'm getting to is how forsaken
> A little cottage this has always seemed;
> Since she went, more than ever, but before—
> I don't mean altogether by the lives
> That had gone out of it, the father first,
> Then the two sons, till she was left alone.
> (Nothing could draw her after those two sons.
> She valued the considerate neglect
> She had at some cost taught them after years.)

I mean by the world's having passed it by—
As we almost got by this afternoon. (32–44)

In these lines, the minister reveals how strange it is to him that this woman actually believed in the political and national principles of freedom and equality. For such principles, the woman's husband was willing to die, even though that choice left his wife a widow. For such principles, one of her children sought his fortune in the West, even though that meant abandoning his mother. For such principles, the woman sacrificed her own happiness. She encouraged her husband to fight and her children to leave, and she refused to follow her sons and be a burden to them—"Nothing could draw her after" them. The fact that they were free, and that she was abandoned, was a price she had decided to pay for her convictions: "She valued the considerate neglect / She had at some cost taught them after years." "Considerate neglect" is a far cry from the fatal neglect Margaret shows to her two children in Wordsworth's poem.

The minister's response to this woman raises the poem's central problem. The fact that he does not even know Gettysburg from Fredericksburg tells us that from his perspective what matters "is how forsaken / A little cottage this has always seemed" (34–35). For the minister, the cottage, in other words, is a metaphor for how skeptical and far removed contemporary life is from this woman's moral theological certainty about just wars. Reading this phrase metaphorically also tells us that, for the minister, the cottage is also representative of the nation itself. At this point, then, Frost's poem becomes a specifically nationalist drama about the American republic's foundations in such theological principles as freedom and equality. As the minister says, the certainty represented by the cottage and, by extension, by these very principles is in such a poor state that:

we almost got by this afternoon.
It always seems to me a sort of mark
To measure how far fifty years have brought us. (44–46)

Frost's poem is set in 1913. Fifty years before, Lincoln had issued the Emancipation Proclamation. The minister's comment refers to the kind of specificity that one also finds in Wordsworth.[14] Furthermore, the specifics

---

14. See Ken Johnston, "The Politics of Tintern Abbey," *Wordsworth Circle* (1983), 6–14 for a discussion of Wordsworth's use of the French Revolution to make a point about nationalism.

here tell us that, as far as the minister is concerned, a kind of devolution has occurred since 1863. Fifty years ago the citizens of the nation, like the man in the crayon portrait, were willing to sacrifice for others. But today would we still? Because the answer, given the context of the poem, would appear to be no, the poem has reached a dead end. Certainty here, as was true in the tale of Margaret, seems to be woefully absent. The minister has made his point that the nation has abandoned its deepest convictions.

Unlike "The Ruined Cottage," however, no transcendental, extra-human "power to virtue friendly" redeems the bleakness of this interpolated tale. Margaret is dead, and the men are left to make sense of her example. Wordsworth solved the problem caused by the excess of meaning latent in Margaret's tale by having his wanderer prove the existence of virtue through the agency of the spear-grass. But this is hardly a solution. Even before he tells the tale, the wanderer had such faith in nature. And before he says anything, the poet, himself, proves such faith by basking in the idyllic landscape that is the current cottage scene. Given the poet's pleasure in the moment of his rest by the ruined cottage, why on earth should the wanderer feel compelled to make him miserable by telling him just what a site for unhappiness and woe this place really is? What compels the wanderer to tell a tale of sorrow? The excess of meaning in this tale, apparently, compels not only the wanderer to tell it to the poet, but also the poet to then tell it to us, his readers. In the end, certitude is discovered in nature but only because the wanderer discovers it there. I have argued elsewhere that the wanderer's own guilt at being a mere witness to Margaret's downfall explains his compulsion to tell the tale.[15] Her story, in other words, implicates him as well as her. The point here, however, is that the meaning of Margaret's faith is so unstable that it demands to be interpreted, and no abundance of spear-grass, shade, good water, and rest will put an end to that need. The wanderer feels obliged to tell the tale if for no other reason than to make sense of it for himself. And, once told, the story proves so striking and ambiguous to the poet that he must write the poem for us. Margaret's story, in short, sets off a chain reaction, presenting to each person who hears it the problem of faith in other people. In the end, the only balm in this Gilead is to be found not in the spear-grass but in the way certain people choose to see certain things.

15. Jonathan Barron and Ken Johnston, "'A Power to Virtue Friendly: The Pedlar's Guilt in Wordsworth's 'The Ruined Cottage'" in *Romantic Revisions*, ed. Robert Brinkley and Keith Hanley (Cambridge: Cambridge University Press, 1992), 64–87.

Similarly, in Frost's cottage tale, we are also given a woman of faith whose tenacious hold on her convictions will not be shaken. And, as with Wordsworth's cottage woman, this woman proves her faith to be so ambiguous, strange, and difficult that it, too, sets off a chain reaction of interpretation. In an age when, in intellectual circles, ambiguity had become the norm, certainty would prove to be the most unsettling of all ethical and moral phenomena. In his poem, then, Frost, rather than trouble the waters of certitude with the problem of stubborn fidelity, troubles the waters of doubt with the problem of faith.

After concluding that the country had forsaken its ideals, the minister realizes that this is really not true. In short, the poem could very well have ended with the minister's conclusion that fifty years have withered away whatever convictions Americans once held. But instead of concluding there, Frost has his minister lapse into an extended monologue that is little more than a severe intellectual critique of his own devolutionary ideas. No sooner does the minister conclude that the country has lost its ideals than he also realizes that he has to be wrong. He reasons that a country is only the sum of its parts, its citizens, and if even one citizen believes in the basic ideals of the republic, then those principles must be true. Moreover, as a minister, he is supposed to believe in those same ideals. So how can he now argue for their fading away? These questions cause the minister to examine his own faith. As an American minister, he incarnates, via Emerson, the connection between politics and theology. Recognizing that he, himself, is supposed to be testament to the same faith incarnate in the woman, the minister begins to acknowledge his own lack of faith. Rather than insist on "a power to virtue friendly," he recognizes only the absence of such a power; he finds only a void. He looks closely at the "crayon portrait" of the woman's husband and begins to talk more to himself than to the poet; he says that the woman (and, by extension, her husband) was an icon of the very principles that define American individualism—the willingness to sacrifice one's own happiness, even one's life, to ensure the freedom and equality of others: "Her giving somehow touched the principle / That all men are created free and equal" (60–61). Such radical commitment to egalitarianism is, says the minister, "a hard mystery of Jefferson's" (64). He asks,

> What did he mean? Of course the easy way
> Is to decide it simply isn't true.
> It may not be. I heard a fellow say so. (65–67)

What amazes the minister is the woman's unshakable faith in those principles. As he says,

> She had some art of hearing and yet not
> Hearing the latter wisdom of the world.
> White was the only race she ever knew.
> Black she had scarcely seen, and yellow never.
> But how could they be made so very unlike
> By the same hand working in the same stuff?
> She had supposed the war decided that.
> What are you going to do with such a person? (73–80)

Here, the minister manifests a deep cynicism toward the meaning of the Civil War itself: he cannot believe the woman is naive enough to suppose the Civil War insured any equality. Nor can he bring himself to believe that anyone really held these principles so dear that she would sacrifice her life for them. Yet, as a minister, isn't he supposed to believe this?

Despite his own cynicism, he cannot help admiring the woman's tenacity:

> Strange how such *innocence* gets its own way.
> I shouldn't be surprised if in *this* world
> It were the force that would at last prevail.
> (81–83, emphasis mine)

"Innocence" is no idle word for a minister to use. This woman's "innocence," her seemingly naive faith in freedom and equality—may in fact be the extra-human, supernatural, "power to virtue friendly" of New England's version of Protestant Christianity, of Jesus. In this instance, such innocence is incarnate in the woman, not in Jesus, not in speargrass. By locating the poem's idealism in this woman Frost returns the idealism of "The Ruined Cottage" to the human sphere. This is particularly appropriate because a minister should be especially responsive to incarnate virtue; as he well knows, this is the definition of Jesus as a Christ. His innocence, so the minister teaches his flock, will cause virtue to prevail in the end. Yet, when faced with this actual woman, and her husband, he cannot possibly accept the implication of his own creed.

The minister's inner turmoil manifests itself at this point in the poem because recognizing the meaning of this cottage and of this woman's life in terms of freedom and equality is also a recognition of the basic premise of his own theology. In the concluding lines of the poem (111–24), the minister reflects on the innocent infant Jesus and imagines his own reaction had he been a witness to Jesus's birth.[16] This is not a sudden and bizarre inward turn but an inevitable extension of the minister's meditation on this black cottage and its former tenants. What would better put an end to the minister's doubt than to be a witness to the birth that defines his faith? His fantasy then is actually an empirical fantasy, a demand for certitude. There are other implications behind this fantasy as well. It may, for example, reveal him to be a very dangerous, potentially destructive man because it indicates a willingness only to observe rather than act or participate. That such a man should be teaching moral certitude is a scandal since he himself is unwilling to act on, or even to hold, the convictions he urges others to uphold. As a witness, this minister need make no choices because, according to his creed, they have all been made in advance for him. Empiricism in this interpretation becomes the worst sort of bad excuse.

III

"The Black Cottage" troubles the connection made between theology and political principles, and even though it does not critique idealism as such, it removes idealism from its Wordsworthian location in nature. Earlier, I suggested that Frost does not necessarily change Wordsworth's poem so much as emphasize its too often neglected social aspects. The most obviously social element of the poem is its diction, which, by definition, invokes a conversational model. And it is this conversational, dialogic dimension of "The Ruined Cottage" that Frost emphasizes in his own poem. This emphasis, in turn, allows Frost to focus on the social aspects of idealism. According to Frost, nature does not reveal to us the truths of freedom and equality; at best, certain people in moments of deep crisis say that it does.

Dramatic monologue with its dependence on the poetic manipulation of diction requires readers to attend as much to the speaker as to the

16. This dream passage has provoked the most discussion about "The Black Cottage," which, it should be said, has not been much discussed and continues to be undervalued. The two most recent critical discussions of this poem both read it, as I do, as a challenge to faith rather than an endorsement of it. **Faggen,** 287–88, takes a Darwinian approach to the poem that differs from mine, but his conclusion is quite similar. Also, Lakritz, *Modernism,* 94, comes to a similar conclusion. Finally, I should mention that although Faggen notes the connection to Wordsworth, only John Evangelist Walsh, *Into My Own,* 47–48, 263, in a footnote, compares the two poems in any kind of sustained and systematic way.

tale. Although "The Ruined Cottage" is a tale told by a particular person, attention to that character is too often ignored. After reading Frost's poem, however, we see that the conversational aspect of Wordsworth's poem becomes all the more crucial. Meanwhile, in Frost's own poem, the diction of a New England minister in the 1910s alludes to the entire social matrix that created that diction in the first place. When Frost attends so carefully in his dramatic monologue to the minister's speech, he inevitably represents a particular time and place. The words themselves, their rhythms, their very timeliness record the loco-specific American context of the 1910s. The dialogic nature of this poem operates on two levels. First, Frost converses with Wordsworth. On this level, Frost's poem is the response to a conversation begun by "The Ruined Cottage." Second, both poems depict conversations between two characters: a poet and a wanderer, or a poet and a minister. This dialogical, intertextual aspect of both poems emphasizes the social over and above the ideal, over and above a transsocial, transhistorical romantic idealism.

Because "The Black Cottage" is so concerned with social matters, I believe its conversational technique was itself a means by which Frost could think through the meaning of conversation itself as a trope, a problem, even a site for ethical, moral principles. When Frost revised "The Black Cottage" for publication, after all, he was engaged in conversations about Wordsworth, and, as I have been arguing, there is every reason to believe that "The Black Cottage" is itself in conversation with Wordsworth. Indeed, these very conversations were most likely focused on the need to be more "hard," less idealistic, more "real" in the depiction of both nature and human community. Wordsworth's *Lyrical Ballads,* and his *Excursion,* therefore, become all the more important in such a milieu; they become literary precedents for the poems of *North of Boston.* For Frost, the main significance of the appeal to nature in "The Ruined Cottage" is the fact that it is a conversational gesture, a means by which two men attempt to regain composure and find comfort when faced with meaninglessness. Meaning as such is not found in the poem. It is, instead, created for a moment in a conversation as recorded in a poem.

When Frost revised for publication "The Black Cottage" the poetic tradition was very much on his mind. Participating in the heated debates about Wordsworth, and entering these debates amidst the brouhaha surrounding Imagism and other modernist poetic movements, Frost found himself compelled to justify and announce his own poetics. In a now-famous letter of poetic independence to his friend John Bartlett, he declared: "I have dropped to an everyday level of diction that even Wordsworth kept above."[17] Notice that Frost emphasizes in his claim how far he has "dropped." He proudly insists on the lack of transcendent aims in his work. He takes pleasure in the fact that rather than elevate his poetry to an ideal state, he can lower it to an even more common level of diction than that found in Wordsworth's own *Lyrical Ballads*.

In another letter, this one written to his friend Sidney Cox shortly after *North of Boston* was published, diction also proves to be central to Frost's poetics and to his theory of language: "the sentence is everything— the sentence well imagined. See the beautiful sentences in a thing like Wordsworth's 'To Sleep.'"[18] In order to prevent Cox from misunderstanding his point, Frost insists that the poetic imagination, idealism, has nothing to do with them; they are material sounds, embedded in the physiology of the body: "Remember, a certain fixed number of sentences (sentence sounds) belong to the human throat as a certain fixed number of vocal runs belong to the throat of a given kind of bird. These are fixed I say. Imagination can not create them. It can only call them up. It can only call them up for those who write with their ear to the speaking voice. We will prove it out of the Golden Treasury some day."[19] Language, for Frost, was, if anything, a quasi-scientific, Darwinian association of sound to sense: it was physiological, not theological. It was in language that ideals like "equality" and "freedom" came to be known, and it was only in society that language itself mattered.

In "The Black Cottage," Frost returns to the material world of actual spoken language as it would have sounded north of Boston in the 1910s. Idealism, in that poem, is located entirely in the social realm of one man's dramatic monologue, his half of a conversation with another man. Why would Frost be so determined to locate ideals in a social rather than a natural or theological context? Specifically, why would Frost not be willing to allow nature or religion to endorse equality, the main issue at stake in "The Black Cottage"? The answer, I believe, has to do with the rising political global tensions in the years 1912 to 1914. In that historical context, the minister, not the cottage, should be read as an analogue to the American individual in 1913, as the devolution of American individuality since the Civil War. Against the minister, Frost posits the absent woman. From

17. Frost to John Bartlett, July 4, 1913, **Letters,** 83–84.
18. **Letters,** 151. Wordsworth wrote three sonnets with the title "To Sleep." Most likely, Frost refers only to the one that appears in Francis T. Palgrave's *Golden Treasury* (New York: Macmillan, 1920) since he refers to Palgrave's work in the next sentence.
19. **Letters,** 151.

this historical perspective, the minister now becomes an example of the weakest sort of unprincipled nationalism. If he is beholden to his religious creed, then he cannot think for himself; if he is not so beholden, then he is at best a hypocrite and at worst a weak and unprincipled man. Rather than simply adhere, as the woman does, to the theological ideals of freedom and equality, the minister doubts the theological ground for those principles, and so refuses to endorse them.

In a 1914 letter written shortly after this poem was published in book form, Frost told his friend Sidney Cox, "Sometime we *must* discuss that minister and his creed. I make it a rule not to take a character's side in anything I write. So I am not bound to defend the minister you understand."[20] Frost should not have worried that he might be mistaken for defending this minister. The poem already argues against him, particularly the final three lines:

> There are bees in this wall. He struck the clapboards,
> Fierce heads looked out; small bodies pivoted.
> We rose to go. Sunset blazed on the windows. (125–27)

In this conclusion, nature does speak. As in Wordsworth's poem, nature is also the voice of conviction, of morality, or virtue but only because I, as a reader, feel compelled to interpret the bees in this way. The spare diction allows for no internal moral connection. The bees shock the minister out of his idle, solipsistic dreams. It is as if, but only as if, nature were telling both men that such dreams are the enemy of the kind of active individualism that a moral certitude would endorse. The spirit of moral sacrifice embodied in the former tenants of this now ruined cottage may be dead and gone, but there are still real bees that do real harm, and ironically, they force the minister and the poet out of the woods and back to town and to the people, where they will have to do more than observe. Ethics are to be located only in the social space of the town, not in the transcendence of religion, not in the immanence of nature.

When, in the final line, Frost's poet reports, "we rose to go" (127), the meaning of Wordsworth's cottage tale is not fundamentally changed. Nature has spoken. And two men who were acquaintances are now, as it were, even more socialized than before. What is different, however, is the absence of comfort. Frost's poem does not tell us how necessary it is to

20. Ibid., 138.

feel better when faced with tragedy; instead, it tells us that, when faced with tragedy, we are obliged to act. In 1915, when Frost explained to an English friend that he "has tried to wish the States into the war" he also invoked, in that same letter, the spirit of the Civil War, which he again said had been forgotten. For Frost, the most pressing issue of the day was how to revive that spirit once more. Yet because "The Black Cottage" tells us that Frost had rejected what he referred to in 1914 as "that Beauty is Truth claptrap," the only place left for genuine ethics, as far as he is concerned, must be the social not the natural and not a theological landscape.[21] From this perspective then, the real tragedy of his black cottage is the fact that it is empty.

On August 20, three months after "The Black Cottage" was published, the Great War began, and Frost announced his feelings about the war to his friend Sidney Cox: "I like the war and the idea of abolishing Prussia, if there is any such thing." Nearly a month later, he raised his "like" a notch: "I love this war regardless of what it does to me personally." Why, when it began, did Frost love this war? Not for the reasons offered by the propaganda machine but rather because it demanded that each individual make a sacrifice, a choice. In an anecdote to still another friend, written in these early months of the war, Frost echoed "The Black Cottage" in remarkable ways: "As for what . . . [the war] is all about: I heard an old cottage woman say this to the proposition that England was fighting for Belgium: 'In a way we are—the same as we would fight for a wall we had put between ourselves and danger.'" To that Frost added, "No sentimental rot there."[22] Deeply considered, deeply felt individual choice, not sentimental rot, defined Frost's nationalism, his morality, and his ethics. If defending walls seems naive to us now, we might recall that the wall itself was never the point. As he said in another poem from the same 1914 collection, "something there is which does not love a wall." That something is Frost.

21. Ibid., 141.
22. Ibid., 132, 134 (September 17), 144.

APPENDIX

FROST	WORDSWORTH
1. "Set well back from the road in rank lodged grass" (4).	"With weeds and rank speargrass" (109)
2. "a front with just a door between two windows" (6)	"a roofless hut; four naked walls" (30)
3. "The path was a vague parting in the grass" (12).	"You see that path, / Now faint" (882–83).
4. "'You see,' he said, / 'Everything's as she left it when she died'" (14–15).	"She is dead, / The light extinguished of her lonely hut / abandoned to decay, / And she forgotten in the quiet grave" (507–10).
5. "Under a crayon portrait on the wall. That was the father as he went to war. / She always, when she talked about the war, / Sooner or later came and leaned, half knelt / Against the lounge beside it" (23–27)	"'I learned, / From one who by my husband had been sent / With the same news, that he had joined a troop / Of soldiers, going to a distant land . . . / —He left me thus—'" (674–78)
6. "Why not sit down if you are in no haste? / These doorsteps seldom have a visitor. / The Warping boards pull out their own nails / With none to tread and put them in their place. / She had her own idea of Things, the old lady" (46–51).	"And, while, beside him, with uncovered head, / I yet was standing, freely to respire, / And cool my temples in the fanning air, / Thus did he speak. 'I see around me here / Things which you cannot'" (466–70).

Sources: "The Black Cottage," in *Robert Frost: Collected Poems, Prose, and Plays*; *The Excursion* Book One, in *Wordsworth's Poetry*, vol. 2, ed. W. J. B. Owen (New Haven: Yale University Press, 1981).

Robert Frost's Liberal Imagination

George Monteiro

POETRY AND POLITICS were very much on Robert Frost's mind when he appeared at the National Poetry Festival, held in Washington in the fall of 1962. That summer he had been to the USSR on a State Department–sponsored visit and, in a lucky turn of events, had been accorded a private visit with Premier Nikita Khrushchev at his dacha away from Moscow. What he had said about that visit to newsmen on his arrival in New York had gotten him in trouble with the State Department and with his friend President Kennedy. It had something to do with whether, in a showdown, a liberal nation would fight, and Frost had declared that Krushchev had said Americans "were too liberal to fight." The president, who had invited him to participate in his inauguration, now spurned him. Frost was not given the opportunity to explain what had happened to the State Department or the president. He was cut out of the conversation and was deeply hurt. "There's nothing so punishing," he once said, "as being left out of the conversation just after you've spoken." Surely he had a grievance, but he would not indulge it. For "poetry is about grief and politics is about grievance," he would insist. Frost then recited a group of poems, culminating in "Provide, Provide," which led him to ruminations about liberals.[1]

I shall return to Frost's considered views of liberals and liberalism, as he offered them to his Washington audience that day in 1962. Those views are critical, playful, apologetic, and sympathetic. They were the fruit of his lifelong conversation with Matthew Arnold and the twentieth-century American liberal critics who were his followers, such as Lionel Trilling, Randall Jarrell, and Carl and Mark Van Doren. The Matthew Arnold of "Dover Beach" became the touchstone for their key concept of American liberalism at midcentury, the replacement of dogma and ideology by human feeling and relations as the guiding principles for moral behavior. For Frost,

---

1. Robert Frost, "'For Glory and for Use,'" *Gettysburg Review* 7 (winter 1994), 93; *Proceedings, National Poetry Festival Held in the Library of Congress October 22–24, 1962* (Washington, D.C.: Library of Congress, 1964), 238.

the worldview expressed in "Dover Beach" was soft and sentimental, and he dismissed the articulators of this Arnoldian version of liberal values as "Dover Beachcombers." But the skeptical Frost was neither ideological nor coldly intellectual, and both his poetry and his remarks on the subject show that he experienced a deep response to Arnold's poetry, particularly "Dover Beach," at some level, enough so that he found it necessary to respond several times within his own poetic terms to Arnold's vision of human significance. "Neither Out Far Nor In Deep" is, in many ways, Frost's response to Arnold and the liberal critics Frost considered his disciples, the "Dover Beachcombers."[2]

I

Two of Lionel Trilling's poetic touchstones for the modern world and its great problems were Matthew Arnold's "Dover Beach" and—much later—Frost's "Neither Out Far Nor In Deep." In a more ironic way, Frost also saw "Dover Beach" as a touchstone for the modern world. For while Trilling saw Arnold's poem as an expression of earned "grief"—"the diminution of religious faith is a reason for melancholy," he explained—Frost saw it as merely a "grievance," deplorably a liberal's lament or complaint. (In this, Frost approaches T. S. Eliot, whose "Love Song of J. Alfred Prufrock" ironizes Arnold's recourse, in "Dover Beach," to whatever personal refuge there might be in the love and truth of a human relationship. But that is a different story, for another time.) As for Frost's "Neither Out Far Nor In Deep," suffice it to say for now that Trilling, describing its "actual subject" as being "the response of mankind to the empty immensity of the universe," argues that "the poem does not affirm that what is watched for will appear. It says no more than that it is the nature of 'the people' to keep watch, whether or not there is anything to appear." But that comes later in the story.[3]

My narrative begins *in medias res* with Frost's presence at the Columbia University commencement of 1932 when he was awarded an honorary doctorate and was the Phi Beta Kappa poet. Before the local chapter he read "Build Soil," describing it as a "political pastoral." That much the *New York Times* reported but nothing more about Frost or his part in

---

2. *Proceedings, National Poetry Festival,* 243.
3. Lionel Trilling, *Prefaces to the Experience of Literature* (New York: Harcourt Brace Jovanovich, 1979), 252, 284, 287.

Columbia's academic festival. Preceding its paragraph on the Phi Beta Kappa poet and his poem the *Times* offered a detailed account of Walter Lippmann's address to the same group of Phi Beta Kappa members and honorees. He spoke on "The Scholar in a Troubled World," insisting that scholars would do best for their world by staying at their scholars' desks and not trying to go out to resolve the crises of the day. Lippmann concludes with ringing remarks about the fate of democracy: "For what is most wrong with the world is that the democracy, which at last is actually in power, is a creature of the immediate moment. Democracy of this kind cannot last long; it must, and inevitably it will, give way to some more settled social order. But in the meanwhile the scholar will defend himself against it. He will build himself a wall against chaos, and behind that wall, as in other bleak ages of the history of man, he will give his true allegiance not to the immediate world but to the invisible empire of reason." There was much in Lippmann's speech that Frost could agree with, particularly if he was warning against socialism as a solution to the world's social and economic problems. But he would never have argued that the scholar was precluded from taking action in the "immediate" world. "Build Soil" addressed that very matter. It took a position that was both political and moral. It implied a strong if unpopular ethic. Against all those who would rush to implant a socialist system by which the government might bring about the greatest good for the greatest number, Frost's spokesman in "Build Soil" says:

> Build soil. Turn the farm in upon itself
> Until it can contain itself no more,
> But sweating-full, drips wine and oil a little.
> I will go to my run-out social mind
> And be as unsocial with it as I can.
> The thought I have, and my first impulse is
> To take to market—I will turn it under.
> The thought from that thought—I will turn it under.
> And so on to the limit of my nature.
> We are too much out, and if we won't draw in
> We shall be driven in. (295)

(To anticipate a theme that I shall later take up in greater detail—linking Frost to Matthew Arnold—it might be noted here that in his discussion of "Build Soil," Laurence Perrine quotes Arnold's "The Function of Criticism at the Present Time": "Let us try a more disinterested mode of seeing [things]; let us betake ourselves more to the serener life of the mind and spirit. This life, too, may have its excesses and dangers; but they are not for us at present. Let us think of quietly enlarging our stock of true and fresh ideas, and not, as soon as we get an idea or half an idea, be running out with it into the street, and trying to make it rule there. Our ideas will, in the end, shape the world all the better for maturing a little.") But let us return to Lippmann and Frost at Columbia in 1932. Like Everett's featured address at Gettysburg, Lippmann's address soon disappeared into relative obscurity. Frost's poem, however, was fated to take on, eventually, a good deal of notoriety. To be sure, the notoriety was not immediate nor locally based, for it would not be until the poem "Build Soil" was collected in *A Further Range* in 1936—that is, after it too had built soil—that it, along with the rest of the volume, became the subject of widespread public criticism.[4]

Reading "Build Soil" at Columbia seems to have been closely calculated. The reading would come a decade or so after Carl Van Doren, teaching at Columbia, had published his influential essay "The Soil of the Puritans," extolling the qualities of Frost's poetry attributable to his emerging out of rich "subsoil" (of the "Puritans"). Understandably, Frost took Columbia to be a not entirely hostile place to air his objections to leftist, socialistic views of mankind that were being adopted left and right by the writers and intellectuals of the depression that emerged out of market crash of 1929. Van Doren had begun his piece on Frost with an impressionistic account of English Puritan migrations first to Europe and then to the New World, resulting ultimately in a New England populated by those descendants of the Puritans who did not move out into the American continent. "Those who remained," observed Van Doren, "tended to be either the most successful or the least successful, the gentry for whom Boston set the mode or the gnarled farmers who tugged at the stones of inland hillsides." "The gentry," he continued, "found its poetical voice first: the sharp-tongued satirists of the Revolution; Holmes, the little wit of the Puritan capital; Longfellow, the sweet-syllabled story-teller and translator; Lowell, learned and urbane, who stooped to the vernacular; Emerson, whose glowing verses had to preach." It was a different story with the "gnarled farmers"—in their case "the Yankee subsoil long resisted the plow." They were joined by Thoreau, "hired man of genius," who "read Greek in his hermitage," and Whittier, who "born to be the ballad-maker of his folk," turned "half politician." And when, "after the Civil War, rural New England was rediscovered by poetry and romance, it was valued largely because it seemed quaint, because it was full of picturesque

---

4. "Democracy Losing, Lippmann Asserts," *New York Times* (June 1, 1932), 18; Laurence Perrine, "The Meaning of Frost's 'Build Soil,'" in **Tharpe I,** 235.

remnants of a civilization." "No wonder the elder Yankees had no voice," writes Van Doren. "Inarticulate themselves, both by principle and by habit, they invited obscurity. Overwhelmed by the rush of the new world which had poured over them, they took to the safer hills." For a century or more the Yankee awaited his spokesman or poet.

> But there were flesh and blood beneath their [the farmers'] weather-beaten garments, as there was granite beneath the goldenrod and hard-hack about which the visitors babbled; and in time the flesh and blood and granite were reached. If it seems strange that Robert Frost, born in California, should have become the voice of those left behind, it actually is natural enough. New England was in his blood, bred there by many generations of ancestors who had been faithful to its soil. Some racial nostalgia helped draw him back; some deep loyalty to his stock intensified his affection. That affection made him thrill to the colors and sounds and perfumes of New England as no poet had done since Thoreau. He felt, indeed, the pathos of deserted farms, the tragedy of dwindling townships, the horrors of loneliness pressing in upon silent lives, the weight of inertia in minds from which an earlier energy has departed; but there was in him a tough sense of fact which would not let him brood. He drew life from the sight of the sturdy processes which still went on. Unable to see these upland parishes as mere museums of singular customs and idioms, he saw them, instead, as the stages on which, as on any human stage however small or large, there are transacted the universal tragedies and comedies of birth, love, work, hope, despair, death.

Among many other canny observations, Van Doren pointed to what might be taken as one of the Yankee poet's limitations. "As a Yankee," wrote Van Doren, "he may have too little general humanitarianism to be a patriot of the planet, but he is so much a neighbor that he can strike hands of friendship with the persons whom he encounters in his customary work." After the publication of "Build Soil" in *A Further Range,* several critics objected to the conservative narrowness of Frost's dedication to New England individualism. In fact, Carl Van Doren himself seems to have turned against Frost, no longer finding him relevant enough to include him among the literary revolutionists of the true American subsoil, as he put it in prepared remarks to the faithful at the opening of a leftist bookstore in New York.[5]

5. Carl Van Doren, "The Soil of the Puritans," in *Many Minds: Critical Essays on American Writers* (New York: Knopf, 1924), 51–52, 53–54; Carl Van Doren, "To the Left: To the Subsoil," *Partisan Review and Anvil* 3 (Feb. 1936), 9.

More so than Carl, Mark Van Doren would become one of Frost's staunchest supporters. "One of my faithful," Frost singled him out in 1962. For decades Mark Van Doren reviewed Frost's books as they appeared. Like Carl Van Doren, he had first praised Frost in 1923, in his case, with a review of *New Hampshire*. Although he did not review *A Further Range*, in the year of its publication he published a global piece in the *American Scholar* entitled "The Permanence of Robert Frost." Without naming him, Mark took issue with his brother Carl's view that Frost was perhaps too much of a Yankee—that he lacked the "general humanitarianism"—to be "a patriot of the planet." Frost was a poet of "dualities," argued Mark Van Doren,

> and the last of his dualities is by no means the least important . . . He is a New England poet, perhaps the New England poet, and reaps all the advantage there is in being true to a particular piece of earth—true to its landscape, its climate, its history, its morality, its tongue. But he is in the same breath a poet of and for the world. One need not have lived in New England to understand him. He has induced, it happens, nostalgia for New England in persons who never saw the place. But what is of greater consequence, his voice is immediately recognizable anywhere as a human voice, and recognizable for the much that it has to say. He has his roots, as literature must always have them; but he grows at the top into the wide air that flows around the world where men and women listen.

Later, in a review of *A Masque of Reason*, Van Doren expanded on the notion of Frost's recognizable human voice—that is to say, as the voice of a recognizably human being, differentiating it from that of a poetizing poet, and warning that Frost had not "escaped the danger there is for a poet in having a voice": "The advantages of a voice are famous—no poet can hope to succeed without one. But there is also the danger that a man who *has* a voice will decline into a man who *is* one. Then he becomes a sage. To be a Voice is not to be enviable, for it means taking whatever you say as valuable merely because you hear yourself saying it. Mr. Frost has been charged with such a decline, and too harshly. But there is this much in it. It has become a bit too easy for him to apply his principle of cussedness in the world. He takes short cuts and applies it in wrong places, defeating thus the principle itself."

One might think from this that Van Doren is complaining about the Frost who wrote the poems of *A Further Range*, notably "Build Soil." But not so, for he concludes this review of *A Masque of Reason* with ten brief quotations from Frost's poetry that are Arnoldian touchstones proving that "the poems he has written have the best chance of any I know these days to live." This list begins with "The fact is the sweetest dream that labor knows" from "Mowing" and "Something there is that doesn't love a wall" from "Mending Wall" and ends with "I bid you to a one-man revolution" from "Build Soil." But he apologizes for taking these lines "out of the poems where they belong" for "Robert Frost's unit is the poem, not the line." " 'The Oven Bird,' or 'Once by the Pacific,' " he informs us, "is as perfect as any poem can afford to be."[6]

In later reviews and pieces Van Doren worked away at his understanding of the sources of Frost's poetic power. Reviewing the *Complete Poems 1949*, he provided another list, this time of the fifty "titles that anthologize themselves as one reader turns the pages of this book": "Into My Own," "Storm Fear," "Mowing," and "The Tuft of Flowers" from *A Boy's Will* (1913); "Mending Wall," "The Death of the Hired Man," "The Mountain," "Home Burial," "A Servant to Servants," "After Apple-Picking," and "The Wood-Pile" from *North of Boston* (1914); "The Road Not Taken," "An Old Man's Winter Night," "Hyla Brook," "The Oven Bird," "Birches," "The Cow in Apple Time," and "The Hill Wife" from *Mountain Interval* (1916); "New Hampshire," "Two Witches," "Fire and Ice," "The Runaway," "Stopping by Woods on a Snowy Evening," "To Earthward," and "The Lockless Door" from *New Hampshire* (1923); "Spring Pools," "Acceptance," "Once by the Pacific," "The Flood," "Acquainted with the Night," "The Birthplace," and "The Armful" from *West-Running Brook* (1928); "A Lone Striker," "Two Tramps in Mud Time," "A Drumlin Woodchuck," "In Time of Cloudburst," "The Figure in the Doorway," "Desert Places," "They Were Welcome to Their Belief," "Neither Out Far Nor In Deep," and "Build Soil" from *A Further Range* (1936); "The Silken Tent," "Come In," "I Could Give All to Time," "The Wind and the Rain," "The Subverted

6. *Proceedings, National Poetry Festival*, 235; Mark Van Doren, "The Permanence of Robert Frost," *American Scholar* 5 (spring 1936), 198; Mark Van Doren, "Why Robert Frost Is Ageless at Seventy," *New York Herald Tribune Weekly Book Review* (March 25, 1945), 1 (Van Doren's complete list reads: "The fact is the sweetest dream that labor knows" ["Mowing"], "Something there is that doesn't love a wall" ["Mending Wall"], "Home is the place where, when you have to go there,/ They have to take you in. I should have called it/ Something you somehow haven't to deserve" ["The Death of the Hired Man"], "With the slow smokeless burning of decay" ["The Wood-Pile"], "Or highway where the slow wheel pours the sand" ["Into My Own"], "All out of doors looked darkly in at him" ["An Old Man's Winter Night"], "Loud, a mid-summer and a mid-wood bird" ["The Oven Bird"], "And miles to go before I sleep" ["Stopping by Woods on a Snowy Evening"], "Great waves looked over others coming in" ["Once by the Pacific"], "I bid you to a one-man revolution" ["Build Soil"]; Van Doren, "Why Robert Frost," [2]).

Flower," "The Gift Outright," "The Lesson for Today," and "Boetian" from *A Witness Tree* (1942).[7]

Lists of Frost poems—each of them constituting an attempt at identifying a lasting canon—seem to have been in vogue, the lead having been taken by Randall Jarrell in "The Other Robert Frost," a piece in the *Nation* in late 1947 that provided a generation of academic readers with "another," an unpopularized Frost canon. On his list were "The Witch of Coös," "Neither Out Far Nor In Deep," "Directive," "Design," "A Servant to Servants," "Provide, Provide," "Home-Burial," "Acquainted with the Night," "The Pauper Witch of Grafton," "An Old Man's Winter Night," "The Gift Outright," "After Apple-Picking," "Desert Places," and "The Fear." Van Doren undoubtedly read Jarrell. Yet he did not include in his own second list, then or later, the poems "The Witch of Coös," "The Pauper Witch of Grafton," "Design," "Provide, Provide," or "The Fear." In the 1960s, after Frost's death, Van Doren made still another attempt to fix the canon, setting his limit at forty this time, and offering as replacements "The Pasture," "Revelation," "The Telephone," "Nothing Gold Can Stay," "Good-by and Keep Cold," "A Masque of Reason," "A Masque of Mercy," "Away!" "A Cabin in the Clearing," "One More Brevity," "In Winter in the Woods Alone," and (a Jarrell favorite) "Directive." But the selections make it clear that it was the Frost whose best politics were the politics of the self—but an ungrieving self—that appealed to him. He would later quote approvingly (but from memory) Frost's remark on poetry and politics made in Washington in 1962: " 'Poetry and politics? They're not quite the same. Poetry is about the grief, politics about the grievances.' I suppose he never said anything better than that," concluded Van Doren.[8]

II

The difference between "grief" and "grievance" that Frost insists upon has a necessary relevance to his relationship to Matthew Arnold. It is

---

7. Mark Van Doren, "Our Great Poet, Whom We Read and Love," *New York Herald Tribune Weekly Book Review* (May 29, 1949), 11.

8. Randall Jarrell, "The Other Frost," in *Poetry and the Age* (New York: Knopf, 1953), 27; Mark Van Doren, "Robert Frost: 1874–1963," in *The Essays of Mark Van Doren (1924–1972)*, sel. with intr. by William Claire (Westport, Conn.: Greenwood, 1980), 241–42; Mark Van Doren, "Recollections of Robert Frost," *Columbia Library Columns* 12 (May 1963), 6.

not commonly noticed that in 1962 at the National Poetry Festival in Washington, just three months before his death, Frost spoke affectionately about Arnold. "I feel a certain affinity for him. His sad old face always haunts me," he said. "And the word about his being a liberal comes to me when he says that we intellectuals 'Dejectedly take our seat on the intellectual throne.' That's a very liberal attitude." "Grievance" and "grief."[9]

What has held sway in criticism of Frost, however, has been his early expressions of dissatisfaction with Arnold's liberalism. Frost's seemingly deprecating lines about Matthew Arnold in "New Hampshire" (1923) have long colored our way of looking at Frost's relationship to one of his most important precursors. For example, Richard Poirier, certainly an able interpreter of Frost, notes that while the Arnold of "Frost's impressionable years" was "the poet of 'Sohrab and Rustrum,' which he later read to his own children, or 'Cadmus and Harmonia,' 'my favorite poem long before I knew what it was going to mean to us,'" he later evoked Arnold "as an illustration of liberal intellectual querulousness about the perils of the age and the terrors of nature. 'Adlai Stevenson's Democrats,' I once head him say, were 'Dover Beach boys.'" He then cinches his case by quoting nearly fifty lines of "New Hampshire." Asked to choose between being a "prude" or a "puke," "mewling and puking in the public arms," the poet, forced to choose, insists:

> I wouldn't be a prude afraid of nature.
> I know a man who took a double ax
> And went alone against a grove of trees:
> But his heart failing him, he dropped the ax
> And ran for shelter quoting Matthew Arnold:
> " 'Nature is cruel, man is sick of blood';
> There's been enough shed without shedding mine.
> Remember Birnam Wood! The wood's in flux!"
> He had a special terror of the flux
> That showed itself in dendrophobia.
> The only decent tree had been to mill
> And educated into boards, he said.
> He knew too well for any earthly use
> The line where man leaves off and nature starts,
> And never overstepped it save in dreams.
> He stood on the safe side of the line talking—

9. *Proceedings, National Poetry Festival*, 243.

> Which is sheer Matthew Arnoldism,
> . . . .
> I'd hate to be a runaway from nature.

But neither would he choose to be "a puke," one

> Who cares not what he does in company,
> And when he can't do anything, falls back
> On words, and tries his worst to make words speak
> Louder than actions, and sometimes achieves it.

That Frost chose Arnold to be his whipping boy might be construed as a way of covering his poetic tracks (or tracts) or, more likely, as another instance in which Frost picks a lover's quarrel with a precursor. His wife, Elinor, testifies in a 1935 letter that Frost knew more of Arnold's poetry by heart than that of any other poet, with the exception of Edgar Allan Poe and John Keats.[10]

Frost's later quarrels with Arnold seem to have centered on Arnold's essential poem, more exactly, the complaint that is "Dover Beach" (1867). As Frost wrote to the *Amherst Student* (the campus newspaper) in 1935 from Key West (where he was almost literally surrounded by the sea): "Speaking of ages, you will often hear it said that the age of the world we live in is particularly bad. I am impatient of such talk. We have no way of knowing that this age is one of the worst in the world's history. Arnold claimed the honor for the age before this. Wordsworth claimed it for the last but one. And so on back through literature. I say they claimed the honor for their ages. They claimed it rather for themselves. It is immodest of a man to think of himself as going down before the worst forces ever mobilized by God." In 1934 Frost would publish his "answer" to "Dover Beach," "Neither Out Far Nor In Deep," written by the shores of the Pacific Ocean in Los Angeles when he was attending the 1932 Olympic Games. Interestingly enough, when Wilbur L. Cross praised the poem, having seen it in the March 1934 issue of the *Yale Review*, Frost followed his acknowledgment of Cross's praise with a reference to Walter Lippmann: "I'm glad if I still can please you. I need all the encouragement you can give me in that kind of poetry to hold me to it. The temptation of the times is to write politics. But I mustn't yield to it, must I? Or if I do, I must burn the results as from me likely to be bad. Leave politics and affairs to Walter Lippmann. Get

10. **Poirier,** 46, 46–48; **Early Years,** 500.

sent to Congress if I will and can (I have always wanted to), but stick to the kind of writing I am known for."[11] Now, to turn to Arnold's "Dover Beach":

> The sea is calm to-night,
> The tide is full, the moon lies fair
> Upon the Straits;—on the French coast, the light
> Gleams, and is gone; the cliffs of England stand,
> Glimmering and vast, out in the tranquil bay.
> Come to the window, sweet is the night air!
> Only, from the long line of spray
> Where the ebb meets the moon-blanch'd sand,
> Listen! you hear the grating roar
> Of pebbles which the waves suck back, and fling,
> At their return, up the high strand,
> Begin, and cease, and then again begin,
> With tremulous cadence slow, and bring
> The eternal note of sadness in.
>
> Sophocles long ago
> Heard it on the Aegaean, and it brought
> Into his mind the turbid ebb and flow
> Of human misery; we
> Find also in the sound a thought,
> Hearing it by this distant northern sea.
>
> The sea of faith
> Was once, too, at the full, and round earth's shore
> Lay like the folds of a bright girdle furl'd;
> But now I only hear
> Its melancholy, long, withdrawing roar,
> Retreating to the breath
> Of the night-wind down the vast edges drear
> And naked shingles of the world.
>
> Ah, love, let us be true
> To one another! for the world, which seems
> To lie before us like a land of dreams,
> So various, so beautiful, so new,
> Hath really neither joy, nor love, nor light,
> Nor certitude, nor peace, nor help for pain;

11. **Letters,** 417–18, 403.

And we are here as on a darkling plain
Swept with confused alarms of struggle and flight,
Where ignorant armies clash by night.[12]

Here is "Neither Out Far Nor In Deep," a poem by one who thought "all ages of the world are bad—a great deal worse anyway than Heaven," but always a place where it is "about equally hard to save your soul":

> The people along the sand
> All turn and look one way.
> They turn their back on the land.
> They look at the sea all day.
>
> As long as it takes to pass
> A ship keeps raising its hull;
> The wetter ground like glass
> Reflects a standing gull.
>
> The land may vary more;
> But wherever the truth may be—
> The water comes ashore,
> And the people look at the sea.
>
> They cannot look out far.
> They cannot look in deep.
> But when was that ever a bar
> To any watch they keep? (274)

To Randall Jarrell, writing in the *Kenyon Review* in 1952, must go the credit for "discovering" this poem. In his influential essay, in the form of an epistle "To the Laodiceans," he singled out five of Frost's poems neglected by readers but worth close attention. Acknowledging that "there is the deepest tact and restraint in the symbolism," he nevertheless finds it to be "flatter, greyer, and at once tenderer and more terrible" than a comparable poem by Housman, "without even the consolations of rhetoric and exaggeration—there is no 'primal fault' in Frost's poem, but only the faint Biblical memories of 'any watch they keep.'" Jarrell has been taken to task, deftly and lightly, by William Pritchard, for working too hard to prove that "Frost's surface simplicity in 'Neither Out Far Nor In Deep'"

---

12. Matthew Arnold, "Dover Beach," in *Portable Matthew Arnold*, ed. Lionel Trilling (New York: Viking, 1949), 165–67; **Letters**, 418.

is really a deep complexity," even as his reading is otherwise confirmed: "[Jarrell] finds the watchers in the poem to be foolish and yet heroic as well; we must feel them as both because of the tone of the last lines, 'or rather, their careful suspension between several tones.' So the poem as a whole is a 'recognition of the essential limitations of man, without denial or protest or rhetoric or palliation'—and that recognition is the usual thing, he says, we encounter in Frost's poetry." Richard Poirier, too, writing in 1977, had assumed much of Jarrell's reading but without criticizing him for violating what Pritchard would later see as the "light tone" of the poem. Poirier writes: "The landscape of these poems [the poems in *A Further Range*] is in every sense impoverished. It gives no sustenance to life; it promises little in the future, and none at all to the imagination. . . . [T]he only hint of metaphoric activity in 'Neither Out Far Nor In Deep,' aside from the mockery in the title, is the observation that 'The wetter ground like glass/ Reflects a standing gull.' These lines, and others in the poem, emphasize the total *un*reflectiveness of 'the people' who merely sit all day and look at the sea. And what is further emphasized is the fact that no detail of the poem mirrors or reflects anything except inertia and conformity."[13]

What Pritchard and Poirier might have acknowledged is Jarrell's recognition that the lightness of tone conveys the poet's tenderness, a fact that strangely enhances what is "terrible" in the poem. But what Jarrell finds "terrible" in the poem is not very much at odds with the readings of Poirier and Pritchard:

> What we do know we don't care about; what we do care about we don't know: we can't look out very far, or in very deep; and when did that ever bother *us*? It would be hard to find anything more unpleasant to say about people than that last stanza; but Frost doesn't say it unpleasantly—he says it with flat ease, takes everything with something harder than contempt, more passive than acceptance. And isn't there something heroic about the whole business, too—something touching about our absurdity? if the fool persisted in his folly he would become a wise man, Blake said, and we have persisted. The tone of the last lines—or, rather, their careful suspension between several tones, as a piece of iron can be held in the air between powerful enough magnets—allows for this too. This recognition of the essential limitations of man, without denial or protest or rhetoric or palliation, is very rare and very valuable, and rather usual in Frost's best poetry.

13. Jarrell, "To the Laodiceans," in *Poetry and the Age*, 39; **Pritchard**, 208; **Poirier**, 269.

It is important to take up Frost's reference in the first line to "the people." We can dispense with the possibility that the reference is honorifically "democratic" in the sense of the 1930s view (to borrow from Sandburg) of "The People, Yes" or, conversely, that "the people" refers to anything like the "mob" that Ezra Pound and T. S. Eliot feared and mocked. What Frost thought of "the people" may be suggested by something else he said in his 1935 letter to the *Amherst Student:*

> There is something we can always be doing without reference to how good or how bad the age is. There is at least so much good in the world that it admits of form and the making of form. And not only admits of it, but calls for it. We *people* [emphasis mine] are thrust forward out of the suggestions of form in the rolling clouds of nature. In us nature reaches its height of form and through us exceeds itself. When in doubt there is always form for us to go on with. Anyone who has achieved the least form to be sure of it, is lost to the larger excruciations. I think it must stroke faith the right way. The artist, the poet, might be expected to be the most aware of such assurance, but it is really everybody's sanity to feel it and live by it. Fortunately, too, no forms are more engrossing, gratifying, comforting, staying than those lesser ones we throw off like vortex rings of smoke, all our individual enterprise and needing nobody's cooperation: a basket, a letter, a garden, a room, an idea, a picture, a poem. For these we haven't to get a team together before we can play. . . . To me any little form I assert upon it is velvet, as the saying is, and to be considered for how much more it is than nothing.

Devoid of the plangent imagery and pervading lyricism that characterize Wallace Stevens's mid–1930s poem "The Idea of Order at Key West," Frost's poem deals only with the flattest, most essential act of "looking" for—order, meaning, form, for once, then, something. The people do not look out far or in deep, not because they lack interest, but perhaps because they cannot do so, for no one can look out far or in deep—not Stevens's solitary singer, not Ramon Fernandez, not even the poet Stevens himself. Again to the *Amherst Student:* "The background is hugeness and confusion shading away from where we stand into black and utter chaos; and against the background any small man-made figure of order and concentration. What pleasanter than that this should be so?"[14]

14. Jarrell, "To the Laodiceans," 39; **Letters**, 418–19.

III

Lionel Trilling's doctoral dissertation became his first book. *Matthew Arnold*, published by W. W. Norton in 1939, was described by its author as "a biography of Arnold's mind." In this reinterpretation of the exemplary if beset Victorian poet and critic, he had neither used nor searched out primary materials, satisfying himself with the use of available secondary materials and Arnold's own published writings. He had taken to heart, it would seem, the essence of Arnold's teachings and would apply those teachings to the study of his mind: "to see the object as it really is." The details of the poet's outward, public life, as well as his more private, emotional life, he took as established by the best sources. Having filed disclaimers and stated his preemptive explanations, he felt free to present his understanding of Arnold. Couched in the "objective" terms of disinterested, if engaged, scholarship, his argument nevertheless can now be seen clearly for its usefulness to Trilling himself. For its lasting and valid claims as a freestanding piece of critical scholarship notwithstanding, *Matthew Arnold* is perhaps even more valuable when viewed as a personally useful self-heuristic study. In certainly important ways, moreover, it is Trilling's most personal book, though its rhetoric and discourse are at least one removal from himself, those of the scholar-teacher he had already become. But like Arnold, Trilling had also started out as a "poet." And although he had had to satisfy himself with a handful of stories published in the *Menorah Journal* in the late twenties, by 1930, if not sooner, Trilling had seen that his poetic gleam had already faded. Like Arnold, who as a poet had seen for what they were the problems of his time and those of the future and would then turn to trying to solve them, Trilling had also turned to his world's cultural, political, and social problems. He could still envy Ernest Hemingway's literary successes, as he confessed to his journals, but by the early 1930s he knew that such successes in "poetry" were not to be his. Of course, he would later achieve a modicum of literary recognition for his stories, "Of This Time, of That Place" and "The Other Margaret," as well as his Cold War novel *The Middle of the Journey*, but by 1930 the die was cast in favor of the critic of Arnoldian high seriousness. Perhaps he, too—like Frost—was always haunted by Arnold's "sad old face."[15]

15. Lionel Trilling, *Matthew Arnold* (New York: W. W. Norton, 1939), 9, 11.

Trilling reviewed none of Frost's books and indeed had published nothing on the New England pastoral poet when he was asked to speak at Frost's eighty-fifth birthday dinner. Obviously, he had been reading his colleague Mark Van Doren as well as Randall Jarrell. But before going on to his unsettling speech in 1959, let us backtrack. It is not known if Trilling (or either of the Van Dorens, for that matter) heard Frost read "Build Soil" at Columbia in 1932. We do know that Trilling heard Frost talk at a conference held at Kenyon College in 1946. He did not much like the performance, as he confided in his notebooks. "Frost's strange speech," he wrote,

> apparently of a kind that he often gives—he makes himself the buffoon—goes into a trance of aged childishness—he is the child who is rebelling against all the serious people who are trying to *organize* him—take away his will and individuality. It was, however, full of brilliantly shrewd things—impossible to remember them except referring to the pointless discussion of skepticism the evening before, he said: " 'Skepticism,' is that anything more than we used to mean when we said, 'Well, what have we here?' "—But also the horror of the old man—fine looking old man—having to dance and clown to escape (also for his supper)—American, American in that deadly intimacy, that throwing away of dignity—"Drop that dignity! Hands up" we say—in order to come into anything like contact and to make anything like a point.

It is hard to say just how much of Frost Trilling had read to this point—not much, one would guess, given his admissions at the birthday dinner in 1959. But there is one other entry in the notebooks, for 1951, that, while not mentioning Frost, nevertheless evokes the poet who wrote "The Wood-Pile." Trilling writes: "A catbird on the woodpile, grey on grey wood, its breast distended, the feathers ruffled and sick, a wing out of joint, the head thrown back and the eyes rolled back, white. Looked so sick I thought of killing it, when another bird appeared, looked at it, took a position behind it, and assumed virtually the same attitude, although not so extremely. To distract me? This it did once more, although with rather less conviction the second time, then flew away. Suddenly the first bird pulled itself together, flew to a tree above, sat there for a moment seeming to adjust its wing, or exercise it, then flew away."

Certainly Frost had no monopoly on the observation of the way birds behave, as Trilling's entry shows. But that entry also shows that Trilling could see no humor in the event. There would have been rather little humor for the first bird had Trilling followed through on his first impulse to kill it—what an un-Frostian thing to consider doing, let alone doing it.[16]

More seriously, however, Trilling's response to the pathos he thought he was seeing reveals his own failure, in Frost's terms, to be sufficiently "versed in country things" (223). Trilling put the matter this way in 1959: "It is a fact which I had best confess as simply as possible that for a long time I was alienated from Mr. Frost's great canon of work by what I saw in it, that either itself seemed to denigrate the work of the critical intellect or that gave to its admirers the ground for making the denigration. It was but recently that my resistance, at the behest of better understanding, yielded to admiration—it is probable that there is no one here tonight who has not admired Mr. Frost's poetry for a longer time than I have."[17]

I shall not go much into the full details of Trilling's speech or rehearse the hullabaloo about it caused largely by J. Donald Adams's account in the *New York Times Book Review* a few days later. Suffice it to say that admitting that only recently had he found in Frost the kind of poetry that mattered to him, Trilling defined a terrifying poet of loneliness, isolation, and cosmic terror. "I think of Robert Frost as a terrifying poet. Call him, if it makes things any easier, a tragic poet, but it might be useful every now and then to come out from under the shelter of that literary word. The universe that he conceives is a terrifying universe. Read the poem called 'Design' and see if you sleep the better for it. Read 'Neither Out Far Nor In Deep,' which often seems to me the most perfect poem of our time, and see if you are warmed by anything in it except the energy with which emptiness is perceived."

Trilling had begun his remarks by greeting Frost "on his massive, his Sophoclean birthday," but he withheld explanation of the eponymous adjective until his conclusion: "And I hope that you will not think it graceless of me that on your birthday I have made you out to be a poet who terrifies. When I began to speak I called your birthday Sophoclean and that word has, I think, controlled everything I have said about you. Like you, Sophocles lived to a great age, writing well; and like you, Sophocles was the poet his people loved most. Surely they loved him in some part because he praised their common country. But I think that they loved him

16. "From the Notebooks of Lionel Trilling," sel. Christopher Zinn, *Partisan Review* 51 (1984–85): 507–8, 514.

17. Lionel Trilling, "A Speech on Robert Frost: A Cultural Episode," *Partisan Review* 26 (summer 1959), 445–52; reprinted in *Robert Frost: A Collection of Critical Essays*, ed. James M. Cox (Englewood Cliffs, N.J.: Prentice-Hall, 1962), 151–58. The quotation comes from page 155 of the latter.

chiefly because he made plain to them the terrible things of human life: they felt, perhaps, that only a poet who could make plain the terrible things could possibly give them comfort." Trilling has offered Frost Sophocles as an honored and valued predecessor for his terrifying universal vision.[18]

Trilling might also have mentioned Matthew Arnold, about whom, in his introduction to the 1949 Viking *Portable* he had written: "It was no academic theory, as people even of his own time were pleased to think, that dictated Arnold's devotion to the Greek tragic poets; rather was it their brilliant sense of the terror of loneliness." Small wonder, then, that Trilling found "Dover Beach" to be "pre-eminent" among Arnold's "wholly successful poems" and "for many readers," "the single most memorable poem of the Victorian age." A poem about "the eternal note of sadness" sensed by the poet as he looks out from Dover, across the channel, and in his mind's eye as far as the Aegean, "Dover Beach" recalls that "Sophocles long ago / Heard it on the Aegean, and it brought / Into his mind the turbid ebb and flow / Of human misery." In his introduction to the Viking *Portable Matthew Arnold,* published a decade before Frost's eighty-fifth birthday dinner, Trilling had written of Arnold's "devotion to the Greek tragic poets" and "their brilliant sense of the terror of loneliness."

> They were fascinated by the man who is set apart from other men by his fate or his own misguided will: Ajax or Oedipus or Philoctetes; or Achilles and Priam, each solitary under his doom, yet able for a moment to meet—the most terrible and most beautiful instant of community that literature has recorded—in the equal and courteous society of grief. And Arnold lived in an age when—it is one of the clichés of cultural history—man was becoming increasingly aware of loneliness. For the Romantic poets, who are the poets Arnold read in his boyhood and youth, the characteristic situation is that of the isolated individual who seeks to enter some communion. The isolation was felt to be not only social but also cosmic. The universe had undergone disruptive changes which the poets from Schiller through Leopardi to D. H. Lawrence have deplored, and in terms which do not much vary; science, they all tell us, has emptied the haunted air and demonstrated a universe in which man is a stranger. It is this double loneliness that makes Arnold's humanism, which was his response to isolation, so complete and so personally stamped.

Arnold's poetic link of himself as the poet of "Dover Beach" with the Sophocles of old (both hear the "eternal note of human sadness") stands

18. Trilling, "A Speech on Robert Frost," 156–57, 153, 158.

behind Trilling's discovery of a Sophoclean (and Arnoldian, it must be said) Robert Frost.[19]

Although the link to Arnold might not have been immediately apparent to Frost, whose own remarks following Trilling's speech were somewhat confused and unsettled, the connection to Arnold soon came to him, for on July 11, 1959, he wrote to Lawrance Thompson:

> Did Trilling have something the other night? I was a little bothered by him but chiefly because I didn't hear very well. We are to have another chance at his speech; it is appearing presently in the *Partisan Review*. At least he seemed to see that I am as strong on badness as I am on goodness. Emerson's defect was that he was of the great tradition of Monists. He could see the "good of evil born" but he couldn't bring himself to say the evil of good born. He was an Abominable Snowman of the top-lofty peaks. But what a poet he was in prose and verse. Such phrases. Arnold thought him a voice oracular. ("A voice oracular has pealed today.") I couldn't go so far as that because I am a Dualist and I don't see how Matthew Arnold could because he was a Dualist too. He was probably carried away by the great poetry. Wisdom doesn't matter too much.

It is interesting that Arnold was still on Frost's mind at this date. For although it is not the poet of "Dover Beach" that he invokes in this letter to his biographer, the reference to Arnold may have been meant to serve as a clue to Trilling's own sources in his birthday speech. Whether Thompson took the clue or even wished to follow the hint remains doubtful, for when he published Frost's reply to Trilling's letter conveying a copy of his remarks as printed in the *Partisan Review* for June 1959, he prefaced the letter: "RF's publisher held an eighty-fifth birthday banquet for the poet in New York City on 26 March 1959. The major speaker of the evening was Lionel Trilling, whose carefully considered remarks in praise of certain 'terrifying' elements in the poetry of RF unintentionally created a teapot tempest, primarily stirred up by J. Donald Adams in the *New York Times Book Review*. Trilling responded in the *Partisan Review* for June 1959 and sent a copy to RF expressing the hope that the after-dinner speech and the subsequent hubbub had not distressed him." While it is curious that Thompson dismisses as a "teapot tempest" the event that Trilling had called a "cultural episode," Frost's letter to Trilling, dated June 18, 1959, offers us a different take on the matter. "Not distressed at all," he assures

---

19. Trilling, introduction to *Portable*, 6; Trilling, *Prefaces*, 250; "Dover Beach," in *Portable*, 166; *Portable*, 6.

Trilling. "Just a little taken aback or thrown back on myself by being so closely examined so close by. It took me more than a few minutes to change from thoughts of myself to thoughts of the difficulty you had had with me. You made my birthday party a surprise party. I should like nothing better than to do a thing like that myself—to depart from the Rotarian norm in a Rotarian situation. You weren't there to sing 'Happy Birthday, dear Robert,' and I don't mind being made controversial. No sweeter music can come to my ears than the clash of arms over my dead body when I am down." There are perhaps private sources for the images and language of this letter, but it is sufficient here to call attention to Frost's evocation of a "clash of arms," a veiled reference, as I see it, to those ignorant armies that "clash by night" on "a darkling plain" in Arnold's poem—a knowing wink in Trilling's direction, one that twits him, perhaps, for having been so long ignorant of the true worth of Frost's poetry. This letter notwithstanding, Trilling's view of Frost, which owed much to Randall Jarrell's usefully "corrective" view aimed at Frost's less demanding readers, remained dangerously one-sided. When Trilling chose poems for his textbook *The Experience of Literature* in 1967 (limiting his choice to twenty-two poems), he included Frost's "Neither Out Far Nor In Deep," as well as Arnold's "Dover Beach." And his section of plays—eight of them—started out with Sophocles' *Oedipus Rex*.[20]

Before putting Trilling's speech to rest, however, it might be useful to acknowledge Mark Van Doren's view of it. On July 16, 1959, just a few days after Frost had written to Thompson, Van Doren wrote:

> You survived Trilling as you have survived all of your commentators. I assume you know he was praising you; Donald Adams made some think it had been an attack. The only trouble was the tone, and the highfalutin business about [D. H.] Lawrence. His praise was for your strength in the face of reality, a good thing to find in anybody, but he leaned too heavily on the word "terrifying," which I fear is a cant word nowadays. It was an article, not a speech, and a *Partisan Review* article at that; between you and me, I can't abide such articles. This one depressed me so much that when I got home that night Dorothy [his wife] looked at me and asked at once what the matter was. I found it hard to say, and I still do.

20. **Letters**, 584, 582–83; "Robert Frost and the Dark Saying," an address, Robert Frost Colloquium to Commemorate the Presentation of the Frank P. Piskor Collection of Robert Frost to the Owen D. Young Library, St. Lawrence University, Canton, New York, October 29–30, 1993. Published in *Friends of the Owen D. Young Library Bulletin* 24 (1994), 13–32.

For Trilling did do his best to prove that you are a poet of great depth, importance, and truth. And so you are, yet there are more beautiful and simple reasons than he found.

Prudently, Van Doren makes no reference to Trilling's comparison of Frost to Sophocles. Both had lived to a great age, Trilling pointed out, and each was "the poet his people loved most." "Surely they loved him in some part because he praised their common country," Trilling allowed. But "they loved him chiefly because he made plain to them the terrible things of human life: they felt, perhaps, that only a poet who could make plain the terrible things, could possibly give them comfort."[21]

Interestingly, Trilling avoids mentioning Matthew Arnold in his tribute to Frost, though Arnold is undoubtedly a gray eminence in everything Trilling said on the occasion, as Frost slyly indicates in the letter quoted above. Rather than the "highfalutin" evocation of D. H. Lawrence, Trilling might have quoted Arnold's "Destiny," a poem Trilling had featured in the *Portable Matthew Arnold*:

> Why each is striving, from of old,
> To love more deeply than he can?
> Still would be true, yet still grows cold?
> —Ask of the Powers that sport with man!
>
> They yok'd in him, for endless strife,
> A heart of ice, a soul of fire;
> And hurl'd him on the Field of Life,
> An aimless unallay'd Desire.

Compare Arnold's poem, along with "To Marguerite in Returning a Volume of the Letters of Ortis," the very next poem in the Viking *Portable Matthew Arnold*, with Frost's "Fire and Ice." All three poems share images and a famous rhyme.[22]

IV

I should like to conclude with a coda in Frost's own words. I quote from his final observations about Matthew Arnold made at the National Poetry

21. *The Selected Letters of Mark Van Doren*, ed. George Hendrick (Baton Rouge: Louisiana State University Press, 1987), 224; Trilling, "A Speech on Robert Frost," 158.
22. Matthew Arnold, "Destiny," in *Portable*, 111–12.

Festival in 1962. In these remarks he defines a liberal Arnold whom he admires and would emulate.

Now, speaking of liberal, my gibes and my jokes—one of them is to call all my liberal friends Dover Beachcombers . . . But now, Matthew Arnold, with all my joking and gibing about him, is one of my "greats." I can tell he is, because I quote him so often—more than Tennyson and more than Browning, more than any of that time. The old schoolteacher, you know, the old school man—not a teacher, maybe—but a school man, and a good deal like me that way, I suppose. I feel a certain affinity for him. His sad old face always haunts me. And the word about his being a liberal comes to me when he says that we intellectuals "Dejectedly take our seat on the intellectual throne." That's a very liberal attitude.

Nearly every liberal that I know of has a tendency when his enemy works up against him, stirs up against him, to try to remember if he isn't more in the wrong than the enemy. I said in two lines of poetry a long time ago that a liberal is a person who can't take his own side in a quarrel. That's all, but I can say better things of a liberal than that. I can say, for this night, part of a poem of Matthew Arnold's of the mighty, sturdy kind. . . . It's on the difficult subject of immortality . . .

> Foil'd by our fellow-men, depress'd, outworn,
> We leave the brutal world to take its way,
> And, *Patience! In another life*, we say,
> *The world shall be thrust down, and we up-borne.*

Too much of that around in poetry at all, this

> Foil'd by our fellow-men, depress'd, outworn,
> We leave the brutal world to take its way . . .

"The brutal world"; the vulgar world, if it isn't the brutal; and then—I'm not going to read the whole sonnet—

> And will not, then, the immortal armies scorn
> The world's poor, routed leavings?

you know—the ones that have talked that way, won't they—won't the great, immortal armies up there want that kind of a skulker from this world? "No," he says:

> . . . the energy of life may be
> Kept on after the grave . . .
> And he who flagg'd not in the earthly strife . . .

Didn't flag, didn't talk stuff about the hard world, blame the world—

From strength to strength advancing—only he,
His soul well-knit, and all his battles won . . .

See, that means little and big challenges—

. . . all his battles won,
Mounts, and that hardly, to eternal life.

That'd be the Greek of it—to the place where the great people live on and nobody else. See how stern that is. He says that "only he . . ."

From strength to strength advancing—only he,
His soul well-knit, and all his battles won,
Mounts, and that hardly, to eternal life.

It's not a Christian doctrine at all—everybody's saved that believes. But that's this—"Mounts, and that hardly . . ."—it's a fight. I just bring that in to show you where I would be.

Later in the evening he settled on "The Gift Outright," the poem he "used," as he put it, at "the President's inauguration." "It has in it something that I want to linger over for the liberals, see," he promised. And then added, with a twinkle, one imagines, "I'm not saying I'm not one myself. That was what the war of our Revolution was."[23]

---

23. *Proceedings, National Poetry Festival,* 243–44, 252.

POETICS

AND

THEORY

Rhetorical Investigations of Robert Frost

Walter Jost

FOR SOME TIME I HAVE been conducting what I call "rhetorical investigations" of the poetry of Robert Frost, attempting to make salient a dimension of practice in the poems overlooked by other critics.[1] By "investigation" I mean a nontheoretical phenomenology of situated language use, aimed at an ethical prudence, and by "rhetorical" I include a variety of concerns, ranging from interest in persuasive argument at one end to philosophic speculations on persuasion and its cognates at the other. These and related matters have been overlooked by critics for the very good reason that it doesn't occur to anyone to find the obvious *re*markable because one assumes, in effect, that the first marking has been enough. In that customary assumption lurks the fallacy that there is only one purpose for marking.

For instance, many critics have noticed that rhetorical arguments occur in Frost, much as arguments exist in other poets.[2] In this regard "The Death of the Hired Man," for example, is usually treated as, in Reuben Brower's

---

1. See my " 'The Lurking Frost': Poetic and Rhetoric in 'Two Tramps in Mud Time,' " *American Literature* 60 (May 1988): 226–40, reprinted in Louis Budd and Edwin Cady, eds., *On Frost: The Best of American Literature* (Durham: Duke University Press, 1991), 207–21; " 'It wasn't, yet it was': Naming Being in Frost's 'West-Running Brook,' " *Texas Studies in Literature and Language* 36 (spring 1994): 5–50; "Lessons in the Conversation That We Are: Robert Frost's 'Death of the Hired Man,' " *College English* 58 (April 1996): 397–442; "Civility and Madness in Robert Frost's 'Snow,' " *Texas Studies in Literature and Language* 39 (spring 1997): 27–64; and "Ordinary Language Brought to Grief: Robert Frost's 'Home Burial,' " in *Ordinary Language Criticism: Literary Thinking after Cavell after Wittgenstein*, ed. Kenneth Dauber and Walter Jost, forthcoming.

2. A good example of rhetorical though not philosophical analysis that takes Robert Frost as *point de depart* is Willard Spiegelman, *The Didactic Muse: Scenes of Instruction in Contemporary American Poetry* (Princeton: Princeton University Press, 1989). For the philosophical dimension of a similar rhetorical criticism, see especially the works of Stanley Cavell, for example, *The Senses of Walden* (Chicago: University of Chicago Press, 1992) and *Disowning Knowledge in Six Plays of Shakespeare* (Cambridge: Cambridge University Press, 1987).

words, an argumentative "debate between opposing temperaments."[3] Yet no one has remarked what is obvious in the sense that it is not hidden, namely that this poem, for all of its arguments, does *not* stage a debate at all, hence that the arguments do not perform in the way that they seem to. A debate, after all—this is obvious—requires an interaction on the same topic, whereas Warren and Mary operate, until the very end of the poem, on different topical planes: Warren defends his choice not to take Silas in, while Mary explores what there is to say about Silas now that he is going to die.

"Death of the Hired Man," moreover, is at once rhetorical and philosophical since the poem reflects on the conditions and limits within which ordinary language can persuasively constitute identity, act, and audience in a specific situation and occasion, which is to say that the poem reflects on the nature of the "ordinary" and "obvious"—vid. Mary's "it all depends on what you mean by home"—in the way that several of this century's most influential philosophers do. In the recovery of the ordinary, of "home," Frost, like James, Dewey, Heidegger, and Wittgenstein, resists metaphysical abstraction and specialist expertise and makes philosophy once again accessible by making it rhetorically conversable. Within his pastoral and domestic scenes, it is true, Frost only indirectly contributes to the very public struggle over the nature of social and political speech being waged at the turn of the present century in this country. But within these same settings Frost reinvents models of social and domestic decorum whose equals have not been encountered since William Wordsworth nor will be seen again until W. H. Auden, and whose *kind* of intelligence provides a powerful complement to the literary high modernism and theory-enchantment still lurking in and around the academy in our own time. The present paper is intended as a kind of progress report of my investigations in the field.

I

Undefined in Front: "The subjects of the other arts are derived from hidden and remote sources while the whole art of oratory lies open to view, and is concerned in some measure with the common practice, custom and speech of mankind, so that, whereas in all other arts that is most excellent which

3. Reuben Brower, *The Poetry of Robert Frost: Constellations of Intention* (New York: Oxford University Press, 1963), 164.

is farthest removed from the understanding and mental capacity of the untrained, in oratory the very cardinal sin is to depart from the language of everyday life and the usage approved by the sense of the community." (Cicero, *De oratore*, 1.12)

Taken too literally or historically, the practice of oratory as it appears in the epigraph above must seem to us impossibly anachronistic. From the perspective of most contemporary literary theory, Cicero's intention that oratory provides nothing short of a holistic intellectual ideal seems, well, quaint. Ralph Waldo Emerson, William James, Mark Twain were orators all, and all worked a sweeping lecture circuit through the 1880s; but by the time Frost began his publishing career a decade or so later, informal conversation, not public oratory, presented a more plausible social orientation for a democratic nation of increasingly crowded and unacculturated urban-dwellers on the move and make. Worry over appropriate modes of talk in politics, religion, commerce and indeed virtually all public and private venues had been considerable throughout the century and remained so even in 1900, in part because forums like Chautauqua and genres associated with an antiquated aristocracy or the higher learning were no longer felt to be appropriate to contemporary experience.[4] Frost's high school sweetheart, covaledictorian, and wife-to-be, Elinor, accordingly, would entitle her commencement address "Conversation as a Life Force," much as Henry James would address the graduating women of Bryn Mawr a few years later on their everyday talk and bearing in "The Question of Our Speech" (1905). Frost built his own career as lecturer on spontaneous conversation, and nominated, as one of the three great things in life along with religion and science, nothing less (or greater) than "gossip." None of which historical *circumstantiae*, however, would have ruffled Cicero, who observed that "the same rules that we have for words and sentences in rhetoric will apply also to conversation," and for whom the important point is that the traditional, large-scale principles of rhetoric ennuciated in *De oratore* may be used as a model across the

---

4. See Kenneth Cmiel, *Democratic Eloquence: The Fight over Popular Speech in Nineteenth-Century America* (Berkeley: University of California Press, 1990); Frederick Antczak, *Thought and Character: The Rhetoric of Democratic Education* (Ames: Iowa State University Press, 1985); R. Jackson Wilson, *Figures of Speech: American Writers and the Literary Marketplace, from Benjamin Franklin to Emily Dickenson* (New York: Alfred A. Knopf, 1989); and Stephen Railton, *Authorship and Audience: Literary Performance in the American Renaissance* (Princeton: Princeton University Press, 1991).

humanities, indeed across all knowledge and modes of communication.[5] As for those "traditional principles of rhetoric," a hundred pages or so of Kenneth Burke's *A Rhetoric of Motives* (1950) still provide not only the handiest brief description but probably the closest thing in our own time to a Ciceronian reformulation of "oratory" responsive to philosophical as well as to more obvious historical changes. Burke's account, we will see, illuminates Robert Frost's pervasive fascination with the powers and limits of rhetorical argument and communication, and is capable of linking Frost with thinkers as diverse as Ludwig Wittgenstein and Martin Heidegger, both of whom gave over their lifetimes to investigating similar mysteries.

On page eighty-six of the *Rhetoric of Motives*, Burke provides a succinct summary of the rhetorical motive wherever it may appear: "persuasion, exploitation of opinion . . . a work's nature as addressed, literature for use . . . verbal deception . . . the 'agonistic' generally . . . formal devices, the art of proving opposites (as 'counterpart' of dialectic)." While it is true that all of these principles can be found to illuminate some part of almost any poet's production, few poets since Donne both use, and reflect on, these and related matters as profoundly and playfully as Robert Frost. For this reason a rhetorical theory as comprehensive as Cicero's and as contemporary as Burke's is required to do justice both to the variety of Frost's rhetorical ideas and methods and to their posed simplicity. Historically, too many accounts of rhetoric have been badly reductive in one way or another, while Burke's theory is comprehensive and searching enough to begin investigating what, since it is *posed*, cannot simply be simple.

Burke's contemporary intellectual power resides in his having reformulated the scope of Cicero's principles and above all in having subsumed conscious, strategic "persuasion" under the more capacious term "identification." Like "persuasion," but allowing now for unintended effects and consequences of our symbol systems, "identification" for Burke involves (a) our actively identifying the nature (or "properties") of some situation, action, person, event—some indeterminacy—from a given evaluative perspective; (b) organizing our own moral and religious growth in terms of such identifications—that is, identifying *ourselves* with those identifications; (c) recognizing that such identifications create disagreement and social discord between ourselves and others; and (d) attempting, in our efforts to identify some person, situation, event, problem and the like, to get others to identify their interests—hence their identities—

5. Marcus Tulio Cicero, *De Oratore*, 2 vols, trans. E. W. Sutton (1975; rpt., Cambridge: Harvard University Press, 1979), 1:37.

with our own (even if we, or they, do so without conscious intent).[6] All identification is, thus, rhetorical more or less, because all identification is more or less situated, perspectival, and interested, ranging from familiar, quotidian problems to life's limit-situations, often those lurking within the quotidian itself.

We will be able to appreciate that last point (strange extremes lurking within the ordinary) when we look at Frost's "There Are Roughly Zones" in the following section. Here we might first try to develop our sense for some generic qualities of Frost's rhetorical consciousness by glancing at the later lyric, "Leaves Compared with Flowers" (1935), which begins almost in sing-song:

> A tree's leaves may be ever so good,
> So may its bark, so may its wood.
> But unless you put the right thing to its root
> It never will show much flower or fruit. (1–4)

On a first encounter we notice nothing very serious here, barely enough in the title to hint at the need for arguing on either side of a question: leaves compared to flowers—so which are better? Soon after, however, and quite characteristically for Frost, the poem comes to recast a meditative introspection into the form of a quasi-public debate, all but belying Mill's claim that rhetoric is (merely) heard while poetry is (as if mysteriously) overheard, as if telepathically eavesdropped upon; for, although the reader is not directly addressed here, she is required to *participate* in an argument by weighing alternatives. The debate gets obliquely introduced in the first two stanzas in alternating voices—the narrator's double-voicing of the commonplaces of others (of our own) in lines 1–4, and then, in line 5, the poet's own counterstatement: "But I may be one who does not care / Ever to have tree bloom or bear":

> Leaves for smooth and bark for rough,
> Leaves and bark may be tree enough. (7–8)

6. Kenneth Burke, *A Rhetoric of Motives* (Berkeley: University of California Press, 1950), 24; cf. 27: "the principle of Rhetorical identification may be summed up thus: The fact that an activity is capable of reduction to intrinsic, autonomous principles does not argue that it is free from identification with other orders of motivation extrinsic from it. Such orders are extrinsic to it, as considered from the standpoint of the specialized activity alone. But they are not extrinsic to the field of moral action as such, considered from the standpoint of human activity in general."

This line of argument is then amplified with further *exempla:*

> Some giant trees have bloom so small
> They might as well have none at all.
> Late in life I have come on fern.
> Now lichens are due to have their turn. (9–12)

And then the issue is given overt rhetorical status and sharpened to a point in the penultimate fourth quatrain:

> I bade men tell me, which in brief,
> Which is fairer, flower or leaf?
> They did not have the wit to say
> Leaves by night and flowers by day. (13–16)

Frost enjoys nothing more than to invite his readers, as he does here, to consider some deliberative or judicial question—which is better, fairer—then to make the question seem to disappear by showing how inadequate argument on one side or the other is to such a matter ("They did not have the wit to say"), only to finish with a rhetorical flourish by reinstating the issue but on a different intellectual and emotional plane. By the end "leaves," "bark," "petals," and "flowers" have become what rhetoricians call "special topics," that is (here) more or less specific terms whose meanings have accrued beyond whatever stable, determinate uses the poet has made of them:

> Leaves and bark, leaves and bark,
> To lean against and hear in the dark.
> Petals I may have once pursued.
> Leaves are all my darker mood. (17–20)

In other words, the rhetorical genre of this poem drifts, as it were, from ersatz deliberation and conclusive judgment on an indefinite issue (what Cicero and other rhetoricians called a "thesis," itself traditionally built on some kind of comparison) to a more inclusive if nonstandard "epideictic" celebration in praise of antithetical virtues ("leaves by night and flowers by day;" or again, in "Fire and Ice," "I hold with those who favor fire" but "Ice is also great;" and elsewhere "Nothing I should care to leave behind"). It also develops from a misleadingly synchronic comparison to a fuller diachronic sense of the appropriateness of all things great and small, according, that is, to their respective *"circumstantiae"*; and from the evocation of "wit," noted by Shaftesbury in the eighteenth century as an important part of the *sensus communis* by virtue of its appeal to recognizable public connections, to a notably nineteenth-century private "mood," a mood transformed at the end, however, to *include* its predecessor in a uniquely twentieth-century, skeptical admixture of both.[7] In this poem, I suggest, our own *sensus communis,* including our sense about speech itself—a comparison of what were once called the "flowers of rhetoric," admired as a product of wit by the learned, to Whitman's democratic "leaves of grass" ostensibly accessible to learned and unlearned alike—comes to be rethought as *neither* an objective social orientation nor yet a subjective personal preference or mood, but as an awareness of the value of inner *and* outer, of backgrounded flowers but also foregrounded leaves. From this perspective, "Leaves Compared With Flowers" is an especially self-conscious, rhetorical performance—a celebration, no less—of many of the themes and tactics historically and intellectually considered central to rhetoric.

I also feature this poem on beginning because its discrimination and joining of both sides of a question is characteristic of Frost's thinking. A similar inquiry and celebration occurs, for example, in "Two Tramps in Mud Time," in which unity of vision is similarly managed from a dual perspective: "as my two eyes make one in sight" (68) = as my (Frost's) two "I's" (the narrator's and the tramps') make one insight. Philosophically the method is not Platonic transcendence to a higher unity but rather Cicero's antithetical operationalism, in which one may as soon end with only one side of a pair of terms as another, with disunion as soon as unity, or with a unity or generalization or rule quite different from what one might have expected on starting: "The Ciceronian debate does not move dialectically from communities and oppositions to an assimilation of lesser truths in the greater. It is controversy, and the debate is only resolved"

> insofar as anyone chooses to adopt one of the conflicting positions or to modify it or to formulate a new position with elements from the alternatives as components. One begins and ends with perspectival diremptions. . . . Philosophy is constituted by this ongoing conversation, the clash of statements and judgments, and the value of the method lies

7. Indeed, in *Wit and Rhetoric in the Renaissance* (New York: Columbia University Press, 1937), W. G. Crane notes that "the critics of the seventeenth century attached much importance to comparison as the [very] *basis* of wit" (14, emphasis mine).

precisely in this discrimination of perspectives and the differentiation of
frames of reference . . . as devices for invention and judgment.[8]

In "Two Tramps in Mud Time" the topical perspectives of "invention"
and "judgment" appear as "play" and "work"; here they are called "flowers"
and "leaves," elsewhere "fire" and "ice," freedom and constraint, working
together and working apart, self and neighbor, and so on. In the abstract
these *topoi* may ring hollow, but in the materiality of their respective poems
Frost keeps complex concepts in play (or at work) without merely reducing
their tensions within some more stable *tertium quid*. Topical invention
deploys and fills up terms and arguments on both sides of a question
circumstantially, while judgment ends only provisionally, often by making
room for both sides.

Equally important, "Leaves Compared with Flowers" presents a mild
sending up, a subtle satire, of classical rhetorical argument and persua-
sion, as well as slight parody of *anti*rhetorical (read "romantic") moods,
for both classicism (and neoclassicism), *and* romanticism presuppose an
unfragmented self in poet and reader that Frost's rhetorical stance belies.[9]
This poem, for example, is replete with humorous verbal deception (e.g., an
assumed voice subverting the subject position) and characteristic rhetorical
showing off ("wit"), and it embodies a further-reaching rhetoric than
even the intellectually promiscuous Cicero knew. In outward form and
parodic purpose it resembles a good many of Frost's most famous poems,
in which explicit argument contends with implicit ridicule or subversion
of argument: "Fire and Ice," with its "Some say . . . Some [others] say"
exploitation of common opinion; "Design," an almost gloating trope of
standard, eighteenth-century theological debate; the ongoing arguments
heard or implied in "From Plane to Plane," "Death of the Hired Man"
and many similar dramatic dialogues; and the recurrence of questions of

8. Michael J. Buckley, S. J., "Philosophic Method in Cicero," *Journal of the History of
Philosophy* 8 (April 1970): 143–54; Michael Leff, "Burke's Ciceronianism," in *The Legacy
of Kenneth Burke*, ed. Herbert W. Simons and Trevor Melia (Madison: University of
Wisconsin Press, 1989).

9. Andrew M. Lakritz puts the first point succinctly: "The paradox of Frost's work
is that it inhabits the movement of reasoned thought in order to take reason apart"
(*Modernism and the Other in Stevens, Frost, and Moore* [Gainesville: University of Florida
Press, 1996], 72); Margery Sabin speaks to the second: reading Brower on Frost, "we
are led to expect two things: first, a kind of coherence of personality; second, a sense of
personality made coherent in relation to an event. Frost's point about the dramatic vitality
of *sentences* promises neither of these things" ("The Fate of the Frost Speaker," *Raritan*
[fall 1982], 130).

interpretation throughout the poems and other writings. A brief glance at another poem—the early dramatic dialogue "The Code" (1914), from Frost's second book, *North of Boston* (1914)—will begin to suggest how Frost actually embodies the Ciceronian rhetorician within a longer pragmatist-rhetorical line extending back to Emerson and forward to Kenneth Burke and Stanley Cavell.

In a letter to Louis Untermeyer, Frost said of *North of Boston* that four of its poems "were almost jokes," and surely "The Code" is one of them, its tale of an attempted homicide merely adding to the fun. Here is a poem *about* persuasion, address, and unfamiliar codes of speech and behavior, in which a passing bit of phatic communication—a worker's suggesting that he and two others "take pains" to cock the hay before it rains—offends to the point of rebuff one of the other two; in which an object lesson intended to prevent future failures fails (the third farmer relates his anecdote about a former boss named Sanders); and in which the unsuspecting reader is left at the end, laughing a little at the slow-witted "town-bred farmer" who misunderstood, but perhaps also as reader failing, like all of the characters, sufficiently to reflect on just what has been said. For "The Code" is less slight, less simply a joke (or less simple a joke) than it appears. Like "Home Burial" or "The Fear," it juxtaposes the fragility of human understanding against the frigidity of mere external codes or internal, emotional ellipses.

Strictly speaking, of course, a linguistic code is not a language, much less a form of life to give words direction and force, but only (from one perspective) "devices for disguising pieces of language so that their meaning is not immediately recognizable without removal of the disguise."[10] This definition is helpful, for though Frost does not use the word strictly, the element of disguise in the form of self-hiding is crucial to this and other poems, as is well known. In "The Fear," for example, Joel is familiar with the code-like speech his wife or lover uses to allude to the difficulties between them (50–54); but he fails to understand *why* a code should be needed at all, why, in effect, she is in disguise from herself and her past. Hence her repeated doubts about his ability to "understand" (50, 88–89)—understand *not* the code itself but its motives.

In "The Code" two different and distinct problems with codes are in play. The first problem is easy to see: the failure of a hired hand to observe a standard of behavior (a behavioral code) out of ignorance of a strange code of communication. The third hired hand has no difficulty explaining:

10. John M. Ellis, *Language, Logic, and Thought* (Evanston: Northwestern University Press, 1993), 17.

"He [James, the worker who walked away offended] thought you meant to find fault with his work" (16), following which

> You've found out something.
> The hand that knows his business won't be told
> To do work better or faster—those two things. (21–23)

In this way a simple misunderstanding arises out of lack of knowledge, which lack now appears to be filled and the confusion allayed.

The second problem is more interesting but has gone entirely overlooked and unremarked by critics: the sheer insufficiency of codes altogether. For the joke of this poem is not, or not simply, the town-bred farmer's first innocence (of the code), nor even his later incomprehension (of the cautionary tale about Sanders), but rather how difficult it is to get anything so humanly vital as standards of life and death (Cicero's "common practice, custom and speech of mankind") into something as inanimate as a linguistic or behavioral code. And *this* joke may be on us, who also have occasion to learn such a lesson in daily life and yet somehow manage to miss it (so Frost writes elsewhere: "Why is [our] nature forever so hard to teach . . . ?") Consider: having accepted his coworker's clear account of the wrong he (the town-bred farmer) innocently committed, the town-bred farmer immediately proceeds further to misapprehend the cautionary tale about Sanders that follows. *Why*, since he had just been told what the code is?

The answer emerges only if we notice that we, too, are tempted to misunderstand this anecdote, I mean to the extent that we accept as reasonable the listener's question at the end, "Did he discharge you?" (113). "Reasonable," because it is a question we ourselves feel that we might have asked, given the fact the farmer who was slighted actually tried to *kill* Sanders. *We* may conceivably even want to call the act attempted murder, or anyway *some* kind of negligence. Strictly to pursue this line of thought, however, is to fail (as the town-bred farmer listening to the narrative about Sanders fails) to place this story into its larger contexts. Where the town-bred farmer fails to judge the meaning and value of his coworker's conduct in the context of unfamiliar mores (having perhaps momentarily *forgotten* the code? It *is* a long tale), we readers are apt to forget to ask after the even larger possible contexts of this tale—namely Frost's poem and its distant, outlying interests, rhetorical and philosophical.

But, then, the point cannot be the *forgetting of the code* by which to judge. For, once the code is recalled, one can still imagine the listener's wondering, perhaps even amazed, whether his coworker did, as he claims, "just right" (114). After all, the code does not dictate its own interpretation, and there is no end to it if we hunt for an Ur-Code to decipher this one. Nor can the point be *our* remembering any code, for we are in the same boat as he (evidenced by the plausibility of our sharing his question at the end). The point is rather just our difficulty in knowing—even when we do recall the code, or recall that this poem is entitled "The Code"—how to go on to judge Frost's meaning and purpose: not merely the farmer's actions toward Sanders, but the whole *exemplum* that just *is* these fellows talking and acting and telling stories. Not, again, that we *cannot* judge, but that *knowing how* (and often being able to say how we know) can be difficult.

On reflection Frost teases and tempts us to rest content (as these fellows in the poem have) with, as it were, a single line of talk or judgment, namely the platitude that communication rests on our knowing or remembering a code, or that a story is (or ought to be straightforwardly codelike, as its teller suggests by his surprise at his listener's reaction). Such a single-minded "moral of the story" is roughly equivalent to the town-bred farmer's (= *our*) assumption that his coworker got fired, or to the coworker's equally confident claim that he himself did "just right," when, in principle at least, he may not have done right at all. For we might ask, Does the code allow you to kill your employer's wife and children, maybe the extended family, too? How far is too far? (And then we may further recall: the country-farmer is *not* offended when his town-cousin breaks the code, though he indicates that any man rightly should be. What then leads us to agree with him, as of course we do, that he ought to overlook that offense, as he does; or to agree with him that he ought to respond, as he does, when the insensitive Sanders breaks the code and insults him?) No code alone tells us such things about itself. *How* then does one know where to stop, or start, in interpreting the code? ("A rule stands there like a sign-post.—Does the sign-post leave no doubt about the way I have to go?"[11] "Washington D.C. 88 miles" doesn't tell me to stay on *this* road to get there.) Again, like Wittgenstein Frost is tempting us, I suggest, in order to *remind* us when our temptation leads us into confusion that we are regularly tempted to overlook the complexity underwriting such codes, that we are frequently confused and do not know our way about.

Exampla such as these, then (the farmer's tale about Sanders, the talk of these workers that constitutes "The Code," "Leaves Compared

---

11. Ludwig Wittgenstein, *Philosophical Investigations*, trans. G. E. M. Anscombe (New York: Macmillan, 1953), sect. 84.

with Flowers"), can serve our purposes in opening up Frost as a distinctly rhetorically minded poet, not because they illustrate any fixed definition of rhetoric (or philosophy, or poetry), but just because they are, in Thoreau's language, "undefined in front": "In view of the future or possible, we should live quite laxly and undefined in front, our outlines dim and misty on that side."[12] Such exempla presuppose what even codes themselves presuppose, namely the possibility for novelty and indeterminacy of ordinary life. And they require a memory not merely for rules but for the larger contexts within which the rules guide us. In short, examples require both rules or codes and the novelty of new experience toward which they point; taken *together,* rule and novel situation (constraint and freedom) constitute just that paradigmatic indeterminacy that rhetoricians from Cicero to Burke would engage.

Taken alone, however, the notion of a code may serve us as a sign for *any* closed system derived, and apart, from the larger open systems of natural language and communication, indeed of human life as a whole. For this reason medieval iconography depicted dialectic as a closed fist, in contrast to the open hand of rhetoric. The latter is, in Cicero's words, "open to view," in the way that what we care about is open to view, is familiar. As Cicero and Frost suggest, the practical world we inhabit is the ferns and lichens, leaves and bark we take for granted without questioning and leave behind without remembering. For just this reason the everyday and ordinary requires our intellectual attention. By walking off some coordinates for this area beneath our feet we will be better prepared to resist reducing rhetoric to one or two of its supporting principles, hence misunderstanding the peculiar nature of the everyday, the familiar order of the ordinary that Frost celebrates.

II. THE ORDER WITHIN THE ORDINARY

Rhetorically we can begin to open up this realm by considering certain *topoi* implied in the opening epigraph and explicitly pursued by later rhetorical philosophers such as Burke and Cavell: "theory" and "practice," "subject matter sciences" (principled inquiries) and "oratory" (rhetoric), freedom and constraint, self-conscious posing and unself-conscious doing, "motion" and "action," and others. In contemporary discussions, problems of interpretation and action often get dangerously reduced to the single celebrated pair, "determinacy" and "indeterminacy," dangerous because

---

12. *Walden,* ed. J. Lyndon Shanley (Princeton: Princeton University Press, 1971), 324.

the temptation is great either to oppose them or to rank-order them, and then to refer all manner of complex phenomena to either oversimplified relation. Instead, I want to begin by relating Cicero's basic distinctions between theory and practice (including reflection on practice in oratory or rhetoric) to several other distinctions, showing how these terms raise a fundamental but overlooked question; and then to work toward an answer to this question by way of Frost's sharp but neglected "There Are Roughly Zones" (1936) and, at the end of the article, his famous "Two Tramps in Mud Time" (1934).

Practical reflection may be be said to stand to the whole of everyday practice as theory stands to some particular aspect of that practice abstracted from the contextual, practical "whole" for specialized purposes. Theory posits an unfamiliar point of departure from which to extrapolate specific observations, inferences, and problems into broader concepts, generalizations, and rules—"unfamiliar," because a product of expert knowledge or skill. So long as one accepts the *points d'appui* (supporting principles) and the concepts and problems identified within a theory's boundaries, the results may be narrow or even wrong, but a degree of exactitude within fixed parameters is guaranteed in advance provided one follows the procedures. This is what Cicero meant when he alluded to "hidden and remote sources," because a theoretically driven, subject-matter inquiry turns on axioms, definitions or hypotheses not immediately available or evident, and demanding the ability to follow their specialized and exact forms. Thus theory puts itself at risk by its temptation to removal, even Cicero's "farthest removal," from common undestanding, the comings and goings of real people in specific activities, although its potential gains—far greater in our own time, of course, than in Cicero's—are conceptual clarity and relative stability, general explanatory power, and increased understanding of rule-governed phenomena.

By comparison practical reflection (should I go to the lecture or work on the stone wall? is this an appropriate insurance policy? the car runs badly but perhaps it's just that right back tire?) is never any great respecter of intellectual boundaries—hence never a single subject matter inquiry—for it is by nature connective and relational, intellectually promiscuous in what it wants or needs to know. Practical reflection is always located somewhere *between* everyday events and the whole range of meanings and entailments possible to them at a given time, aiming at projecting plausible (though sometimes, as we have seen, vague and undefined) lines of solution to some more or less situated issue or problem. Its unique power is its ability to circle slightly above particular facts and below general rules, accumulating various views from which to proceed. Practical reflection is thus holistic in a nontotalitarian way, for it is posed not to exhaust phenomena but rather to react to them *appropriately*—provided that the canons of the "appropriate" are worked out not in advance but only as one goes. Thus, what practical reflection loses in exactitude or depth it gains in versatility, specificity, and human significance. As Cicero notes, "common practice, custom and speech" (and reflection on these as a whole) are "open to view," not in the sense of being transparent in their meanings but because they just are what we do, how we act, and how we achieve meaning and value (however problematic that "we" can become).

Of course, practical reflection is always theory-laden, at least in the weak sense that it is guided by prejudgments (otherwise how could it reflect?), just as any theory is a mode of practice, in the sense that we human beings theorize out of some specific location in time and space (otherwise what could be the point of our reflecting?). Yet current arguments over theory and practice are apt to occlude the relations between these two. Against nineteenth-century reifications of philosophy and science as determinate theories of motion and action (Mill, Comte, Freud, Marx), late-twentieth-century practice of theory often considers science itself as merely a reification of the indeterminacy of action and at bottom a matter of power, choice, desire, or decision (Rorty, Foucault, Lacan). Paradoxically, in other words, this current ascendancy of action is itself skewed toward the protocols of science, for those who investigate the vicissitudes of indeterminacy begin from some determinate principle, axiom, or definition laid down and more or less confined to an *aspect* of the whole (psychoanalytic, Marxist, feminist, and so on), allowing practice and practical reflection as a whole to go a-begging.[13] To be sure, so long as we recognize the requirements that we subscribe to posited principles and confine ourselves to the circumscribed precincts of the theory under view, contemporary theory can shed light on specific parts of that whole. Nevertheless, a most troubling question arises: what has happened to the everyday and ordinary understood from the holistic orientation of practical reflection? Or more pointedly: what is the nature, or the *ordo*, of the ordinary as such?

In his essay "The Over-Soul," Emerson invokes a romantic notion of the whole of life contrary to what I am trying to bring into view when he pursues a metaphysical variant on nineteenth-century philosophic holism

---

13. For a useful collection of essays on these matters, see W. J. T. Mitchell, ed., *Against Theory: Literary Studies and the New Pragmatism* (Chicago: University of Chicago Press, 1985).

(e.g., Kant, Hegel, Green), "the wise silence, the universal beauty, to which every part and particle is equally related; the eternal ONE."[14] It is well known that Frost undermines all such transcendental romanticism, as in his well-known "For Once, Then, Something" (1920), whose deferral of closure anticipates (it might be argued) later deconstructions of identity, "metanarratives," and totalities of any kind. The now-familiar argument by which this may be said to happen holds that any appeal to unit identity or a "one" commits the fallacy of the metaphysics of presence by failing to acknowledge the differential structure of identity, whereby "A" is "A" only because we can distinguish it within a larger set of "B," "C," and so on. While this argument about difference, however, is penetrating (though hardly new), it is difficult to understand how it is supposed to follow that identity, and reflection on it, therefore disappears into difference. For may we not say, on the contrary, that reference to "the whole" is always made under the sign of difference, and that the term is used functionally not absolutely? A military general needs to think of the "whole" army or "entire" battle (hence his title, "general") at some specific time and place, just as a judge in law can imagine how society "as a whole" may be affected by her decision in some specific case—without, that is, any necessary illusions about his or her having exhausted (made present) the whole.

As it happens Emerson offers another description of the everyday and ordinary that uses the trope of judicial judgment, calling ordinary life "one wide judicial investigation of character" ("Over-Soul" 220). This is a provocative description that helps us to consider that, when we investigate the order of the ordinary, we may find *ourselves* investigated, ourselves both the subject and object of investigation. That this should be so is in line with Kant's turn to transcendental categories and Burke's account of the grammar and rhetoric of "identification" of some part or aspect of the world, which is, recall, at once a naming of a thing's properties from out of our *own* antecedent situation, and thus also a naming of ourselves, an identifying-with what is named. Emerson further notes that such an investigation is somehow "wide" (in my terms, connective and holistic; in Cicero's terms, "the practice of mankind") in the way that a judicial proceeding is never fully in charge of the turns it will take, the facts it will uncover or reappraise, and the judgments it will make. And the ordinary is, lastly, a "judicial" investigation, which I take to signify a matter of

---

14. Ralph Waldo Emerson, "The Over-Soul," in *The Portable Emerson*, ed. Carl Bode in collaboration with Malcolm Cowley (New York: Penguin Books, 1981), 210–11.

discrimination, conducted within accepted codes of speech and behavior, and involving judgment.

Frost's "There Are Roughly Zones" (1939) seems to me at once a commentary on and a further case falling under Emerson's constitutional ruling about the ordinary (line 7 of the poem even adverts to an over-soul). "Zones" offers a further probing (= "proving") of those "leaves and bark" we walk past without seeing, in part by further investigating the nature of such rhetorical proof and judgment, in part by investigating just what is to be tried and proved, that is, ourselves and our world.

"There Are Roughly Zones"

We sit indoors and talk of the cold outside.
And every gust that gathers strength and heaves
Is a threat to the house. But the house has long been tried.
We think of the tree. If it never again has leaves,
We'll know, we say, that this was the night it died.   5
It is very far north, we admit, to have brought the peach.
What comes over a man, is it soul or mind—
That to no limits and bounds he can stay confined?
You could say his ambition was to extend the reach
Clear to the Arctic of every living kind.   10
Why is his nature forever so hard to teach
That though there is no fixed line between wrong and right,
There are roughly zones whose laws must be obeyed
There is nothing much we can do for the tree tonight,
But we can't help feeling more than a little betrayed   15
That the northwest wind should rise to such a height
Just when the cold went down so many below.
The tree has no leaves and may never have them again.
We must wait till some months hence in the spring to know.
But if it is destined never again to grow,   20
It can blame this limitless trait in the hearts of men.

"There Are Roughly Zones" is, from a certain angle, an almost classical piece of judicial rhetoric *in utramque partem* (on either side of a question), for if the house and tree are "tried" (tested; line 3), the speaker and those inside the house undergo in their own minds a legalistic trial, if not for murder then for reckless endangerment or perhaps wrongful death. Frost likes this genre of rhetorical accusation and defense (consider "Not Quite Social," also from *A Further Range* [1936], "Home Burial" [1915], "The Star-Splitter" [1923], "The Thatch" [1928]), not because justice is a settled-on object but because character is exposed, its justification probed, and its contextual limits tested. In this poem we might say that law and order is the order (*ordo*) of the ordinary, even one "whose laws *must* be obeyed" (13, emphasis mine). But this is an order that holds "loosely," as Frost says in "Not Quite Social," "as I would be held" (10). Frost's little auxiliary verb "must" here is on the order of Stanley Cavell's "Must we mean what we say?"—which is not the "must" of logic but of the kind of necessity that runs our ordinary lives, where what is at stake is our being human (our *ethos*, our character) in the specific but loose ways that we do, in fact, go about being human. When a cop says "you must move this car," he or she means it in the way that we have to move our king when he's put in check and we can't interpose another piece: it's how we go on, what we do when we play chess (of course we can also tip the king over or walk away—take the ticket, get towed—thereby ending the game; but then we can *always* do that, even when it's not our turn). The point is to get on with whatever it is we are doing when we're out in the car: it is what we do, the kind of person we admit to being.

In this poem-qua-legal proceeding we begin with an admission in line 6, perhaps not an outright admission of guilt ("very far north" is not necessarily *too* far north) but certainly one that is self-incriminating. Things seem to turn from bad to worse in lines 7 through 13, when the defendant himself tries to account for his own apparent lawlessness by appeal to the age-old motives of desire and ambition. But then matters grow murky (15–18), for there seems to have been an agreement that has gone bad, the weather has betrayed our coconspirators, and, far from confessing, the defendant seems to shift the blame, first to the wind and cold, finally to some indefinite trait in "the hearts of men" (21) that came over him and them. All of which amounts, if I hear this correctly, to a kind of insanity defense.

But then, of course, this is far too lucid and thoughtful a speaker simply to be pleading insanity (anyway, nothing has even happened yet!), and we may want to reconsider. If the tree does die, the fact of the speaker's having identified what was in the mind, soul or heart may be taken rather as guilt, not innocence—*unless*, of course, we accept his claim that such desire and ambition mark us all, in which case perhaps we have reason to think of such forces as mitigating factors, like epilepsy, and the defendant(s) as unwitting participants (or some such). Of course someone on our jury will object that a trait so pervasive in the nature of (all) human beings can hardly mitigate anything, for it is just the sort of tendency a "reasonable person" should be aware of and compensate for—and we are back to the possibility that the speaker, in effect, has confessed, witnessed to further by his own talk of betrayal.

Undefined in front and back, then, Frost's "Zones" are zones of meaning as well as moral judgment, for we readers must negotiate competing arguments, stated or implied, to try to establish facts, weigh the speaker's guilt, and speculate on the poem as a whole. In fact just those competing arguments act out, as we consider them, our *own* drive to get those meanings and values straight, even to take one side or the other "clear to the Arctic," as if establishment of interpretive certainty were our rhetorical goal. Frost's frustration of this drive leaves the matter as undefined and unclear as the drive itself in his treatment of "soul" and "mind" and "heart," perhaps because clarity and explanation are not his goal.

In fact what is far more interesting than these indifferently treated metaphysical categories is our own recognition that we cannot attain such interpretive clarity of the poem as a whole without quitting the game that the poem opens up, a game conducted, I have suggested, along the lines of Emerson's definition of the ordinary. First, the *kind* of judicial investigation the poem conducts invites judgment, even sharpens our desire for drawing fixed lines between right and wrong, fact and speculation, aesthetic value and pragmatic meaning—only to blunt this desire in a haze of possibilities and counterstatements until the jury hangs. *Not* because "we the jury" believe that anything, at all times, *logically*, "must" be argued two ways (as in deconstruction), but the contrary: because *these* specific matters—defendant's possible guilt, the plausibility of his claims, our acknowledgement of factors mitigating or not, our need to weigh the arguments, our struggle to understand Frost—wander in and out of *familiar* zones of right and wrong. These zones are not proved to us to exist, but *shown* to us as we struggle with the proofs and arguments.

Second, it is, of course, finally the *reader's* character that is under investigation, not (only) the speaker's. For the trait in the "hearts of men" must be *our* trait if it is a trait at all, and it "must" be our trait in the way that we must move our king, or car, when we are checked or told. Confronted with our own desire for interpretive clarity in the act of seeking it in Frost's poem, we must acknowledge that we, too, exist within zones of interpretive gaming whose codes, even less clear than No Parking or the rules of check, nevertheless restrain us. We can, of course, simply walk away from the critical game and suffer the consequences, or make claims about the contingency of codes and the radical open-endedness of games under their jurisdiction. But this is not what *Frost* says or does.

Finally, if Frost has checked our own desire for limitlessness he has done so by appeal to the ordinary zones of right and wrong in which we live. This is not the same thing as saying that our own conventions are right because they are ours, or that convention cannot itself be checked: the latter because "our" conventions just are "zones," which implies an "outside" to our inside, hence an "other" in which our right becomes no longer right; and the former because no clear appeal is made to any soul, mind, or heart to justify either our desire to escape our zones of meaning and value or our need to exist within them. Frost does not justify but rather (as in "Leaves Compared with Flowers" and "The Code") tracks down the limits of argument and *shows* us where and who we are by showing us what we do. Hence the *ordo* of the ordinary is not law and order, rules and codes *simpliciter;* it is, rather, the interplay of code and act, rule and practice, limitlessness and limits.

These three dimensions of the ordinary—an "investigation" combining argument and showing-by-example; our own character as unstable struggle between limitlessness and limits; and "what we do" in daily life, or in criticism, or in poems, as an interplay of what we "must" do, and when, how, and where we must do it—require, I think, an explanation less involved in just a few poems as this has been if we are to be able to make use of them to show what Frost is up to philosophically and rhetorically. But it is my hope that the preceding provokes others to conduct rhetorical investigations of their own of our most philosophic Frost.

Frost in Transition

Andrew Lakritz

I. LITERATURE, NATION, FROST

IN THE LAST QUARTER of the twentieth century, the study of American literature in the United States has begun to shift. It is no longer to be taken for granted that Robert Frost and other canonical writers of American modernism will continue to be studied or even enjoyed in the next century. One shift has been the severe question, as marked in the anthologies, as to what is American literature: *The Norton Anthology of American Literature*, for instance, no longer begins its trek across U.S. literary history with the Puritans, but instead begins with the "literature" of exploration and conquest (Columbus, Cortes, Cabeza de Vaca, and so on).[1] Paul Lauter's *Heath Anthology*, similarly, begins with "Native American Oral Literatures," and was the pioneer anthology in 1990 to so reorganize the teaching of the American canon. In making these adjustments, these and other anthologies ask teachers of American literature not only to reexamine the word *American*, but also to rethink the notion of "literature" itself. Lauter's push has been to examine canonical texts alongside writing by minority authors, but while these changes in the survey course have had a real impact on teaching American literature, still the scholarship in many ways lags behind the promise of critical integration envisioned by Lauter and his colleagues. Indeed, Werner Sollers has recently called for taking a critical look at the narrowness of the American canon, not only in terms of authors, but also in terms of language itself.[2]

During the recent history of criticism, in addition, scholars and critics have increasingly relied on literary theory as a surrogate for the practice of criticism, in many cases to the exclusion of literary study itself, although

---

1. Nina Baym et al., eds., *The Norton Anthology of American Literature* (New York: W. W. Norton, 1994) vol. 1.
2. Werner Sollors, "The Blind Spot in Multiculturalism: America's Invisible Literature," *Chronicle of Higher Education* (October 30, 1998): 78.

it is not certain we can even agree on a definition of the literary. One question that emerges under these conditions is whether writers who once held canonical roles in the definition of American literature—Eliot, Frost, Pound, Williams, Crane—can continue to hold the interest of English departments and their scholars, even with cagey and disruptive interpreters reimagining their roles and rethinking some of the canonical work itself in new ways.[3] For Frost to survive as a writer of importance he will have to be studied seriously in both classroom and monograph for what his work means and accomplishes in relation to new figures who have arrived on the scene of criticism: African American writers, women poets and novelists, Asians and Hispanics, Native American poets.[4] Traditionalists and Frost loyalists may argue that Frost will survive on his merits, or not at all, but we know from Barbara Hernstein Smith's work *Contingencies of Value* that value in literature may only guarantee a marketing strategy—not necessarily a sale. One still has to get students to read American literature, and that is by no means a given in today's climate.

How Frost will be read in the next century will be determined by how he was read in the last century, and one key to understanding that reading has to do with the question of nationalism. Frost has been seen by many, by detractors as well as by supporters, as important in the same degree that he is "American." This association, furthermore, has developed during the very century when national identity came into its own as a phenomenon, when the modern concept of nation established itself as the sine qua non of mass identity. The nation, as an imagined community in Benedict Anderson's resonant phrase, is not so much a matter of false consciousness—as many critics of nationalism would have it—as it is a matter of an entire cultural, social, and religious consciousness that preceded the formation of a national consciousness. It is true that at political functions and in times of crisis such consciousness may be simplified into symbols, shortened into sound bites, and even hypostatized in ways that suggest false consciousness or ideology. Lech Walesa, when he ran for the president of Poland in

---

3. Philip Fisher makes just this point, for example, in arguing that Henry Louis Gates, Jr., and Richard Poirier write literary criticism designed to return literature (Hurston, Frost) to its "cultural location" as against the more sentimental criticism of an earlier generation. "American Literary and Cultural Studies since the Civil War," in *Redrawing the Boundaries: The Transformation of English and American Literary Studies,* ed. Stephen Greenblatt and Giles B. Gunn (New York: MLA, 1992), 238.

4. An excellent model for this sort of criticism is John Edgar Tidwell's recent article on Sterling Brown and Robert Frost: "Two Writers Sharing," *African American Review* (fall 1997): 399–409.

1990, authorized a television campaign advertisement in which he strode like a giant from the mountains of southern Poland to the shipyards of Gdansk, embodying, in a way many intellectuals felt was absurd, the figure of an old Polish myth. Likewise in the United States during the elaborate arrival ceremonies at the White House for visiting heads of state, the military intermingles its contemporary forces and bands in ceremonial dress alongside a fife and drum corps playing "Yankee Doodle Dandy" alongside a troupe of long-trumpeters with draped ensigns playing "Ruffles and Flourishes" and "Hail to the Chief." In other words, the symbolism of state and nation collapses representation into what Walter Benjamin called "homogenous empty time," with elements from military and social history overlaid with religious and cultural history.[5] Anderson's idea in *Imagined Communities* is that—without being scholars—everyone in the nation recognizes these elements as their own, as part of the consciousness that makes them "American" (or Polish) for example, and connected to people who may live in communities far removed in both space and time but who are unacquainted with one another. Anderson's most radical idea may be that this conception of the nation holds true for all modern nations, from the Philippines to Cape Verde, and from Nigeria to New Zealand. Frost has been called an American poet partly for the way his work gathers together the stands of an identification that marks him as American, and we, as readers, partake of the imagined community he helps to represent in his work. However, while we have had many individual articulations of what makes Frost an American poet, even a quintessentially American poet, we have not yet had much analysis of what it means to identify him in that way, and how those identifications have been made. What the following essay attempts to outline for future study is Frost and nationalism. I do not here have the space to study the history of that designation, with its twists and turns, and I will have to let go important formulations and articulations in the interest of space. (Harold Bloom's work from the 1970s comes to mind as important for this effort, but I do not treat him here.) Instead, I want to isolate a recent expression of this notion, published in the popular press, in order to make some preliminary remarks on the phenomenon. I am less interested in debunking the notion—Frost as quintessentially American poet—as in understanding the imagined community behind the designation, and what goes into that imagination. It strikes me that the work to be done in Frost studies of the future, as well as in literary studies

5. Walter Benjamin, "Theses on the Philosophy of History," in *Illuminations*, ed. Hannah Arendt (New York: Schocken, 1969), 253–64.

generally, may well be to write the history of the multiple nationalities that the literary has helped to define, both for general (or common) readers and for critics and scholars.

In writing about the question of the nation in Frost I want to be clear about what I am not going to explore here. At the end of this essay I make clear, however, that the following prohibition I outline is not done arbitrarily or out of mere annoyance at the current state of the literary academy. Ezra Pound wrote sometime early in the century that all criticism should be personal, and by now, at the other end of the century, it seems as if all anyone can focus on is the biographical, even literary critics who are busy spinning their memoirs at a feverish pace. In the community of Frost criticism, biography has been for many the main issue, especially since the appearance of Lawrance Thompson's first eagerly anticipated volume of his three-volume biography. Frost's life has been rewritten many times over since his death in 1963. Even literary criticism—especially literary criticism—has taken the life as key to understanding the lyric. For better or worse, this interest in the life comes at a time when the life, under the sign of subjectivity, has suffered itself to come into question. Once Michel Foucault announced the end of the subject, the postmodern rushed in with a vengeance, calling fundamentals of epistemology into question, along with much that follows from such epistemology. Younger critics came to ask wryly Who Comes After the Subject? and many other critics—such as feminist and cultural critics—took the concept of the end of the subject as an article of faith. The individual is not so much a person (or in literature, a character), as an effect of a given social (and, in Foucault's terminology, epistemic) structure. Biography, under these conditions, cannot be the delineation of a life or experience so much as the tracing of their aftereffects and the articulation of those structures, institutions, and rules that make such effects possible. Real experience—experience of the real—is not so much a quaint notion like a marriage vow as a thing against which critical theory no longer has the tools to measure. What we call discourse has unmoored itself from the real and taken off into a realm something like pure wish-fulfillment, except that for much of the day such wishes are entirely anticipated by the culture industry: advertising, popular music, sports, politics. The interest in Frost's biography comes at a time when, as the subject has evaporated, the biographical search seems all that's left to restore the man. Except that, in Frost's case, it was biography itself that removed "Frost" from our view, creating the need for ever-more-competitive biographers to come along and give us the "real"—or rather, the real—Frost.

Biography can teach us no more about Frost's work. The time for biography in Frost studies is past, though it will come again for another generation with new questions to ask and another time with different concerns. For now, I want to argue, the work to be done in Frost criticism has to return to the poetry itself, and not as the New Critics elaborated that turn to poetry "itself," nor as new New Critics would elaborate that turn to linguistics, but rather to the poetry as cultural artifact. This essay assumes that poetry lives in the world as other discourses and other art forms. The poem is shaped by the world around it, made up of other poems, bits of language and imagery from popular culture, by the experience of an individual immersed in a given social and political context. In addition, the poem shapes—to the extent that we let it, either as individuals or as a culture—how we see the world. To return to the poem, then, is to return to the world. Not long after World War II, Theodor Adorno suggested that only a philistine could take poetry seriously after the great human tragedy of that war, after the Holocaust, and he seemed to be referring to poetry in that context as the most rarified and purest exemplar of the aesthetic, which in post-Kantian terms refers to formal modes of thought and language perfectly untethered from rational thought. The aesthetic is a luxury we simply can no longer afford, not in dark times. For this reason the novel has come to be the preeminent literary form in the late twentieth century, as a form with roots in journalism. My point is not that Kant got it wrong, or that Adorno's dismay over interest in the aesthetic in the face of mass state-sponsored murder is somehow misplaced with regard to poetry. Instead, my feeling is that what matters is how you read the poem, with what resources you bring to your reading, and what grounding assumptions you allow for the aesthetic. After Kant one can say that poetry has nothing to say about politics, and no role to play in the larger social context, but to say this is to recognize via a kind of negative dialectics the deep nexus that binds poetry and society.

II. FROST IS AN AMERICAN POET

One way to get at the nexus of poetry and society with regard to Robert Frost is to interrogate the nationalism behind and in his status as a U.S. poet. This question need not lead us back to biography, though his life is full of incidents and events remarkable in this regard, from the first two books published in England to his involvement as a cultural ambassador during the Cold War. Instead, we can think of the construction of Frost as a poet one calls "American." In order to do this I will examine the critical designations of three contemporary poets.

In 1996 Farrar, Straus and Giroux brought out a little volume of critical essays called *Homage to Robert Frost*.[6] The volume contains essays published previously in magazines by three Nobel laureates: Joseph Brodsky's *New Yorker* article "On Grief and Reason" (first published in 1994); Seamus Heaney's "Above the Brim: On Robert Frost," first published in *Salmagundi;* and a review by Derek Wolcott of the Library of America edition of Frost's writings published for the first time in the *New Republic*. All of these poets agree that Frost is quintessentially "American." And all of these Nobel laureates were born "elsewhere."

Brodsky believes he has arrived not only at the essence of Frost's meaning as a writer, but in the process he has taken the measure of what it means to be American. To distill this quintessence, one presumes, is the service that Frost performs for his "kind." He satisfies one's need for a definition of selfhood, on a national level, and does so in the context of his poetry. Brodsky's essay concerns, in the main, "Home Burial," a poem that is considered by most critics to be one of Frost's great triumphs. It is a narrative poem that orchestrates the voices of a farm couple suffering from the death of their first child. Part of the brilliance of the poem has to do with the way Frost embeds the psychological position of the two in the rhythm and metaphor of their language, yielding by implication and indirection an understanding of their predicament. But part of the impact the poem has comes from the bleak and tragic conclusions the poem suggests about its subject.

Brodsky suggests that Frost is American, and this poem is American, because it is terrifying, a term he borrows from Lionel Trilling, who used the word to describe Frost back in the terrifying 1950s, during a birthday party fete for Frost. The term, and the event, are loaded with meaning. There may be some readers and critics of Frost for whom this notion is more symptomatic of Trilling and his New York Jewish context than an apt description of Frost's work, and certainly, to some extent, the ambiguous and freighted role that Freud has played in twentieth-century thought might lurk in the background of this discussion. Brodsky's version of this assignment, however, is much more specific than Trilling's, more focused. Brodsky writes that European literature is tragic while American literature is terrifying, and in making this distinction he assigns to American consciousness the idea that once one recognizes the negative

6. **Homage.**

potential of the individual, one must live in terror of what that might bring. The European, by contrast, lives in a world always already accomplished and done with; the tragic is the recognition that evil has always and already been done. There may be terror yet, in the stages and surprises by which the evil event unfolds, but the European knows already that no good end will come to the king or his son, around whom swirl the forces of their undoing in their retainers, rivals, and even in their relatives.

The American knows nothing of the story, and this is Brodsky's larger point, one borrowed from the British poet Auden. One of Harold Bloom's revisionary ratios is *askesis,* which he borrows from Christology, the idea that the strong poet is one who has the will to empty the poetic self out of traditional form in order to power ahead with new forms and a wholly original poetic conception. Brodsky refers to the conventional topos in American literary criticism which holds that American writers, like Americans, write and live in a place totally without history. Up to a certain moment in history, these Americans were completely under the sway of what they left behind, their British or German or French ancestors and traditions. But once the American poet (and the American scholar) turns his back to the old shore and looks deeply into the new continent— as Emerson counseled in "The American Scholar"—an opportunity for making a wholly original art and culture presented itself. Brodsky writes that European trees "stand rustling, as it were, with allusions."[7] American trees, on the other hand, stand "free of references," and this free-standing autonomy Brodsky finds terrifying. You don't have the story beforehand, the narrative map of events, but what you do have is a (Puritan?) sense that since evil lurks in the hearts of men, a good chance exists that no good may come of the encounter.

Americans are those people for whom history is a sometimes pleasant and perhaps curious and often dangerous characteristic of the old world, and the tragedy, for Americans, is that Europeans cannot seem to escape from history, from Verdun and the Maginot line, from the beaches of Normandy, from Sarajevo and Ulster, from Jerusalem and Algiers. European entanglement seems to play itself out with nauseating repetition while Americans look on, often as not disengaged from it, puzzled by a European inability to unstick themselves from the tar baby of history. This is familiar stuff. Those critics who see this as a willfully constructed definition of the American psyche, I believe, are on firmer ground than Brodsky, who buys these notions as plain truth uncritically. Still, Brodsky follows in a long and

7. **Homage,** 8.

American tradition of critics who claim that American writers come out of the Puritan, antinomian tradition of saying no to society in order to create, Adam-like, culture anew from scratch. Compare Brodsky's comments with those of Roy Harvey Pearce writing in 1961 in the opening pages of his book *The Continuity of American Poetry:*

> the American poet again and again imaged himself—in Emerson's and Whitman's word—as an Adam who, since he might well be one with God, was certainly one with all men. The continuity of this narrative is that of the antinomian, Adamic impulse, as it thrusts against a culture made by Americans who come more and more to be frightened by it, even as they realize that it is basic to the very idea of their society: one (in Whitman's words) of simple, separate persons, democratic, en-masse.[8]

In order for there to be the opportunity, or the imaginary, of such an Adamic impulse, one has to conceive of the very ground on which one stands to be unprepared, open, empty. And to accomplish that bit of imagination, one has first to "remove" from the land the humans and the civilization already there, that Frost's forebears found inhabiting the new world, for instance, and the colonial life that existed long before Americans were invented. The imaginary blank in the landscape is paired with an imaginary act powerful enough both to clear the forest of meaning, and stock it again, perhaps not with the same meaning as that cleared away, but with a meaning for Americans to take, to hold, and to use as self-defining. One meaning with which Frost might have filled the bare common of the landscape is a terrifying emptiness, such a blank as would have been unfamiliar to Keats, for instance, whose English nightingale reminds him of Greek myth and "Provençal song" or Wordsworth, for whom Nature "speaks" of Lucy, giving breath to a dead girl in an act of poetic imagining.

Brodsky also later in the essay writes that Frost, in terms of what American poetry is like today, is not American at all. But he finishes with a reassertion of his central premise, now taking a slightly different tack. Brodsky's central insight concerning Frost is that "Home Burial" is an autobiographical poem, that it concerns the success of language to wreak havoc—the husband and wife's language entangling and disrupting each other's private pact with their different emotions in response to

8. Roy Harvey Pearce, *The Continuity of American Poetry* (Middletown, Conn.: Wesleyan University Press, 1987), 5.

the child's death—by placing incompatible drives in proximity with one another (grief and reason). I think what Brodsky finds terrifying, in the end, and American—that is, alien to his own sensibility, and the sensibility of European poetry—is that Frost is even capable of imagining this dialogue, of thinking through this terrible experience (the loss of a child, the couple's response to that loss, and their subsequent alienation from one another), and then composing it as if he were beyond it, above it, to use Brodsky's term, "autonomous" from that experience (he says "utter autonomy"). For if this is Frost's autobiography, to write blank-verse dialogue on the experience, with the form's dull matter-of-factness, then he must be even more cold, more aloof, more cut-off in his own darkness than even Emerson is said to have been by many. Brodsky ends the essay by attributing this kind of autonomy not just to Frost as a singular U.S. poet, but to Frost as a representative American poet.

Seamus Heaney is less interested in designating Frost American, yet he, too, recognizes Brodsky's main argument, takes it as an article of faith, but goes on to say why Frost's poetry at its best might be rescued from a negative vision of this utter autonomous and aloof character. Heaney writes that "Frost was prepared to look without self-deception into the crystal of indifference in himself where his moral and artistic improvisations were both prefigured and scrutinized." He admires Frost because the poetry "is 'genuinely rescued' from negative recognitions, squarely faced, and abidingly registered."[9] Heaney never explains that phrase, nor is it clear why the phrase "genuinely rescued" is in quotation marks. It would seem that what he admires is Frost's ability to look realistically at himself, even if that self he looks at contains qualities one might otherwise not wish to celebrate. The "crystal of indifference" he mentions: this is another way of talking about what Brodsky identifies as Frost's "utter autonomy" from the moral and emotional dilemma of his suffering couple in "Home Burial," and this is what is dark in Frost. At bottom, indifference is what Brodsky has identified as the essential characteristic of the American.

Wolcott discusses the American element of Frost in connection with his early work, when Pound recognized something powerful and positive in Frost's first book, *A Boy's Will*. This is another way of getting at what is American in American poetry, to discuss the turn away from nineteenth-century forms beholden to English poetic forms and subject matter, and to turn toward the vernacular.

9. **Homage,** 63.

Pound gave *A Boy's Will* a good review because, for all his aggressive cosmopolitanism and campaigning for the classics and "the new," Pound was as much a vernacular regional poet as Frost, and the genuine Americanness of Frost must have stirred a patriotic claim in him as much as the tonal authenticity of Eliot did. He derided the falsely modern and saw a classic shape in Frost that made "it" (poetry) new by its directness and vigor: Frost's writing achieved a vernacular elation in tone, not with the cheap device of dialect spelling or rustic vocabulary, but with a clean ear and a fresh eye.[10]

Wolcott, unfortunately, never gets further than merely asserting that Frost represented something genuine, something American. (In this, Wolcott repeats the gesture of Pound eighty years before: Pound, in his review of Frost's first two books, praises Frost for his honest and unadorned approach to rendering "American life with sober fidelity." What both Pound and Wolcott do is to conflate "American life" with New England, in a move that recapitulates the myth of America as an emanation of Puritan New England life and thought.) He mentions "directness" and "vigor," and he uses the term *vernacular,* but without going on to add much detail or to distinguish these qualities from the poetry of other nationalities. Later in the review essay he claims that "America likes its sages ordinary but reclusive, and without sexual passion or desire of any kind, as much as it likes them—Dickinson, Jeffers, Frost, Hopper—cynical of material progress, and the more cynical the more revered."[11] An odd list that, and it may be that Wolcott's attribution of American Puritan asexuality is as much a product of Wolcott's own experience as an "outsider" in New England; it could hardly be a result of careful reading, of either Dickinson or Frost. Having left Whitman out of that list, then, is understandable given what Wolcott wants to assert. To include Whitman would mean that America doesn't like him, nor any of Whitman's progeny (Hart Crane, Henry Miller, Allen Ginsberg).

What do all three poets share in their assessment of Frost? They have in common a recognition that Frost is somehow and in some way America's poet. Brodsky goes furthest in wanting to establish something essential about Frost as an American poet, though Heaney also takes for granted, tacitly, central insights established by Brodsky. And Wolcott, who is writing a review and is, therefore, less interested in drawing out his analysis,

10. Ibid., 98.
11. Ibid., 109.

finds it necessary as well to say something about America by way of its poets. My sense is that one reason Frost has had so much trouble with the critical academy, what Heaney calls the "critical resistance" against Frost, might in some measure be taken as an index of this very issue. In other words, the more patriotic Frost can be made to seem, the more "American" in his themes, strategies, language, and reputation, the less kindly is the critical establishment likely to regard him.

III. READING FROST, READING AMERICAN

Brodsky employs "Home Burial" to retell this narrative. I want to use a lyric to test something similar, but to tack in another direction. "Home Burial" contains those powerful images of the husband who digs his own child's grave and brings the dirt of the child's death into the home on his shoes, along with his spade. In other words, this poem has one of these Adams who scars the earth with his labor yet is incapable of seeing what his wife sees, that terrifying image of sexuality coupled with death he makes in the burial.

> I saw you from that very window there,
> Making the gravel leap and leap in air,
> Leap up, like that, like that, and land so lightly
> And roll back down the mound beside the hole.
> I thought, Who is that man? I didn't know you. (57)

As Richard Poirier has written convincingly, these are lines freighted with the shock of a sexuality seen, in the moment, as bestiality by the stunned woman. The lines demonstrate a recognition—but she is really only speaking in a dreamlike incomprehension—that her husband's sexual act is somehow to be conflated with the act of burying their dead child. The starkness of these lines, the rawness with which the mother's perceptions are stated, and the recognition that neither she nor her husband is fully aware of the extent to which they have been torn from each other by this event: these features suggest how Frost has been (self-)constructed as a sort of primitive who, in Brodsky's words, walks out of his house and meets nature face to face: "Man and tree face each other in their respective primal power, free of references."[12] As Pound put it in his review of *North of*

12. Ibid., 8.

Boston, "even Emerson had sufficient elasticity of mind to find something in the 'yawp.'"

These are powerful and self-confirming images for the American community. They define the American as one who went out into the wilderness on a spiritual errand and planted a civilization, meeting face to face the radicals of human experience:

> Where my imaginary line
> Bends square in woods, and iron spine
> And pile of real rocks have been founded.
> And of this corner in the wild,
> Where these are driven in and piled,
> One tree, by being deeply wounded,
> Has been impressed as Witness Tree
> And made commit to memory
> My proof of being not unbounded.
> Thus truth's established and borne out,
> Though circumstanced with dark and doubt—
> Though by a world of doubt surrounded. (301)

The witness tree of this poem, "Beech," from Frost's 1942 volume *A Witness Tree,* is a tree the surveyor marks to establish the parameters for a homestead. In this poem, the tree is "deeply wounded" as a companion to the iron spine-marker and the pile of rocks. The middle sentence in this three-sentence poem is the longest (six lines), and when you come to the final two lines of this middle passage the rhythm turns abrupt and rocky: "My proof of being not unbounded" has an extra hard or accented syllable (five) to jolt the regularity of tetrameter verse. In fact, the "not" comes along and nearly stops the flow of the language dead in its tracks, making one hear, if perhaps in an undertone, the suggestion of "being not," or naught. Perhaps lurking in the line is proof of nonbeing: the violent mark, the axe cut on the tree, this incision, memory itself, and thus human culture, is in doubt and subject to erasure. The phrase "made commit to memory" is curious as well: made and commit are redundant. One need only say "commit to memory" or perhaps "made me memorize"—yet "made commit" suggests again the anxiety in the act of making the poem memorializes. It is a fictionalizing act, a creative act, the line of poetry syncing up with the imaginary line in the woods, but it is an act with an uncertain, herky-jerky origin. And finally, the double negative of "not unbounded" also slows the reader down, as if it were a trip line set in the woods. The sounds of the line, while slowing down and tripping up, give us a kind of chiasmus or crossing: BEE + N/ N BOUNDED. The last three lines trip lightly away, back to regular tetrameter verse, allowing the reader to take a nice concept home with her, to feel comfortable again after the moment of anxiety has passed. The idea that you need to scar violently the trees in our wilderness in order to preserve some measure of civilization in a "world of doubt"—this notion is hard to swallow. The last two lines offer another chiasmus with "circumstance and doubt / doubt" and "surrounded" (both of these words suggest the circular roundness of the world itself). The function of chiasmus in rhetoric is to set up neat relationships with circular logics, the logic of tautology. Chiasmus offers an image of completion and resolution, like the musical structure that ventures from the dominant chord to another territory and back again to the original dominant. What the poem underscores, for me, is the act in this poem of constructing truth, committing memory, marking and impressing the witness tree, all of these acts lead to one truth? What is the proof or truth this poem raises? "Being not unbounded" suggests the notion that the speaker, far from walking out into the wilderness and getting lost in the boundless wild, is, in fact, nicely bounded, fits well into the confines of the structure the speaker himself has created for himself, in the woods, in the world, in the words. Yet at the very same time the poem offers this "proof" and the establishment of house and truth, it also takes away the certainty one might have in the foundations of these truths: the lines can just as surely speak of nonbeing and a terrifying blank, not so much of nature as of the mind, as they can speak of the triangulation of imaginary lines that help the speaker, and the reader, to get bearings. What is remarkable, then, about this poem of founding and foundations, marking and memory, is that at its heart the proof is at best ambiguous, an act of violence that renders and sunders as much as a constructive act founding a corporate identity.

Frost's "The Road Not Taken" moves in this direction as well, and one question I think these characteristic Frostian moments ask us to consider is whether we can ever be so sure of the territory Frost's poems manage. If we are to think of him as a great or important "American" poet, as perhaps the American poet of the twentieth century, then what exactly is the territory we are talking about. Is it an empty space to be filled with human culture and the spiritual quest of the Puritans? Or is it, rather, a place "made commit to memory" by violent acts of men and women who went into the woods to conquer it? And if the latter, what do those acts prove? Do they prove our bounded existence, or do they rather prove our contingency with the place marked out and possessed? The "Road Not Taken" has to be one of Frost's most beloved poems, one of those poems every schoolchild reads, or has read to them. It is a comforting poem, because it seems so clear, and its lovely conclusion, offers a wonderful self-congratulatory kernel of wisdom for the schoolchild to take home, as much a phoneme of American corporate identity as we are likely to get:

> I shall be telling this with a sigh
> Somewhere ages and ages hence:
> Two roads diverged in a wood, and I—
> I took the one less traveled by,
> And that has made all the difference. (103)

When confronted with the fact that this poem also contains the lines "the passing there / Had worn them really about the same" indicating that one road couldn't possibly be said to have been "less traveled by," many students, in my experience, just throw up their hands. The final stanza says it all, and the earlier lines, well, just don't have the same importance. What interests me in this context is "The Road Not Taken" as a kind of foundation myth for nation building, or for building a national identity. The poem gives as much as it takes away, and in the same breath: American exceptionalism is built on the notion that we have taken, as a nation, a new path, one not taken by other nations. Frost's poem credits that narrative in this allegory of walking through the uncharted woods, but it calls the narrative into question at the same time by undercutting the evidence supporting the allegory of pioneering.

Another key figure in Frost poetry is the ruin. In an earlier study I examined ruins in Frost for the way they figure a critique of U.S. attachment to notions of progress, and showed how the ruin figures an allegory of the family and more generally human relations under attack by social and economic relations during the first half of the twentieth century.[13] Frost's poetry is a scattering of structures ruined and about to be ruined: fences of stone and wood, houses ("closing like a dent in dough," 342), clear-cut forests, communities and farms, woodpiles rotting in the forest, marriages, and even the frail human body. In part this wreckage and ruin scattered across the Frostian landscape is a testament to the state of things in New England during the years Frost was writing, after the failure of the industrial base and the closing of mills and milltowns, as well as the decay of farming as a viable economic activity in the stony and cold Northeast. It has

13. Andrew M. Lakritz, *Modernism and the Other in Stevens, Frost, and Moore* (Gainesville: University Press of Florida, 1996), 69–121.

a connection too, however, to nation and the corporate myth of nation I am exploring. The ruin of the founder's house and evidence of what was there is a powerful symbol for nations and for national mythology. Frederick the Great even built a new Greek ruin on the grounds of Sans Souci, his residence in Potsdam, in order to signify his connection—to make "literal" his imagined connection—to the magnificent historical ground of ancient Greece. In his thesis XIV on the philosophy of history, Benjamin writes that

> history is the subject of a structure whose site is not homogeneous, empty time, but time filled by the presence of the now [*Jetztzeit*]. Thus, to Robespierre ancient Rome was a past charged with the time of the now which he blasted out of the continuum of history. The French Revolution viewed itself as Rome reincarnate. It evoked ancient Rome the way fashion evokes costumes of the past. Fashion has a flair for the topical, no matter where it stirs in the thickets of long ago; it is a tiger's leap into the past. This jump, however, takes place in an arena where the ruling class gives the commands. The same leap in the open air of history is the dialectical one, which is how Marx understood the revolution.[14]

Benjamin here is contrasting at least two ways of thinking about history: historicism tends to see the past in the form of a once upon a time, belonging in an unproblematic way to the so-called "continuum of history." Homogeneous empty time is that sort of thinking about history Benjamin wishes to critique; he admires the way political tacticians use the past to "blast" that continuum, that homogeneity. We may ask the question, then, whether Frost's appeals to origins, political and social and on behalf of something like a notion of American nationality, participate in the dialectical history Benjamin prefers or rather in a historicist version of history.

Frost's ruins serve a similar function to that of Frederick the Great's ruins, that of signifying the ground on which the nation stands, the many ruins on top of which one builds a modern civilization. In every case, however, his ruins are modest: the simple farm in "The Need of Being Versed in Country Things," the child's broken toys in "Directive," the family home now just a cellar hole in "The Generations of Men." These images name parts of the same constellation of images having to do with colonial pioneers and their attempts to create a life where nothing before

---

14. Walter Benjamin, *Illuminations*, 260.

existed. The ruin is evidence of an origin, an original birth, and acts in nationalist terms as guarantee of the identity of the American, as against any other claims for identification. The little site of ruin in Frost's well-known poem "Directive" is so near the spring, the source of the river, that it is too "lofty and original to rage," a phrase that suggests the even temper and maturity of the site of origins. In another well-known Frost poem of ruins, "The Need of Being Versed in Country Things," the burden of the poem appears to be to articulate a proper because natural response to the tragic fire that brought the farmhouse to ruin: what came in the wake of the fire was a happy habitation for the phoebes. Not only is Frost always trying to lay out what can be made of diminished things; in a way, his poetic strategy might be said to lend a sheen to the life Americans have made based on the humble sacrifices made on near-barren ground by the generations before the contemporary age.

Contrast this strategy of poem making with that of Pound: in the early poetry of Pound, as in his later epic poem, *The Cantos*, often one has a kind of analogue to the ruin of Sans Souci, in which Pound has collapsed time by identifying a contemporary event with one from Homeric epic, for example. Eliot's *The Wasteland* attempts to accomplish something similar: by overlaying images and plot elements from ancient fertility rituals and symbols onto contemporary life, Eliot can show how degraded the modern world has become and suggest possible routes out of the degradation. Pound was a utopian in his belief that contemporary language use was corrupt, and that by returning to ancient forms—like the Chinese ideogram or the distinct line of the Greek artists—he could literally heal both language and culture. Frost's poems, like his sayings on the subject, never allowed him to even think that something like human progress was possible, either by increments or through imposition, through the application of power on the part of some Poundian or Eliotic strongman.

However that may be, we still have the enigma of a poet whose major idiom is plain English, resolutely antimodernist in tone and subject matter, who nevertheless is a major figure for people who don't live on farms and cannot possibly identify with the poetry on the grounds that it speaks to their lives. Frost's poems speak of "what was in the darkened parlor" for a readership and audience that by and large no longer experiences the death of loved ones in that way. Frost's poems speak of ruins to an audience fast becoming universally insured, changing the very concept of loss from something individual and private to something corporate and shared. What Joseph Brodsky finds absolutely terrifying more than anything else in "Home Burial" is the way the poet, who he believes is writing about his own loss, and that of his wife, can step back two and three steps and observe the ruin of the small family, the death of the child and that death's effects on the couple. Is it that we don't have much infant mortality here in the United States anymore, and these scenes are less likely? No, not exactly: what I think is shocking about the poem is that in a small way the wife, who is not "his people," not from that farm and probably not a farmgirl at all, brings to the world of the poem something of the perspective of the future. She is shocked that her husband, after losing his child, could go out to the graveyard and with his own hands bury the child. The world of Frost's audience is not a world where fathers bury their own children in the backyard (except perhaps in horror stories and crime blotters).

What I am pursuing is the idea that in Frost's work the archaic is just as much present as in Pound's or Eliot's modernist poetry, but Frost uses the archaic differently. He does not collapse that archaic world with the modern world as if in homogeneous empty time; he does not make of time a binary, of good and bad images or elements. He does not hold with the notion that our own time is the worst time in the history of humanity. Rather, he allows the images of his poetry to seek their place dialectically by being activated in the audience. The audience can if it so desires make self-congratulatory identifications with the images in the poetry: yes, I took the harder road, the road not taken before me, and that has made all the difference! This reading of Frost suggests the possibility of a nationalism uncomplicated and free of conscience, in a way one that indeed does conflate our present with the past. A fife and drum corps accompanies the modern U.S. Marine Corps marching band to presidential events welcoming ceremonies of heads of state, an image that telescopes the present to the past of the revolutionary war. Frost's poetry also, however, renders those identifications hard to make, particularly for those who listen carefully and read well. One of the reasons Pound's and Eliot's poetry is often so difficult for the common reader is just that they write as if there were some perfect continuity between the past and the present, and of course the modernists were famous for condemning their common readers for their ignorance. Eliot's statement that a poet who gets a popular following too quickly is probably not writing important poetry is only the most obvious one in this connection. Frost's use of the archaic moves in the opposite direction. It lulls the reader into seeing him or herself in the obvious and self-congratulatory light of a corporate, because national, recognition. Frost's poetry may not be revolutionary in the manner of Benjamin's Robespierre. However, in many poems Frost uses the archaic to lull us into territory we might think, at first glimpse, as familiar, only to throw that recognition into doubt. In other words, in Frost's best work, if we get the "quintessential American" characteristic Brodsky outlines, the individualist who stands beyond history and memory, an "American Adam," we get that image on the way toward its severe qualification and critique. It might be clear, by now, how I think this works in a poem like "The Road Not Taken," but how does it work in "Home Burial," the archetypal American poem for Brodsky?

For Brodsky, "Home Burial" is a document that maps with "utter autonomy" the poet's own loss and that of his wife, the loss of a child. The poet does this as if he were skin meeting the bark of a tree: that is, he does it unflinchingly, without sentimentality, without any intervening text, history, memory. The poet happens upon the thing itself and is able to see it without allegory: that appears to be the terrifying element that Brodsky, the European, finds in Frost. My sense is that biography is getting in the way of Brodsky's reading of this poem, because what's crucial for me is that the wife in the poem is not of the farmer's world, even if she married into it and moved to the farm. I read the poem as an allegory approximating the narrative of the materialist historian of Benjamin's text: the wife's confrontation with death, and with her husband's experience of that death, gives us a very precise analogue of the modern approach to death, as opposed to an archaic approach. In this allegory, the wife more or less represents the reader, who looks at the burial ground as through a window, and from a certain height and distance: in any case, removed from that death. The death of the child is the event that marks the sudden, violent separation of these two views of life, conditioned as they are by different world-historical conceptions of death. The terrifying shock of recognition embodied in the couple's abrupt conflict is akin, I would argue, to the "blast" that Benjamin writes about in which the "continuum of history"—history as if it were a smooth progression of past to present—is blasted by the fullness of his so-called "now-time" (*Jetztzeit*). The poem, as in much of Frost's writings, puts into dramatic action the collision of the archaic with the contemporary, and the importance of Frost's best work is that it can mark, often with great elegance and beauty, the sharp line between our own time and the past. The poetry accomplishes this for an audience too often caught up in the sense of history as homogenous empty time, in the sense that time represents a continuity or merely a progression. Only through a new kind of close reading can the poem be returned both to itself as aesthetic object, and to its cultural moment—the social and economic contexts during the first half of the twentieth century. The poem is a document embedded in history: if Frost is to have significance in the next hundred years it will be for how he looked forward and backward at the same time and put the collision of those worldviews, those windows, into dramatic relief.

"By Pretending They Are Not Sonnets"

The Sonnets of Robert Frost at the Millennium

Richard J. Calhoun

ROBERT FROST WOULD have been pleased to know that he would be discussed in retrospect at the millennium. He let his audience know that he liked to envision himself taking part in such momentous occasions. I have a strong memory of Frost playing cryptically with the idea of witnessing the millennium. He was speaking at Chapel Hill in 1957, and after reading "It Is Almost the Year Two Thousand," he said, "You know some of us are looking forward to it." Some members of the audience laughed, and he responded, "You don't laugh. I thought you had laughed at me for saying that." Then he added softly, "I was about to weep."[1]

At the century's end I also remember all too well Robert Frost's unsettled reputation with critics back at midcentury. I was at the Kenyon School of English in the summer of 1949, learning how to read modernist poetry in the light of the formalism of the New Criticism. The status of Robert Frost came up at a breakfast discussion being dominated by one of his "enemies," Yvor Winters, known for categorizing Frost just the year before as an Emersonian "spiritual drifter."[2] On Winters's neohumanist ethical scale, this placed Frost about as low as one could register. Frost's friend among these critics, John Crowe Ransom, was not present. I was the only one foolish enough to risk defending Frost by suggesting that a formalist reading would disclose complexities masked by apparent simplicity. To the New Critic sophisticates, I might as well have been advocating Carl Sandburg, with whom Frost was equated, but I remained convinced of the applicability of New Critical techniques to Frost's poetry. I was only

---

1. Richard J. Calhoun, ed., "Frost in the Carolinas," *South Carolina Review* 7 (November 1974): 10–11. This is the transcript of a talk I recorded in 1957 and published with permission of the Frost estate.

2. Yvor Winters, "Robert Frost, or the Spiritual Drifter as Poet," *Sewanee Review* 56 (1948): 64–96.

vaguely aware in 1949 that Frost wrote sonnets, and so I was unable to use this achievement to give him status. The only consolation I had then was the consensus recognition that Frost was better than Edgar Guest.

Any witness to what Robert Lowell, in his sonnet on Frost, called the "great act" of "saying" his poems might have suspected that his difficulty with the modernist establishment did not come only from his uncommon popularity as a stringently American poet. Frost could not resist dispensing to audiences occasional witty verbal barbs in what was almost a public quarrel with T. S. Eliot. There were reasonable suspicions that the sonnet "The Broken Drought" was aimed at Eliot in response to a lecture by the chief modernist before fourteen thousand people in Minneapolis. Eliot had, in his own quintessential style, expressed his opinion of Frost publicly as early as 1922: "His verse, it is regretfully said, is uninteresting, and what is uninteresting is unreadable, and what is unreadable is not read. There, that is done."[3] Fortunately, it was not done, and the relationship between the two poets improved. But Frost appeared to be Eliot's direct opposite—American and traditional, a poet whose poetry was personal, not impersonal. Honors came, even Pulitzer Prizes, but Frost remained sensitive to a reputational discrepancy between popular adulation and a critical cold shoulder from much of the establishment intelligentsia. Frost at Harvard came to know his enemy simply as the "Pound, Eliot, Richards gang."[4]

Half a century later, I am confident Robert Frost would be pleased with his standing among critics at the millennium. Frost criticism has come far in promoting what has been designated the "rehabilitation" of Robert Frost. The traditional term would be "apologizing," a cause obligatory for all the faithful in the prolonged aftermath of Lawrance Thompson's biography. My regard in this process is for an appreciation of what has yet to be sufficiently appreciated: Frost's sonnets. Frost rightfully belongs in the company of poets who have managed to write highly acclaimed poems in this deceptively demanding form. I am also concerned with a minor puzzle. Frost is known as a traditionalist in poetry who sought form and could not abide free verse, and yet he wrote some perplexingly irregular sonnets.

An assessment of Frost's approaches to the sonnet that confirms his technical expertise may be the most tangible contribution left for any further appraisal. William Pritchard, Stanley Burnshaw, Jay Parini, and

3. T. S. Eliot, "London Letter," *Dial* 72 (May 1922): 513.
4. There is a good discussion in **Pritchard,** 201–2.

even Jeffrey Myers have apparently managed to exorcise the "monster of egoism" that Lawrance Thompson's demythologizing of the myth of Frost as a New England shaman farmer had fabricated.[5] The discrepancy between Frost's positive popular reputation and his negative reception by establishment critics has been narrowed. By the end of the 1980s Jay Parini could announce the good news in a new literary history that "book-length studies" had "permanently settled the question of whether or not Frost was a major poet in the sense that we apply the term to say Eliot, or W. B. Yeats."[6] All owed a debt to their predecessor Randall Jarrell, who appreciated Frost from the perspective of a poet as well as that of a critic. Surprisingly, Jarrell did not, in his assessment of the "other Frost," include Frost's accomplishments with the sonnet. Nor did Parini.

Even overdue recognition as a major poet did not necessarily mean that Frost would also be by the millennium universally acknowledged as either a serious thinker or a poet of exceptional skill and creativity. Mark Twain faced much the same ordeal in finding respect for his thought and his craft. Popular writers with sometimes unpopular politics, either too liberal or too conservative, are among the usual suspects for lack of depth. At the 1997 Winthrop University International Frost Conference, a position paper for a panel on biography professed that substantiating Frost's intellectual and artistic powers was the next responsibility for Frost scholars. Some understanding of Frost's craftsmanship has come out of work by Rueben Brower, Richard Poirier, and William Pritchard, and later by Frank Lentricchia, Judith Oster, and Mark Richardson. Homage was paid by three Nobel Prize winners—Seamus Heaney, Joseph Brodsky, and Derek Walcott—to one of the most conspicuous nonwinners.[7] Still Frost at the millennium is probably better recognized as a thinker, which he prudently never claimed to be, than he is as craftsman, which he always proclaimed himself to be. Mark Richardson's significant study *The Ordeal of Robert Frost* convincingly describes a Frost who was much more aware of significant issues for the poet in his time than had been suspected.[8] My

5. Stanley Burnshaw, *Robert Frost Himself* (New York: George Braziller, 1986) is personal testimony; there is Jay Parini's biography *Robert Frost: A Life* (New York: Holt, 1999); **Meyers** is factual but controversial among Frost scholars.

6. "Robert Frost," *Columbia Literary History of the United States* (New York: Columbia University Press, 1988), 937–46.

7. Reuben Brower, *The Poetry of Robert Frost: Constellations of Intention* (New York: Oxford University Press, 1963); and **Poirier** remain two of the best overall studies with good readings of poems. **Homage** provides a fascinating shock of recognition of the craft of Frost by three of his peers.

8. **Richardson.**

caveat is that we must be careful, as Richardson is, to know Frost, first of all, as a poet dedicated to understanding his craft. A careful reading of what Frost thought on and did with the sonnet should suggest a substantial knowledge of that form and a serious interest in poetics that contributed to a remarkable craftsmanship.

There is interest in Frost's poetics, but there are few formal essays, no philosophical treatises, and we never got the book of prose that he joked about writing. We know that he rejected the late Victorian view that music was the essential element in poetry and turned instead to the realism evoked by the spoken voice. Equally well known are his definition of a poem, "it begins in delight and ends in wisdom," and his contention that the wisdom might provide temporary stability—"a momentary stay against confusion." "The background in hugeness and confusion shading away from where we stand into black and utter chaos; and against the background any small man-made figure of order and concentration. What pleasanter than that this should be so?"[9] Frost valued any amount, however small, of control that form and structure could bring to a poem, or to a life for that matter. He was fond of saying about form, "it'll have to do for now" and then, "you'll have to get another one." Form was as necessary for the poet to write as the net was for the tennis player to play his game. I heard Frost use what he called "another analogy": the game of hop, skip, and jump. The "hop" and "skip" provided the form that was necessary for the ultimate value, the creative "jump." It is not surprising that the prescribed forms and conciseness of the sonnet were a challenge to conform and to resist. The sonnet is also, as Helen Vendler has demonstrated in her splendid new study of Shakespeare's sonnets, the most "voiceable" of poetic forms.[10] Poetic voice was a specialty in which Frost excelled.

Frost's prose commentary, especially that taken from tapes of his readings, has only recently been read as useful observation on his own and other poetry. We are becoming more aware, as the inclusion of prose in the Library of America edition evidences, that many of these comments contribute to an understanding of his own ideas about poetry. "The Constant Symbol" is one of Frost's best-known published comments. But it has not been read for its insights into the difficulties a poet may have with the sonnet form, especially in fitting what he wants to say into the anticipated fourteen lines. In Frost's view the sonneteer is never entirely a free agent;

9. "Letter to *The Amherst Student*," in **Prose,** 107.

10. Helen Vendler, *The Art of Shakespeare's Sonnets* (New York: Belnap Press of Harvard University Press, 1997), 17–21.

on the contrary, he may even be deprived of the "say of how long his piece will be, whether he will outlast or last out the fourteen lines." He can even "appear to finish in 12 lines and not know what to do with the last two." The sonnet raises a matter of concern about irregularities, just how much control a poet has over the writing of his poem once he has begun.

What is most pertinent to the sometimes irregular structure of Frost's sonnets is the tension between a need for form and the corresponding need for a freedom from form. Mark Richardson sees as central in Frost's "poetry, poetics, and vocation" the need to balance "the tendency towards conformity on the one hand and towards extravagance and difference on the other." In "The Figure a Poem Makes" there is a cryptic discussion of the "wildness" that Frost, no doubt influenced by William James, found in himself and realized the need for in his poetry. He believed that wildness was necessary to balance form, just as he knew the irregular rhythm of the spoken word had to break across the regular beat of the meter. For emphasis, perhaps because readers had failed to see it, Frost even exaggerates the importance of wildness: "If it is a wild tune, it is a poem."[11] No poetic form was more adaptable to this kind of tension or dualistic balance than the sonnet. It is long enough for meditation, too short for much narrative, and a challenge through its concise prescribed forms to the poet's formal skills. It has tradition behind it. It also permitted Frost a choice of two time-tested versions, Petrarchan, or Italian, and Shakespearean, or English. Each of these has variant forms and offers an opportunity to contest with some of the greatest poets in Western civilization. Frost preferred the Shakespearean sonnet but risked writing the Petrarchan, which most critics regard as the more difficult form. When Frost needed form to balance wildness, he provided it often by the insertion of rhyme to make a couplet. When he needed even more wildness, he could, as he liked to say, "cut loose," especially from the expected rhyme scheme or by moving toward a freer "speech sound" similar to the blank verse he used so effectively in longer narrative. On occasion this was simply a matter of going with the syntax of things—on to the end of the sentence.

As for influence, Frost admired Wordsworth's sonnets and surely shared with him the views in "Scorn Not the Sonnet."

> Scorn not the Sonnet; Critic, you have frowned,
> Mindless of its just honors; with this key
> Shakespeare unlocked his heart. . . .

11. **Prose,** 18.

Wordsworth's sonnets are sometimes regarded as "loose sonnets," an in-
dication that Wordsworth had his own "wildness." The traditional sonnet
did provide a structural skeleton and served as a formalizing device. But
Wordsworth, like other major poets, did not adhere strictly to all the
prescriptions of the Italian sonnet. Most obvious, his diction was less
formal, and his major breaks may occur within lines.

The standing of Frost's sonnets at near millennium echoes the question
raised by Wordsworth of "just honors." Unjustly, no major critic has
persuasively verified that Robert Frost wrote a significant number of the
best sonnets in English in the twentieth century. He is rarely mentioned in
accounts of the twentieth-century sonnet, unlike his contemporary Edwin
Arlington Robinson. In fact, Frost's sonnets are his least-known success,
as attested to by how few of them have been explicated in any detail.
Critical articles have been infrequent and not comprehensive enough to
do justice to either the quantity or the quality of Frost's sonnets. The only
book-length study, H. A. Maxson's *On the Sonnets of Robert Frost: A Critical
Examination,* is more valuable for the explication of individual poems than
it is as a definitive study of Frost's theory and practice of sonnet making.[12]
Maxson does recognize that the troubling factor in assessing Frost as a
sonneteer has been that he created irregular variants. Consequently, his
sonnets have been undervalued as near sonnets and even judged as "failed"
sonnets. Instead of perfecting a trademark sonnet of his own, Frost seems
to have regarded writing sonnets as an opportunity to experiment with
familiar prescribed forms. He recognized that the sonnet structures, as
their history discloses, could either provide the structural pattern *within*
which the poet might write or present a framework *against* which the poet
could work. Frost could write within the pattern, but he also was attracted
to writing against the pattern. The quotation most apropos surfaces in
a letter to Louis Untermeyer: "The sonnet is the strictest form I have
behaved in, and that mainly by pretending it wasn't a sonnet."[13]

Prior to Maxson's book the most valuable study was Oliver H. Evans's
article " 'Deeds that Count': Robert Frost's Sonnets."[14] Evans understood
that the irregular sonnets are products of Frost's serious play with re-
strictive, prescribed forms. The deeds that count are the "liberties taken

---

12. H. A. Maxson, *The Sonnets of Robert Frost: A Critical Examination* (Jefferson,
N.C.: McFarland, 1998).

13. **Untermeyer,** 381.

14. Oliver H. Evans, " 'Deeds That Count': Robert Frost's Sonnets," *Texas Studies in
Literature and Language* 23 (spring 1981): 123–37.

with the conventions." Critics have tended to judge Frost's sonnets rather strictly in comparison with the best of conventional sonnets. Even Frost enthusiasts have, on occasion, doubted Frost for not conforming to certain expected modes and not competing directly with the best work in regular sonnet forms. What was overlooked was what Frost seemed well aware of—the flexibility of the sonnet form as evidenced by the practice of the great sonnet-makers in producing numerous variants of the original Petrarchan form. Evans makes the valid and important claim for a grand occasion like the millennium: "Frost wrote some of the greatest sonnets in American poetry." An appropriate reply to Eliot and other doubters would be: "There, it has been done."

Critics have long noticed Frost's obsession with form to counter chaos. Frost never made a more germane statement about his life in art than in "To the *Amherst Student*": "When in doubt there is always form to go on with."[15] And one might add: the greater the doubt, the more intense the fear, the greater the need for more form. The maximum seven rhymes in "Once by the Pacific" would be appropriate for a poem Frost always made clear was based on terrifying experiences of his youth. An essay by Karen Rood on Frost's Italian sonnets deserves attention because she focuses on his need both for form and variants like his characteristic three to seven rhymes, rather than the usual four or five.[16] She prefers the norm, neither too much nor too little form, but she admits that some of Frost's most powerful poems are those in which the "confusion" is so strong as to require maximum form to maintain "a momentary stay." She notes that where regularity is expected Frost often introduces a new rhyme, makes a couplet, or (her major interest) allows sentence sounds and syntax to intrude on regular meter. She also links Frost's variations to his dualistic belief in an opposition between form that renders meaning and the wildness that mirrors the confusion of his world. Her study is the kind we need to explain the irregularities but limited too much to the effect of sentence sounds.

Aware of his reputation as a poet who scorned free verse and most tenets of modernism, Frost, on occasion, felt challenged to declare his own identity, unorthodoxy, even audacity, as a serious modern poet. Early in his career he wrote to his friend John Bartlett of his discovery of the "sound of sense": "I am one of the great craftsmen of my time."[17] The importance

---

15. **Prose,** 106.
16. Karen Rood, "Wildness Opposing 'Sentence Sounds': Robert Frost's Sonnets," **Tharpe II,** 196–210.
17. **Letters,** 79.

of "the sound of sense" crashing across regular meter to Frost's poetry is now pretty well understood. But the intricacies of the struggle with both form and wildness have not been adequately explored, even by the few critics who have discussed his sonnets. Elaine Barry's succinct account of the sonnet tells only half the story: Frost's search for form rather than his need for both form and wildness.[18] We know that Frost never intended a sonnet sequence, but he did a better thing. He produced, as one of the great craftsmen of his time, a body of sonnets remarkably diverse in subject and complex in form—not modernist but certainly modern.

Helen Vendler reminds us that the usual conception of the sonnet is simpler than the diversity a history of all its variations reveals. Actual practice specifies that a sonnet is a poem "usually" in iambic pentameter and "most often" fourteen lines long. The reality is even that there have been sixteen-line sonnets (George Meredith wrote them), seventeen-line sonnets (especially in Renaissance France), and sonnets in tetrameter. Of the two principal kinds of sonnets, Frost preferred the Shakespearean but risked the more difficult Petrarchan. He also liked to use elements of both in the same poem. The Italian is normally a two-part poem, usually with an eight-six division, rhyming originally abba abba cde cde; and the English sonnet, a four-part poem, with three quatrains and a couplet, rhyming abab cdcd efef gg. Variants were quickly developed, beginning with cdc, dcd for the Italian. Frost's favorite variant was to insert a couplet or two. The Italian sonnet usually poses a question or problem in the octave and provides an answer or resolution in the sestet. Frost may ask a question that has no satisfactory answer or suggest a problem but supply no resolution. The English sonnet may follow this pattern or utilize either repetitions or variations of the question and answer form. The Italian sonnet usually has a rhetorical turn in thought in line nine, at the beginning of the sestet. The Shakespearean sonnet usually has its turn at line thirteen, the beginning of the couplet. But there is sometimes a turn at line nine, following the Italian version. Frost also varies his turn based on whether he wants balance or imbalance between the parts. Vendler adds as structural elements the key word and the "couplet tie," which is simply the key word reappearing in the final couplet. The repetition of the word "water" in "Once by the Pacific" would be a striking example by Frost, as would the recurrrence of some form of "whisper" in "Mowing." If the Petrarchan sonnet features a problem-and-solution schematic, it may also be put out of balance with a twelve-two division characteristic of the Shakespearean sonnet. Another

18. Elaine Barry, *Robert Frost* (New York: Ungar Publishing Co., 1973).

variation, often overlooked, is in what some critics call the Spenserian sonnet, which links each quatrain to the next by a continuing rhyme: abab bcbc cdcd ee. Frost's skillful "Putting in the Seed" has this sestet form. What is important to record is that Frost employs most of these variations and adds some of his own, including letting natural speech alter meter.

The number of sonnets Frost wrote is sufficiently impressive to command attention if we accept Maxson's count of thirty-seven and add, as I would, "Mowing" and "Hyla Brook." Frost's practice was to write several sonnets, take leave from the form for a few years, and then return with three or more additional sonnets. Since there are questions as to which poems are actually sonnets, I shall list my thirty-nine. Frost began with four in *A Boy's Will* (1913), "Into My Own," "A Dream Pang," "The Vantage Point" and the "virtual" sonnet "Mowing"; five in *Mountain Interval* (1916), "Meeting and Passing," "The Oven Bird," "Putting in the Seed," "Range-Finding," "Hyla Brook"; six in *West-Running Brook* (1928), "Acceptance," "Once by the Pacific," "The Flood," "Acquainted with the Night," "A Soldier," "The Investment"; four in *A Further Range* (1936), "The Master Speed," "Design," "On A Bird Singing in its Sleep," "Unharvested"; three in *A Witness Tree* (1942), "The Silken Tent," "Never Again Would Birds' Song Be the Same," "Time Out"; seven in *Steeple Bush* (1947), "Etherealizing," "Why Wait for Science," "Any Size We Please," "The Planners," "No Holy Wars for Them," "Bursting Rapture," "The Broken Drought"; nine in the Library of America edition (1995), "Despair," "When the Speed Comes," "The Mill City," "Pursuit of the Word," "The Rain Bath," "On Talk of Peace at This Time," "The Pans," "Trouble Rhyming," "A Bed in the Barn." These sonnets were previously uncollected and unpublished prior to the Library of America Edition. I find only "The Mill City" interesting. There were no sonnets in *North of Boston* (1914) and only one, "On a Tree Fallen across the Road," in *New Hampshire* (1926). Frost's sojourn in England did not promote the writing of sonnets. The Georgians there did not share the Victorian taste for Italian sonnets as a part of their interest in things Italian. *Palgrave's Golden Treasury* was a better resource for Frost.

The diversity of these sonnets, their range in subject and theme, has never received the notice merited. There are several conventional lyric sonnets, including the traditional compliments to a woman, beautifully formulated in "The Silken Tent" and "Never Again Would Birds' Song Be the Same." I find in the latter sonnet a line that, taken in the context of the poem, is one of his most graceful: "And to do that to birds was why she came." At the other extreme, Frost used the sonnet form for humorous and satirical play on the concept of progress, as in "Why Wait for Science" and "Etherealizing," both crowd-pleasers at his readings and marvelously suited to his voice. Then there are traditional nature sonnets, like the extraordinary "The Oven Bird"; Emersonian poems, like "Hyla Brook," with man on the natural scene, finding there truth, even if only modest or ambiguous truth; and celebrations of work performed in nature, in poems like "Mowing." Significantly, there are also Frost's great dark sonnets: "Once by the Pacific," "Acquainted with the Night," and "Design," which Lionel Trilling, in a consequential half-truth, called one of Frost's "terrifying" poems.

There is diversity in type of sonnet. Karen Rood finds twelve Italian sonnets among the collected poems. These include the most often explicated, "Design"; the most orthodox, "Why Wait for Science," and two of the most underrated, "The Vantage Point" and "Range-Finding." Others are "The Flood," "A Soldier," "The Investment," "A Dream Pang," "Meeting and Passing," "Any Size We Please," "The Broken Drought," and "Bursting Rapture." Three could be added from the uncollected poems, "Pursuit of the Word," "The Rain Bath," and "Trouble Rhyming." I find seventeen to be basically Shakespearean. Among these are his first sonnet, "Into My Own," "Putting in the Seed," "On a Tree Fallen across the Road," "Acceptance," "Once by the Pacific," "Acquainted with the Night," "The Master Speed," "On a Bird Singing in Its Sleep," "The Silken Tent," "Never Again Would Birds' Song Be the Same," "Time Out," "Etherealizing," "Any Size We Please," "No Holy Wars for Them," "On Talk of Peace at This Time." Among those formerly uncollected are "The Mill City," and "Pursuit of the Word." There is striking variety. Three of Frost's Shakespearean sonnets are formed from seven rhymed couplets, while one, "The Planners," actually employs four rhymed triplets, followed by a couplet in only near rhyme. There are borderline cases of poems with elements of both the Italian and the Shakespearean sonnet forms; these could be classified, following Evans, as "compromise sonnets."

In passing judgment on the quality of Frost's sonnets, I would borrow a metaphor (as Frost would urge) of Randall Jarrell's that suggests judging the greatness of a poet by the number of times he was "struck by lightning" in the creative process.[19] In my judgment, lightning energized the poet at least seven times and came close three or four more. My choices for the best of the group would include "Mowing," "The Oven Bird," "Once by the Pacific," "Acquainted with the Night," "Design," "The Silken Tent," and "Never Again Would Birds' Song Be the Same." I would list as near

---

19. Randall Jarrell, *Poetry and the Age* (New York: Vintage Books, Inc., 1959), 134.

strikes the sonnets "The Vantage Point," "Range-Finding," and the much underrated "Putting in the Seed" and "A Soldier." Jarrell required a dozen or more poems for poetic greatness. I believe Frost nearly attains that status on the merits of his sonnets alone. These best sonnets are mostly poems that critics have admired but explicated as dramatic lyrics rather than as sonnets. Space limits my own comments on reading them as sonnets.

Frost's first sonnet, "Into My Own," was, according to him, written in 1901 though not published until May 1909 in the *New England Magazine* and republished in *A Boy's Will* as the initial poem. It was displaced in the *Collected Poems* by "The Pasture," which would introduce Frost's New England version of pastoral verse. The earlier poem, however, is important because it provides an introduction to the Frostian voice. It is also mildly experimental, as Maxson notes, the first of "experiments calculated to discover just how far the poet could stray, and the form could flex to accommodate." As Frost strays from the norm in the sonnet form, there is a parallel desire for the speaker to stray from civilization. He would wish that "those dark trees . . . stretched away unto the edge of doom" in case he should one day actually venture into that unknown. He would not expect to return but would rather invite those "who would miss me here" to follow and join him, finding him altered only by an increase in self-confidence.

The experiment is, as most often in Frost, with the rhyme scheme. The basic structure is the three quatrains and a final couplet of the Shakespearean sonnet, but this is also a Shakespearean sonnet written entirely in couplets, a form also used in three of his finest sonnets, "Once by the Pacific, " "The Oven Bird," (irregularly) and "On a Bird Singing in Its Sleep." Through the use of couplets Frost retains the seven rhymes of the Shakespearean sonnet but arranges them in quatrains according to his own scheme, often determined by the thought pattern or a speech rhythm. Frost also does something else distinctive by employing "sentence sounds" against the prescribed iambic pentameter of the sonnet form. The opening line of "Into My Own" is couched in such natural speech rhythms: "One of my wishes is that those dark trees. . . ." In the Shakespearean sonnet the rhetorical turn is expected at line thirteen, initiating the final couplet, which in this poem is

> They would not find me changed from him they knew—
> Only more sure of all I thought was true.

The turn in this reading is from the speaker's wish to his certainty that he would be found "not changed" except to have become "more sure." But the turn might also occur in line nine ("I do not see why I should e'er turn back") as the speaker suggests that those he left behind follow his tracks. If the turn is at line nine, I do not see the poem as specifically declaring either his future success as a poet or his reassurance to himself and to Elinor that, should he run away in youthful despair to the Dismal Swamp again, he would emerge the better for it. The borrowing of the phrase "edge of doom" from Shakespeare's great Sonnet 116 would support this view. His bold assertion of confidence is made in a poem that requires the restraining form of a sonnet of seven couplets and possibly an ambiguity as to the rhetorical turn. While retaining the quatrain and final couplet pattern and preserving the maximum rhymes of the Shakespearean sonnet, "Into My Own," if the turn is at line nine, may have also adopted the octave-sestet structure of the Italian sonnet to compose what Evans calls a "compromise" sonnet.

Another early sonnet, "Once by the Pacific," serves as a reminder that the "momentary stay against confusion" a poem might provide was not just for the reader but also for the poet. Anyone who witnessed Frost's reading of this poem might testify that it was based on his great traumatic fear of facing an ocean storm alone, which he did as a child when he felt abandoned at the Cliff House beach. He also had a re-curring fear of losing his father to the ocean on one of his long swims from this beach. "Once by the Pacific" was, consequently, one of his sonnets requiring maximum form for a fourteen-line poem, a sonnet in seven couplets. Frost increases the effect of the terror by personifying the natural forces ("The clouds were low and hairy in the skies") that threaten. Frost depersonalizes his fears by universalizing the storm's effect into a danger for everything water can threaten, even the shore itself. Frost liked to recall that the poem has been regarded as "prophetic" but actually was based on an event that happened long before the two world wars. It was most likely written during 1906 or 1907 at Derry Farm, and it is more immediately a vision of ultimate destruction than a prophecy.

In this sonnet, too, the place of rhetorical turn is ambiguous. It could occur at line twelve ("Someone had better be prepared for rage") as the poet's tone becomes admonishing, stressing the human need for prepara-tion just as nature has provided a cliff for the ocean, which may not be sufficient. But he also restates in lines thirteen and fourteen the extent of the danger, in a final couplet that stands out from the rest of the sonnet because it alone has feminine end rhymes. The same God who said "Let there be Light" will give the command to "Put out the Light."

> There would be more than ocean water-broken
> Before God's last *Put out the Light* was spoken.

Frost does leave the rhetorical structure open to interpretation. The turn could even be in the run-on of line eight into line nine, when the speaker turns from the threatening scene to compare, in grammatically parallel clauses, the need for preparation by human kind as well as in nature.

> It looked as if a night of dark intent
> Was coming, and not only a night, an age.

A reading of an earlier poem, "The Oven Bird" (1916), reveals that the sonnet can be an effective medium through which to express major themes of Frost's poetry, in this case his acceptance of the diminished view that science (Freud, behaviorism, etc.) has left for the imagination. The oven bird, a midsummer bird, comes late to song, and it sings not from the darkest, deepest woods but from midway into the woods. Its location in time enables it both to remember the fresher spring and to sing of decline into autumn, voicing in "all but words" a major Frost theme, "what to make of a diminished thing." The story of Frost's unhappy response to Sidney Cox's assumption that the oven bird was Frost as poet is well-known vintage Frost. Frost preferred to see the poem as about endurance.

Only Maxson has analyzed the poem as a sonnet, noting its "hidden intricate rhyme" and "technical brilliance." According to him, the first two "He says" lines introduce irregularities into the poem by changing the rhyme scheme. An attempt to approximate speech toward the colloquial leads to irregularities in rhyming. I would point out that Frost's rhyme scheme in this sonnet—aa bcb dcd ee fgfg—resembles neither Shakespearean nor Petrarchan practice, except that it has the seven rhymes of the former. Playing against the structure of "He says" statements, the poet opens with a couplet and then inserts another couplet as lines nine and ten:

> And comes that other fall we name the fall.
> He says the highway dust is over all.

Maxson considers these to be key lines, interpreting "the fall" as the failure of technology ("highway dust"). But, since the "petal fall" of spring is mentioned earlier in the poem, the "other fall" logically would be autumn, with possible overtones of that Fall in Eden that brought death to humankind. The sonnet's rhetorical turn is also irregular, appearing between the key internal couplet and the closing quatrain, between line ten and line eleven. Closure comes, atypically, in a quatrain (fgfg) as we are told the meaning of the oven bird's song. He knows "not to sing" about midsummer but rather to ponder "what to make of a diminished thing."

Another poem that lends itself to structural analysis is "The Vantage Point." The first eight lines of this irregular Petrarchan, perhaps Wordsworthian, sonnet are emotionally detached from the scene of men's homes and their cemetery; the last six are committed, as the speaker turns around to experience sensually the natural elements surrounding him. Frost manages the transition through meter, as regularity of meter in line nine is followed in the next line by one lone trochee in the midst of iambic regularity.

> And if by noon I have too much of these,
> I have but to turn on my arm, and lo,
> The sun-burned hillside sets my face aglow. . . .

It is as if the reader is forced to participate through an almost physical bodily turn.

If a fifteen-line sonnet can be justified by theory and logic, "Hyla Brook," in spite of Maxson's rejection, has to be a sonnet. The final two lines have both the force and terminal punctuation of joint closure. The last line is a summation of what has been said, a necessary addition for emphasis in order to make explicit what is implicit. The point that is being made in the fourteen lines of the sonnet proper is that this is not the conventional brook celebrated in poetry. To be explicit, to justify his concern, Frost adds the fifteenth line: "We love the things we love for what they are." In the additional line he justifies for himself why he has remembered this unremarkable brook. Such things may not be sufficient, traditionally, for celebration in song, but they are, as this brook is, adequately interesting to be recorded for memory.

The rhyme scheme of this poem is, on the surface, too irregular to be taken as a sonnet. It seems to begin with a Petrarchan quatrain but develops into the pattern abb acc add, coming to closure at a full stop. The middle triplet, describing the vanished "Hyla breed," is enclosed in parentheses. Then follows the couplet ee, which brings to a climax the description of the brook in summer. The couplet stands out in the poem both by the strength of its metaphor and by the slowing of pace through meter in its second line.

> Its bed is left a faded paper sheet
> Of dead leaves stuck together by the heat—. . . .

The final quatrain (12–15) rhymes fgfg, as the speaker sums up the value of his brook to those "who remember long." The form is complex but, arguably, functional. Maxson has trouble with placing the turn in line twelve. I see this turn leading into the explicit statement in the additional lines required for satisfactory closure. The poem is concerned with why we like ordinary things.

"Acquainted with the Night" is one of Frost's more daring and best-known experiments with sonnet form—a sonnet in terza rima. Its pessimism is highly unusual for Frost, and the form is unique. The setting is atypical, a city at night, perhaps based on Frost's residence in Ann Arbor. This poem conveys a sense of loneliness more characteristic of Edwin Arlington Robinson, a master of the sonnet in his own right, than of Frost but still within his range. Both Elaine Barry and William Pritchard devote some time to reading this poem as a sonnet in terza rima. For the standard Shakespearean three quatrains and a couplet Frost skillfully substitutes four tercets and a couplet aba bcb cdc dad aa. The internal line of the last tercet returns with "height" to the "a" rhyme of the first, creating a circular pattern but also enabling the couplet to employ an "a" rhyme in the couplet so that it can close the sonnet with a repetition of its first line, "I have been one acquainted with the night." There is metrical repetition also, as five of the seven lines beginning "I have" continue with two stressed words—"walked out," "outwalked," "looked down," "passed by," and "stood still"—before returning to iambic meter. Since line twelve runs swiftly on into the couplet, a possible turn might take place with the image of the "One luminary clock" on its "unearthly height," which appears at line eleven.

In "The Silken Tent" Frost definitively demonstrated that he could write a conventional sonnet on a traditional subject, a compliment to a lady. It may have been a compliment to two women, perhaps begun as a tribute to Elinor and, upon her death, redirected to pay homage to his private secretary, Kathleen Morrison. I would agree with Elaine Barry's judgment that the poem is worthy of comparison with the great Elizabethan love sonnets in its sheer tonal beauty. The woman is admired for her poise in the context of the speaker's stormy life. She is the tent's "supporting central cedar pole," only loosely bound by its silken guy ropes. The poem is a tribute to this woman's ability to remain responsive to others' needs while, at the same time, experiencing only "the slightest bondage" when one tie goes "slightly taut." The sonnet's form is appropriately Shakespearean in its rhyme scheme, but the final couplet is a run-on from line twelve, thus avoiding any possibility of a rhetorical turn at this point. Frost does this in a half dozen of his Shakespearean sonnets. It is also unusual that the entire poem is one sentence, the verb for its second clause, whose subject occurs in line five, not appearing until the last line.

On the other hand, in Frost's other great poetic compliment, "Never Again Would Birds' Song Be the Same," the turn at the couplet seems obvious in its definitive restatement of the sonnet's title. Maxson finds ambiguity in two possible readings, dependent on whether we find an octave and sestet, as in the Petrarchan structure, or three quatrains and a couplet, as in the Shakespearean. Whether or not the man and woman of this poem refer to someone in particular, it is "the daylong voice of Eve" that has added a "tone of meaning" to birdsong. Woman has significantly enhanced the Garden. We have, in this perfectly regular Shakespearean sonnet, Frost's lyric voice at its best.

"Design" is Frost's most explicated sonnet, more often read as a dramatic lyric than as a sonnet. It is one of those dark sonnets singled out by Lionel Trilling and a model of how Frost's apparent simplicity may be deceptive. Many readers have remarked upon how the poem begins with nursery-rhyme simplicity and moves upward to Miltonic questioning of responsibility for evil. The tone of the poem changes in line three with the first hint of death in the word *rigid,* suggesting rigor mortis. There is then a gradual build up within the octave from "death and blight," to "witches' broth" and "dead wings." The scene of spider, heal-all, and moth now set up, three questions are posed about the meaning of this coincidence of whiteness. "Steered" becomes a key word here, suggesting a directive from some outside force. There are two conclusions. The first is terrifying: "What but design of darkness to appall?" But the second is deconstructive of the entire argument: "If design govern in a thing so small." We have within the explicit form of a sonnet an implied epic theological debate.

Only three different end rhymes—the minimum—are utilized in this sonnet. There are two Petrarchan quatrains in the octave and a variant rhyme pattern in the sestet: abba abba ac aa cc. The return to an "a" rhyme in line nine, with "white" echoing the end of line one, while "heal-all" at the end of line ten anticipates "appall" and "small" in the concluding couplet. The question and response of the remaining four lines in the sestet are composed as two couplets, allowing a secondary rhetorical turn at the beginning of the final couplet, when the third question implies its own answer. The three dashes in the poem require pauses that possibly add suspense. Although "Design" has the eight-six division of the Italian sonnet, it is with a marked difference. Questioning comes not in the octave but in the sestet, coinciding with the rhetorical turn.

"Putting in the Seed," considered by Maxson to be a masterpiece, is a sonnet in which the boundaries between narrative and the lyric are obscured. This poem is solidly Frostian, an activity poem spoken by a husband to his wife. The speaker wonders whether he can quit work when his wife calls him for supper and then seems to invite her to share his "springtime passion for the earth." A dramatic shift develops through the course of the sonnet. Beginning in natural speech rhythms, with two contractions and the colloquial "fetch me" and "leave off," the lines slow metrically to describe the work of planting seeds that are intermixed with petals of fallen apple blossoms.

> (Soft petals, yes, but not so barren quite,
> Mingled with these, smooth bean and wrinkled pea) . . . .

Then, cued by language in line nine, specifically, "Slave" and "passion," the concluding sentence surges both emotionally and metrically from "How Love burns" to the birth of a seedling, whose "arched body comes / Shouldering its way and shedding the earth crumbs." The poet inserts sexual overtones into his work as a seed planter by personifying the emerging sprout. The rhyme scheme is, basically, Shakespearean (abab abab cdcd ee), made with five instead of seven rhymes because the second quatrain repeats the rhymes of the first. As for a rhetorical turn, although it seems to occur at line nine as in the Petrarchan sonnet, syntactically that line belongs with the preceding quatrain.

Finally, there is the question of "Mowing." Maxson rejects the poem as a sonnet, not only because it is irregular in rhyme scheme and meter, but also because he cannot discern a pattern or find an acceptable rhetorical turn. I cannot regard this poem as having failed in any way. I prefer to retain it as a sonnet in as much as many readers have accepted it as such and because it is one of Frost's finest lyrics. It is a product of the Derry Farm days, when Frost was writing his first sonnets. It is also helpful to know that Frost regarded "Mowing" as a talk song, his first. This perhaps helps explain its irregularities. There are more three-syllable feet than usual, functionally interrupting the traditional iambic flow. Moreover, the poem certainly possesses a key word, one of Helen Vendler's signs of the sonnet form. "My long scythe whispered" in line fourteen echoes "My long scythe whispering" in line two, while "whispered" reappears in lines three and six.

Perhaps a pattern can be extracted from the poem's rhyme scheme (abc abd ec dfeg fg) by coordinating it with its rhetorical and syntactical structure. The first three lines, ending in a semicolon, set up the question of what the scythe may be whispering. The next three lines, beginning "Perhaps it was something about the heat of the sun" and ending with a full stop, suggest a possible answer. The next two lines (rhymes "e" and "c") tell what the scythe does not suggest, a dream of leisure or hoard of fairy gold. Then, at what must be regarded as a rhetorical turn, at line nine as in the Petrarchan sonnet, we are told, in an unrhymed quatrain that

> Anything more than the truth would have seemed too weak
> To the earnest love that laid the swale in rows. . . .

Resolution appears in line thirteen in an unrhymed couplet closure, in what Frost once claimed could be a definition of poetry: "The fact is the sweetest dream that labor knows." Some ambiguity remains as to whether the fact is work itself or the hay left "to make" is the product of the mower's work.

It should not be overlooked that Frost could write humorous or satirical sonnets. I mentioned "Etherealizing" and "Why Wait for Science" as good specimens that allowed Frost full use of his voice for emphasis and for a bit of wildness. Both poems ridicule abstracting, theorizing, faith-in-progress in an age of technology. Frost's idea is similar to Eliot's stress on a Cartesian split between thought and feeling; his ridicule is of the idea that we could become all mind in "Etherealizing," or of the idea that we need to wait for science when we already have common sense as a guide.

As I try to comprehend Frost at the millennium my thoughts go back to 1959. It was a time when there was excitement about Robert Lowell, a longtime admirer of Frost, and his book *Life Studies,* the beginnings of confessional poetry. As Robert Frost was thumbing through his poems for one more selection, he looked up from his text at the audience and said in the most confidential of tones, "There's all sorts of things in here." I would say the same of his sonnets. There is more than one can cover short of a book. It is evident that, not being fully happy in harness with all the prescribed forms, Frost wrote both within and against the required patterns. Perhaps he liked the conciseness, even being forced to be concise himself, and took special delight in the ambiguities that the brevity helped create. Some demands, especially in the rhyme scheme, he did not meet but departed from, with a special delight in adding couplets. He stayed pretty close to the prescribed fourteen lines, but "Hyla Brook" shows that in a good poem an extra line may be added to finish a thought, a sentence, or a rhyme. This is even more justifiable if the extra line accomplishes all three purposes. Evans finds a few sixteen-line sonnets. I do not. The theory would be that the thought outlasts the poem, requiring a quatrain instead of a final couplet. Frost's sonnets, successful with their variances, provide ample evidence that in Frost we had one of the greatest craftsmen of his time. With that done no further apology is needed, perhaps only a reminder of the importance of play to Frost. There is one role that American writers, Emily Dickinson and Mark Twain among them, played in going against convention. When he got to certain poems Frost couldn't resist playing it, especially when reading to mostly student audiences. Perhaps there is also a slightly devilish play in pretending the sonnets were not sonnets while knowing that his audience would not know anyway.[20] Framing his remarks in a political context that could correspond to his literary role, Frost warned,

> See you're going to use some analogy that leads up to something. Someone says, "You aren't much of a New Dealer, are you?" Well, I'm a Democrat. . . . I am not New Deal. I'm *auld diel*. You don't know what that means, do you? *D I E L.* [So spelled by Frost and then so softly said it was not transcribed] *old devil.*

20. "Frost in the Carolinas," 11.

ABOUT THE AUTHORS AND EDITORS

JONATHAN N. BARRON is Associate Professor of English at the University of Southern Mississippi and is coeditor of *Jewish American Poetry: Poems, Commentary, and Reflections*. Beginning in 2001, he will be editor in chief of the *Robert Frost Review* and Director of the Robert Frost Society.

RICHARD J. CALHOUN, Alumni Distinguished Professor Emeritus, Clemson University, was for twenty-six years editor of the *South Carolina Review*, in which he established a special issue on Frost for each spring; he has published books on the poets James Dickey and Galway Kinnell, and for six years he reviewed contemporary poetry for *American Literary Scholarship*. Professor Calhoun has been a Fulbright professor five times, has lectured on Frost in Europe for Arts America, and is a past president of the Frost Society.

DAVID HAMILTON has for the past twenty years edited the *Iowa Review*. His essays have appeared in the *Huntington Library Quarterly, Michigan Quarterly Review,* and *Gettysburg Review*.

WALTER JOST is Associate Professor of English at the University of Virginia. He is the author of *Rhetorical Thought in John Henry Newman* and coeditor of *Rhetoric and Hermeneutics in Our Time: A Reader* and *Rhetorical Invention and Religious Inquiry: New Perspectives*. He has just finished a book entitled *Rhetorical Investigations: Ordinary Language, Everyday Life in Poems of Robert Frost*.

KATHERINE KEARNS has published *Nineteenth-Century Literary Realism: Through the Looking Glass, Psychoanalysis, Historiography, and Feminism: The Search for Critical Methods,* and *Robert Frost and a Poetics of Appetite*.

KAREN L. KILCUP is Professor of American literature at the University of North Carolina at Greensboro. She received a U.S. National Distinguished Teacher award in 1987 and was recently the Davidson Eminent Scholar Chair at Florida International University. She is President of the American Humor Studies Association and editor of its journal. She has published numerous essays and books on American literature and culture, including "Soft Canons: American Women Writers and Masculine Tradition."

ANDREW LAKRITZ is an independent scholar living and working in Arlington, Virginia. He is the author of *Modernism and the Other in Stevens, Frost, and Moore*. With his wife, Eileen, and daughter, Ania, he volunteers with the Washington, D.C., chapter of Partners of the Americas, which is linked with Brasilia, Brazil.

GEORGE MONTEIRO is the author of forthcoming books *Fernando Pessoa and Nineteenth-Century Anglo-American Literature* and *Stephen Crane's Blue Badge of Courage*. He has published *Robert Frost and the New England Renaissance, The Presence of Camões,* and *The Presence of Pessoa,* and edited *Conversations with Elizabeth Bishop* and *Critical Essays on Ernest Hemingway's* A Farewell to Arms. He teaches at Brown University.

MARK RICHARDSON is Associate Professor of English, Western Michigan University. He is author of *The Ordeal of Robert Frost: the Poet and the Poetics* and coeditor, with Richard Poirier, of *Robert Frost: Collected Poems, Prose, and Plays.* He can be reached at mark.richardson@wmich.edu.

LISA SEALE is Associate Professor of English at the University of Wisconsin, Marathon County, where she teaches courses on Robert Frost and Emily Dickinson, Asian American literature, and literature about the Vietnam War. She has studied the public talks and readings of Robert Frost for many years and hopes someday to see the bulk of them in print.

PETER J. STANLIS has written more than a dozen significant essays on Frost in addition to being a scholar of Edmund Burke. He has been editing the *Burke Newsletter* and *Studies in Burke and His Time,* and his most recent work on Burke is *Edmund Burke: The Enlightenment and Revolution.* His interest in Frost has a personal dimension: he met Frost at Bread Loaf in 1939 and continued to be his friend for twenty-three years. He is currently writing on book on the intellectual life of Frost.

EARL J. WILCOX is founding editor of the *Robert Frost Review* and for the past fifteen years has been Director of the Robert Frost Society. He is the editor of two previous collections on Frost. A cofounder of the Philological Association of the Carolinas, he has also been Executive Director of the College English Association, President of the Jack London Society, and remains an avid baseball fan.

INDEX

This index includes only primary works discussed in the text.